the Pacific Crest Trail

Volume 2: Oregon & Washington

Jeffrey P. Schaffer
Andy Selters

Maps drawn by
Jeffrey P. Schaffer and Kenneth R. Ng

Acknowledgments

During the summer of 1973, Jeff Schaffer mapped all of the Oregon PCT and some of the Washington PCT: Columbia River to White Pass and Stevens Pass to Rainy Pass. Bev and Fred Hartline mapped the rest of the Washington PCT: White Pass to Stevens Pass and Rainy Pass to Manning Provincial Park. Both parties went back in the summers of '75 and '76, and Schaffer went back in '78, '82 and '85, most of these excursions being for the purpose of mapping newly built PCT segments. Along such trips Schaffer would try to spot check as many roads, trailheads, trail segments and resorts as possible. The Hartlines moved away from the area, so in 1985 Schaffer asked Andy Selters, a professional alpine guide operating out of Bellingham, Washington, to become a co-author. Selters remapped and rewrote the PCT description from White Pass to Stevens Pass.

If one has only a very limited time to do field work on the PCT, he must know what stretches need to be mapped or field-checked. For this information we have relied on the U.S. Forest Service, the National Park Service, the Bureau of Land Management and our readers. We don't have the space to acknowledge all those who helped us in previous editions, but we can acknowledge a few of those who helped with the current edition. Arranged by governmental agency, from south to north, these folks are: Jack Darnall (Klamath N.F.); Phil Akerman, John Czemerys and Margaret Holman (Rogue River N.F.); William Deese (Winema N.F.); James Wieman (Umpqua N.F.); Walter Schloer (Deschutes N.F.); Howard Rondthaler—who has always been very helpful and very critical (Mt. Hood N.F.); Donald Smith (Wenatchee N.F.); and Gail Ross (Manning Provincial Park). Among those in the private sector who who wrote us were Dan Atkinson, Jan Benson, Richard Greve and Ed Patterson. John Larsen of Tualatin, Oregon, deserves special mention, for over the years he has supplied us with every bit of PCT information he's come across.

Once we knew where to hike and what to verify, we were often faced with the problem—as many PCT hikers are—of arranging a shuttle service. At times Ken Ng provided Schaffer with extensive shuttle service and also recorded data on roads, campgrounds, available services and anything else he saw. In like manner Jeff MacDonald and Margaret Wilson provided shuttle service for Selters. Jill Fugate also provided such service, and on top of that, she reviewed Andy's manuscript.

Finally, credit must be given to Thomas Winnett, publisher of Wilderness Press, who conceived the idea of a *detailed* PCT guidebook, and who, despite the many problems of cost and production, strove for increasingly higher guidebook standards while other publishers settled for less. Without him, this book never would have become the "PCT hikers' bible" that it is today.

Jeffrey P. Schaffer
Hercules, California

Andy Selters
Bellingham, Washington

May 1986

First edition 1974
Second edition 1976
Third edition 1979
Fourth edition 1986
FIFTH EDITION 1990
Copyright © 1974, 1976, 1979, by Jeffrey P. Schaffer and Bev and Fred Hartline
Copyright © 1986, 1990 by Jeffrey P. Schaffer and Andy Selters
Library of Congress Card Catalog Number 89-70744
International Standard Book Number 0-89997-113-X

All photos by Jeffrey P. Schaffer except as noted
Cover photo © 1990 by Ed Cooper: **Mt. Jefferson**
Title-page photo: **Glacier Peak from the north**

Wilderness Press, 2440 Bancroft Way, Berkeley CA 94704

Library of Congress Cataloging-in-Publication Data

Schaffer, Jeffrey P.
     The Pacific Crest Trail / Jeffrey P. Schaffer, Andy Selters ; maps
drawn by Jeffrey P. Schaffer and Kenneth R. Ng. -- 5th ed.
          p.   cm.
     Includes bibliographical references.
     Contents: -- v. 2. Oregon & Washington.
     ISBN 0-89997-113-X (v. 2)
     1. Hiking--Pacific States--Guide-books. 2. Hiking--Pacific Crest
Trail--Guide-books. 3. Pacific States--Description and
travel--1981- --Guide-books. 4. Pacific Crest Trail--Guide-books.
     I. Selters, Andrew. II. Title.
GV199.42.P3S33 1990
917.97'043--dc20
                                        89-70744
                                          CIP

Contents

Introductory Chapters

Trail Chapters

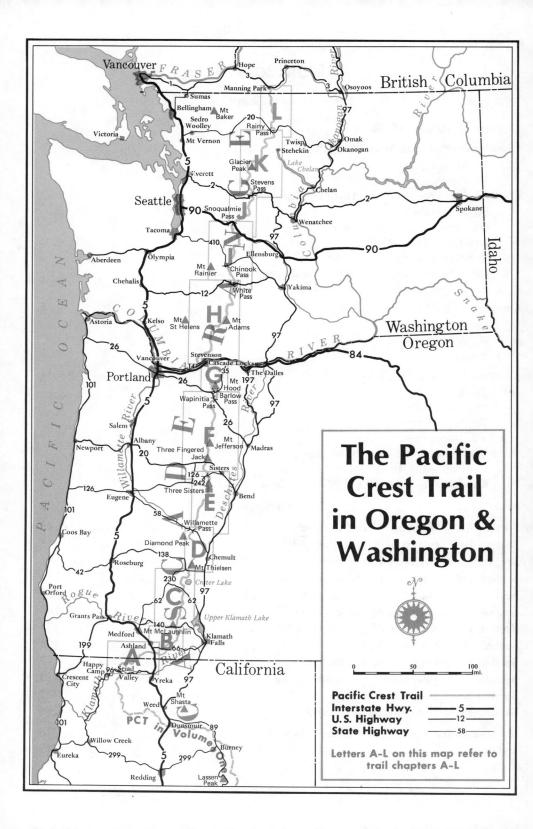

The Pacific Crest Trail in Oregon & Washington

Pacific Crest Trail
Interstate Hwy.
U.S. Highway
State Highway

Letters A-L on this map refer to trail chapters A-L

0   50   100 mi.

Chapter 1: History of the PCT

The first proposal for the creation of a Pacific Crest Trail that we have been able to discover is contained in the book *Pacific Crest Trails,* by Joseph T. Hazard (Superior Publishing Co.). He says that in 1926 he was just ending a business interview with a Miss Catherine Montgomery at the Western Washington College of Education in Bellingham when she said,

"Do you know what I've been thinking about, Mr. Hazard, for the last twenty minutes?

"Just what have you in mind, Miss Montgomery?

"A high trail winding down the heights of our western mountains with mile markers and shelter huts—like those pictures I'll show you of the 'Long Trail of the Appalachians'— from the Canadian Border to the Mexican Boundary Line!"

To go back six years in time, the Forest Service had by 1920 routed and posted a trail from Mt. Hood to Crater Lake in Oregon, named the Oregon Skyline Trail, and with hindsight we can say that it was the first link in the PCT.

Hazard says that on that very night, he conveyed Miss Montgomery's suggestion to the Mt. Baker Club of Bellingham, which was enthusiastic about it. He says that soon a number of other mountain clubs and outdoor organizations in the Pacific Northwest adopted the idea and set about promoting it. Then, in 1928, Fred W. Cleator became Supervisor of Recreation for Region 6 (Oregon and Washington) of the U.S. Forest Service. Cleator proclaimed and began to develop the the Cascade Crest Trail, a route down the spine of Washington from Canada to the Columbia River. Later he extended the Oregon Skyline Trail at both ends so that it too traversed a whole state. In 1937 Region 6 of the Forest Service developed a design for PCT trail markers and posted them from the Canadian border to the California border.

But the Forest Service's Region 5 (California) did not follow his lead, and it remained for a private person to provide the real spark not only for a California segment of the PCT but indeed for the PCT itself. In the early Thirties the idea of a Pacific Crest Trail entered the mind of Clinton C. Clarke of Pasadena, California, who was then chairman of the Executive Committee of the Mountain League of Los Angeles County. "In March 1932," wrote Clarke in *The Pacific Crest Trailway,* he "proposed to the United States Forest and National Park Services the project of a continuous wilderness trail across the United States from Canada to Mexico. . . . The plan was to build a trail along the summit divides of the mountain ranges of these states, traversing the best scenic areas and maintaining an absolute wilderness character."

The proposal included formation of additional Mountain Leagues in Seattle, Portland and San Francisco by representatives of youth organizations and hiking and mountaineering clubs similar to the one in Los Angeles. These Mountain Leagues would then take the lead in promoting the extension of the John Muir Trail northward and southward to complete a pathway from border to border. When it became evident that more than Mountain Leagues were needed for such a major undertaking, Clarke took the lead in forming the Pacific Crest Trail System Conference, with representatives from the three Pacific Coast states. He served as its President for 25 years.

As early as January 1935 Clarke published a handbook-guide to the PCT giving the route in rather sketchy terms ("the Trail goes east of Heart Lake, then south across granite fields to the junction of Piute and Evolution Creeks"—this covers about 9 miles).

In the summer of 1935—and again the next 3 summers—groups of boys under the sponsorship of the YMCA explored the PCT route in relays, proceeding from Mexico on June 15, 1935, to Canada on August 12, 1938. This exploration was under the guidance of a YMCA secretary, Warren L. Rogers, who served as Executive Secretary of the Pacific Crest Trail System Conference (1932–1957) and who continues his interest in the PCT by publishing new information on the trail and conducting trip-planning seminars about it.

During World War II, the Pacific Crest Trail was generally ignored and its completion remained in a state of limbo until the 1960s, when backpacking began to appeal to large numbers of people. In 1965 the Bureau of Outdoor Recreation, a Federal agency, appointed a commission to make a nationwide trails study. The commission, noting that walking for pleasure was second only to driving for pleasure as the most popular recreation in America, recommended establishing a national system of trails, of two kinds: long National Scenic Trails in the hinterlands and shorter National Recreation Trails in and near metropolitan areas. The commission recommended that Congress establish four Scenic Trails: the already existing Appalachian Trail, the partly existing Pacific Crest Trail, a Potomac Heritage Trail and a Continental Divide Trail. Congress responded by passing, in 1968, the National Trails System Act, which set the framework for a system of trails and specifically made the Appalachian and the Pacific Crest trails the first two National Scenic Trails.

Meanwhile, in California, the Forest Service in 1965 had held a series of meetings about a route for the PCT in the state. These meetings involved people from the Forest Service, the Park Service, the State Division of Parks and Beaches, and other government bodies charged with responsibility over areas where the trail might go. These people decided that so much time had elapsed since Clarke had drawn his route that they should essentially start all over. Of course, it was pretty obvious that segments like the John Muir Trail would not be overlooked in choosing a new route through California. By the end of 1965 a proposed route had been drawn onto maps. (We don't say "mapped," for that would imply that someone actually had covered the route in the field.)

When Congress, in the 1968 law, created a citizens Advisory Council for the PCT, it was the route devised in 1965 which the Forest Service presented to the council as a "first draft" of a final PCT route. This body of citizens was to decide all the details of the final route; the Forest Service said it would adopt whatever the citizens wanted. The Advisory Council was also to concern itself with standards for the physical nature of the trail, markers to be erected along the trail, and the administration of the trail and its use.

In 1972 the Advisory Council agreed upon a route, and the Forest Service put it onto maps for internal use. Since much of the agreed-upon route in California, southern Oregon and southern Washington was cross-country, these maps were sent to the various national forests along the route, for them to mark a temporary route in the places where no trail existed along the final PCT route. This they did—but not always after field work. The result was that the maps made available to the public in June 1972 showing the final proposed route and the temporary detours did not correspond to what was on the ground in many places. A common flaw was that the Forest Service showed a temporary or permanent PCT segment following a trail taken off a pre-existing Forest Service map when in fact there *was no trail* where it was shown on that map in the first place.

Perfect or not, the final proposed route was sent to Washington for publication in the Federal Register, the next step toward its becoming official. A verbal description of the route was also published in the Federal Register on January 30, 1973. But the material in the register did not give a center line which could be precisely and unambiguously followed; it was only a *route,* and the details in many places remained to be settled. Furthermore, much private land along the route remained to be acquired, or at least an easement secured for using it.

A portion of the Federal Register describing the PCT is reproduced below together with one of the register's PCT maps.

OREGON

At the south end of the Bridge of the Gods is the community of Cascade Locks, elevation 100 feet. This is the lowest elevation on the Pacific Crest Trail between the Canadian border and the Mexican border. A quarter of a mile south of the Bridge of the Gods, the Trail enters the Mt. Hood National Forest and ascends the rugged south side of the Columbia Gorge and quickly attains an elevation of 4,000 feet on Benson Plateau. It continues south, past Chinidere Mountain and Wahtum Lake, traversing the slopes high above Eagle Creek, the West Fork of Hood River and Lost Lake. The Trail then descends gently into Lolo Pass, crosses Forest Road N12 and ascends Bald Mountain where it is joined by Timberline Trail on Mt. Hood. Traversing Mt. Hood, the Trail then descends into the Muddy Fork, passes beneath Ramona Falls, and crosses the main fork of the Sandy River. Two miles south of the Sandy River, the Trail enters Mt. Hood Wilderness near Paradise Park at an elevation of 6,000 feet. It descends and crosses Zigzag Canyon, leaves the Mt. Hood Wilderness, and turns easterly to regain 1,000 feet in elevation and crosses just north of Timberline Lodge and the Mt. Hood Ski Area. It

At the time of the Register's publication, the Pacific Crest Trail was more or less continuous from Canada's Manning Park to Highway 140 near Lake of the Woods in southern Oregon. However, southwest from that highway, the 73-mile PCT route to the California border was *entirely* along roads. (Before the Register's publication of a route, the PCT route coincided with the old Oregon Skyline route, which headed south 40 miles from Highway 140 near Lake of the Woods over to the California border. Only 5 miles of trail existed along this older route.)

Of great importance, then, was the construction of PCT to replace the 73-mile temporary route. In 1973 the PCT in the southern Sky Lakes Area was relocated so that it ended on Highway 140 near Fish Lake. Then, from 1974 until 1978, the trail was built southwest toward Interstate 5. During this time, another stretch of trail was built northeast from Seiad Valley toward Interstate 5. However, as late as 1985 private property stood in the way, and 3½ miles of route were still along roads.

Likewise, private property prevented the PCT in Washington from extending its last few miles south to the Columbia River. Its predecessor, the Cascade Crest Trail, had in fact been completed to the river in 1935, seven years after work on it had begun. However, that old trail ended 12½ miles east of a suitable river crossing, namely, the Bridge of the Gods. Likewise, the Oregon Skyline Trail ended not at a river crossing but rather at a trailhead 3 miles east of the bridge. An Oregon route to that bridge was built in 1974, but its Washington counterpart, across lands outside the National Forest, was not completed until 1984. This Washington stretch, making a roundabout route, takes 44 miles to reach Big Huckleberry Mountain; the old Cascade Crest Trail reached it in 20½ miles.

During the 1970s the existing PCT also underwent changes. In May 1971 the Forest Service produced a *Pacific Crest Trail Guide for Location, Design, and Management*,

Trail specifications, steep slope (from F. S. *PCT Guide*)

NATURAL GROUND

48"

30"

TRAIL BED

30"

24"

TREAD

Steep side slope providing horse pack clearance

which stipulated specific characteristics of the final trail. Perhaps the two most significant ones were that the trail should stay close to the crest and that its grade should not exceed 15 percent (a 15-foot rise for 100 horizontal feet). The old Cascade Crest and Oregon Skyline trails veered away from the crest in places, and in many places they were too steep.

In order to reduce the steepness, the trail had to either go around ridges rather than over them, or else it had to have switchbacks added to reduce the grade. Both changes led to increases in the PCT's overall length. The best example of such lengthening is along a stretch from Highway 138 north past Mt. Thielsen to Windigo Pass. Originally 24½ miles long, it was stretched to 30¼ miles by 1977, an increase of 23 percent. North of Windigo Pass a new section of PCT was built because the old Oregon Skyline Trail veered too far east from the crest. This change also increased the overall PCT route length, replacing a 21-mile stretch with a winding, 30½-mile one, an increase of 45 percent! However, not all realignments are longer. For example, in the Goat Rocks Wilderness, minor trail relocations in 1974 and 1978 both led to a small reduction of the PCT's length, as did a relocation in the northern Sky Lakes Wilderness.

The PCT has also been relocated to avoid wet areas. One such area that gave hikers mosquito bites and muddy boots was a short stretch south from southern Washington's Sawtooth Huckleberry Field. The trail was rerouted along slopes above the area's boggy flats.

Publicity about the PCT, especially through Eric Ryback's popular, if inaccurate account, inspired new waves of backpackers to trek along the route. Some parts of the route, however, were overused, and therefore had to be relocated. One such area was the Twin Lakes area, just north of Oregon's Wapinitia Pass. In Crater Lake National Park, a trail stretch was relocated for a similar reason. The Park's most scenic stretch crossed the Pumice Desert and gave the hiker views of both the Crater Lake rim and Mt. Thielsen. Decision makers, however, felt that hordes of hikers would trample the "desert's" fragile wildflowers into ruin—not very likely. Right or wrong, they relocated the trail to conform with the rest of the park's PCT—an essentially viewless, mosquito-infested traverse through a lodgepole forest.

To the consternation of PCT hikers, the decision makers did *not* relocate the stretch of Crater Lake PCT that circumvents Crater Lake. This route, along abandoned roads, stays several miles away from the lake's view-packed rim, and therefore backpackers rarely take it. Surely, if any stretch of PCT deserves to be relocated, it is this stretch, which should be rebuilt so that it *at least* touches or approaches the rim in several places.

After new sections of the PCT were built and many others rebuilt or relocated, the Forest Service turned its attention to trailhead parking lots. Most PCT hikers, after all, do short stretches such as the 12 sections (A–L) found in this book and virtually all of them park their cars near the PCT. In 1977 and '78, the Forest Service constructed several large lots, just off the PCT and major roads, to fill the need. In the 1980s, most work was in the form of new trail construction in southern California. We hope the PCT will be completed, so it exists as one continuous filament threading its way along the tops of mountain ranges from Mexico to Canada.

The trail's place in history is certainly minor when compared with today's world events, but generations from now, future historians may ponder its significance. During the middle of the 19th century, pioneer trails were blazed across the continent to open up new lands and resources for a growing, young America. About a century later, trails of another kind appeared, which we now call National Scenic Trails. These are about as long as the pioneer trails, but unlike them, they serve no economic purpose. At trail's end no fertile valleys, no gold mines, no thriving ports are reached. The Pacific Crest Trail, like the other National Scenic Trails, is not a corridor to an economic end but rather is a process for individual change and growth. Although the trail's end is a desirable goal, it is not a necessary one, for the traveler is enriched in a nonmaterial sense with every step he takes along the way. Clinton Clarke saw the trail as a way to "lead people back to a simpler and more natural life and arouse a love for nature and the outdoors." The trail, then, is a prescription to improve one's understanding of his place in the world. In a way, the trail is like a Norman Rockwell painting. This illustrator painted American land and life not as it was, but rather, as it *should* have been. So, too, the Pacific Crest Trail paints impressions on the hiker's mind, not of a world ravaged by man, but rather of a timeless, largely forgotten world where nature still exists as it was meant to be.

A trail-location drawing (from F.S. *PCT Guide*)

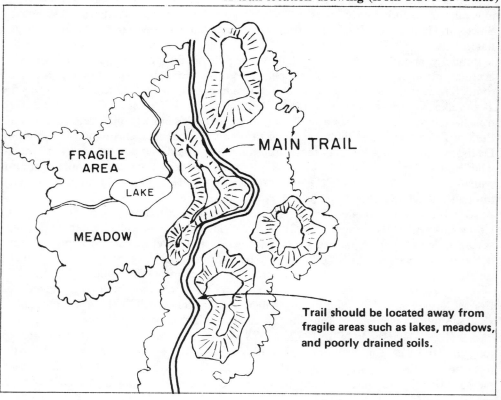

FRAGILE AREA

LAKE

MEADOW

MAIN TRAIL

Trail should be located away from fragile areas such as lakes, meadows, and poorly drained soils.

Chapter 2: Planning Your PCT Hike

What to Expect

Of the thousands of backpackers who will taste wilderness along the Pacific Crest Trail each year, probably a hundred or less will complete the Oregon-Washington section and a few dozen will complete the entire tri-state route. Several hundred may hike either all of Oregon, which takes about 3½ weeks to hike, or all of Washington which, being more rugged, takes a few days more. Probably the vast majority of the trail's travelers will confine their wilderness visit to two weeks or less and therefore will be able to carry all their needs on their backs without having to use resupply points. This guidebook divides the Oregon-Washington PCT into 12 convenient backpack trips (Sections A through L), each starting and ending at a highway. The shortest trip, Section B, is usually done in 2½ to 4 days, while the longest ones, Sections H and K, are usually done in 6 to 12 days.

Some readers will walk the whole trail, Mexico to Canada. This takes 5–6 months to complete if you do 14–17 miles per day *nonstop*. Since most long-distance PCT hikers take layover days and also short side trips to supply points, they usually have to average about 20 miles per day when hiking along the trail. In past editions, we said that we hoped some readers would walk the whole trail in one long season. Some did and some more certainly will. However, for several reasons, we no longer recommend it. Hiking 20 miles a day, you'll be too exhausted to appreciate the scenery. Also, during the first two months and the last month, you are likely to encounter plenty of bad weather, lots of snow-covered ground, or both. These detract from your enjoyment of the scenery as well as impede your progress. Finally, the human body was not meant to carry heavy packs continuously over a rugged 2600-mile distance, and some hikers attempting this feat developed serious bone and ligament problems in their feet and legs.

Those still determined to hike the entire PCT continuously should start in early May (or sooner, if the Sierra Nevada snowpack has been light). The California section takes expert hikers about three months. You should try to complete the hottest part, south of the *southern* Sierra Nevada, by early June. However, you won't want to get into the High Sierra too early, for bad storms occurring as late as mid-June can bring your progress to a halt—or worse. If you're on schedule, you should cross into Oregon in early August and pass through the Sky Lakes Wilderness and the southern Three Sisters Wilderness in mid-to-late August. If you pass through these areas before late July, their seasonally superabundant mosquitoes will drive you almost insane. Perhaps by Labor Day your labor of wilderness love will be celebrated with your entry into Washington. One month later you should hope to consummate your hike, probably under the threat of rapidly deteriorating weather, in British Columbia's Ernest C. Manning Provincial Park.

If you are planning a short stretch and expect to encounter snow, hike from south to north. This way you'll encounter more downhill snow slopes than uphill ones, since snow lingers longer on north slopes—the ones you'll be descending. It's more fun to slide down a snowbank than to climb up one.

If the Cascade Range in Oregon and Washington were a uniform, continuous range, you could expect the snowpack to retreat uniformly northward as the summer wore on, and you could plan a month-long trek north so that you would always have a dry trail yet always have an adequate water source. However, this plan could have an undesired effect if you began at the height of the mosquito season: you'd have a continuous cloud of mosquitoes accompanying you north. The Cascade Range, however, is far from uniform, and often you will find yourself descending a snowbound pass into a warm, soothing, lake-dotted basin. If you are hiking the entire PCT, you are bound to encounter both pleasant and adverse trail conditions. If you want to avoid snow-clad trails, incessant mosquitoes and severe water shortages, then hike the following segments at these recommended times (remembering, of course, that weather patterns vary considerably from year to year).

Seiad Valley, Siskiyou Mountains, southern Oregon: *June through mid-September*
Mt. McLoughlin, Sky Lakes basin, Seven Lakes basin: *mid-July through late August*
Crater Lake: *July*
Mt. Thielsen, Windigo Pass, Diamond Peak: *mid-July through late August*
Three Sisters: *late July through early August*
Mt. Washington, Three Fingered Jack: *late June through mid-July*
Mt. Hood: *late July through mid-August*
Columbia River gorge, southern Washington: *mid-June through early September*
Mt. Adams, Goat Rocks, White Pass, Mt. Rainier, Stampede Pass, Snoqualmie Pass, Stevens Pass: *mid-July through mid-August*
Glacier Peak, North Cascades, Manning Provincial Park: *late July through early August.*

There are, of course, advantages and disadvantages to hiking in any season. In the North Cascades, for example,

- early June will present you with spectacular snow-clad alpine scenery—but also soft-snow walking and a slight avalanche hazard;
- early July will present you with a riotous display of wildflowers—plus sucking mosquitoes and biting flies;
- early August will present you with the best trail conditions—and lots of backpackers;
- early September will present you with fall colors and ripe huckleberries—but also nippy nights and sudden snow storms.

Weather

With the foregoing information plus a scan through the introduction of each of this guide's 12 hiking chapters, you should be forming in your mind a vague idea of where and how long you expect to hike. Let's sharpen that idea by looking at the weather. The warmest temperatures are in mid-July through early August; they can vary from the 90s in southern Oregon to the 70s in the North Cascades. During this period night temperatures for the entire two-state route are usually in the 40s, but at times can be in the 50s or the 30s, and occasionally in the 20s.

In late June, with its long daylight hours, the maximum and minimum temperatures are almost as high as those in midsummer. In addition, you can expect to be plagued with mosquitoes through early August. A *tent is a necessity*—preferably one large enough for you and your friends to prepare meals in. During these warm summer nights, you'll want to sleep *atop* your sleeping bag, and although the mosquitos abate somewhat after dark, without a tent you won't get a mosquito-free sleep until later on in the season when the nights are cooler. Only when the wind picks up (late morning through late afternoon) or when a storm sets in are you afforded partial relief from these cursed insects. In Washington you will also be exposed to at least three species of biting flies—Ouch! But they are slower and easier to swat.

By late August the days have got considerably shorter and the temperatures lower. The evenings and nights in southern Oregon are comfortable but those in northern Washington are nippy, if not freezing. Expect to see morning frost on your tent and prepare for brisk, "autumn" days. Too, there's likely to be a water shortage, particularly in most of Oregon. The national forests may be closed to backpacking or they may require the backpacker to refrain from building campfires and use only a stove. A stove is also useful for boiling stagnant water and for melting snow. An advantage of a hike at this time, however, is that both Oregon and Washington will have a variety of berries ready for picking.

Another consideration is storms. Storm frequency increases northward. Northern California is virtually storm-free from mid-June through early September. In central Oregon the period of good weather is only July through August, and even then occasional storms may be expected. If you visit southern Washington, be prepared for bad weather, even though you might get to hike a week or two at a time in beautiful midsummer weather. Expect bad or threatening weather in northern Washington. It is possible to hike two solid weeks in the North Cascades without receiving a drop of precipitation, but don't count on it—you might just receive a month of rain, as hikers did in the summer of 1978. Here, a tent is necessary to keep out the rain as well as as to keep out the seasonal mosquitoes and flies.

Like storm frequency, lake temperature is influenced by the sun's apparent seasonal migratory pattern. Lakes are generally at their warmest in late July through early August. Also affecting a lake's temperature are its latitude, elevation, size, depth, inflow source and the side of the mountain, if any, that it is on. Below are some representative *maximum* temperatures you can expect to find at certain lakes and rivers, south to north.

Klamath River, northern California	80°F
Emigrant Lake, near Ashland	78
Margurette Lake, Sky Lakes Wilderness	75
Dumbbell Lake, Three Sisters Wilderness	73
Scout Lake, Mt. Jefferson Wilderness	67
Wahtum Lake, northern Oregon	65
Eagle Creek, Columbia River gorge	57

Columbia River	65
Shoe Lake, Goat Rocks Wilderness	65
Pear Lake, Henry M. Jackson Wilderness	63
Lake Janus, Henry M. Jackson Wilderness	72
Mica Lake, Glacier Peak Wilderness	33
Stehekin River, North Cascades National Park	50

After you decide which segment of the PCT you want to do, next comes the question of transportation. Unlike round trips and loop trips, a hike along part of the PCT does not take you back to where you started. So if you take a car and leave it at the trailhead, you have a transportation problem. The solution may be any of several:

- walk back to where you started
- take a bus back to where you started
- hitchhike back to where you started
- arrange for someone to drop you off and pick you up
- arrange with another group to meet halfway along the trail and exchange car keys, or have duplicate sets made in advance.
- take at least 2 people and 2 cars, and leave one car at each end of your trek
- take a bicycle or motorcycle in your vehicle, ride it to your trailhead, and after walking your section pick it up with your vehicle, which you left at the other trailhead.

After you have decided on a solution to the car problem, write it down and put it in your pack. You might forget if your trek is a long one.

Logistics for the Long Distance Backpacker

How can a book describe the psychological factors a person must prepare for . . . the despair, the alienation, the anxiety and especially the pain, both physical and mental, which slices to the very heart of the hiker's volition, which are the real things that must be planned for? No words can transmit those factors, which are more a part of planning than the elementary rituals of food, money and equipment, and how to get them.

—Jim Podlesney, in *Pacific Crest Trail
Hike Planning Guide,* edited by Chuck Long
(Signpost Publications)

The authors agree with that quotation. Furthermore, they do not believe a trail guide is the place for an extensive explanation of basic backpacking techniques, and in any event the PCT end-to-end is no trip for novices. However, the peculiar problems of an *expeditionary* trek do warrant a few pages.

If you are going to be on the trail for more than a couple of weeks, you will want to have supplies waiting for you at one or more places along the route. For this you can mail packages to yourself. Alternatively, you can drive to a place and leave a package with someone, if you are sure that person will be responsible for it. You can also hide caches in the wilderness, if you are willing to carry the heavy load in from the nearest road and carry all the packaging out—and if you trust the wildlife. There are a few towns near the PCT which will perhaps have adequate supplies and equipment—Ashland, Sisters, Cascade Locks, Stevenson and Chelan. However, even those towns may not have an adequate selection of lightweight backpacking food. It is best to depend on post offices. A list of post offices on or near the trail appears on page 15.

SUPPLIES

This discussion of supplies attempts to tell you what you will need, and how best to get it. The discussion relies heavily on the experiences of Ben Schifrin (co-author of Volume 1) during his hike of the entire PCT.

The first thing to know about supplies along the PCT is that they are scarce. Too many young people try to do the PCT without pre-planning their food and other supplies. So they get to a resort and find that there is no white gas, and its store is so limited that they will have to eat the same macaroni and cheese for the next five days. If one wants to go light, the *only* choice is to pre-plan your menus and the rest of your needs, and mail things ahead to yourself.

Food

The main thing to have waiting your arrival at a post office is food. When hiking long-distance on the PCT, food is the main concern. It causes more daydreaming and more bickering than anything else, even sex. As for the bickering, most people hike in groups, and much of the friction in a group is due to different eating habits. Some hikers don't eat breakfast; others won't hike an inch until they've had their steak and eggs. Some people eat every hour; others take the traditional three meal breaks. Many of these problems can be cured if each hiker carries his own food, and suits his own prejudices. This arrangement also allows flexibility in pace and in hiking partners.

As for the daydreaming, it comes to focus on delicious food, and lots of it. Schifrin's first rule is that it won't hurt to take too much, because it will turn out to be too little anyway. He and his two companions ate over 6000 calories a day out of their packs, and still lost weight. The mental stresses, as well as the obvious physical ones, use up energy. So food serves two purposes: to provide fuel, and to bolster morale. Take the things you crave. Most goodies—Hershey bars, beer, double fudgies, fresh cheese, mint cakes—are great energy sources, as well as providing variety and what Schifrin calls a "body con". At the bottom of some horrible ascent, you say to yourself, "You get a double helping of Hershey bar when you get to the top." It's something to sweat for.

Then there's the usual egregious gluttony upon reaching a town (which are so scarce along the Oregon-Washington PCT)—steaks, quarts of ice cream, gallons of chocolate milk, giant shrimp salads. Besides being good for morale and filling you up, these binges can give you a good idea of what's been missing from your diet, namely, whatever you craved and stuffed yourself on. For the next trail segment, correct the deficiency, insofar as you can. And for the whole trek, take a supply of multivitamin pills, just in case your diet is deficient in important vitamins.

The only time people told Schifrin they had brought too much food was when they thought they had brought too much of a *certain item*. One attractive young lady carried only soybeans and powdered milk. She made it—but only after she'd stopped at each ranger station along the route for a few days, and made it with the ranger in exchange for palatable food. Two men, carrying soybeans and something else unpalatably organic, got so sick of this menu that they ripped off a ranger station. (They didn't finish the trail; the ranger caught them two days later, and they went to jail.)

Other hikers seem to think that wild foods are theirs for the taking. Berries—huckleberries in particular—certainly are, but they won't sustain you. Remember that Indians spent most of their waking hours in search of foodstuffs, not just an hour a day.

Besides, if hikers gorged themselves at every berry patch, there would be that much less for other hikers and the wild animals. Sample the berries, don't feast on them. Similarly with trout: don't plan to live off trout—they may not be biting during the time you have free to devote to fishing. View a fresh catch as a bonus, not an essential.

You won't have to rely on "Mother Nature" in Oregon or Washington since, if you're an "average" long-distance PCT hiker, you'll never have to carry more than an 8-day food supply, even on the longest stretches between supply points. Therefore, with careful shopping, you can buy all the food you'll need at your local supermarket rather than buy expensive freeze-dried food. (In California's John Muir Trail section of the PCT, lightweight freeze-dried food is a *must*.) Freeze-dried food, despite its high cost, is preferred by some hikers since, in the Oregon-Washington PCT, using it can cut your pack's weight by 5–15 pounds, depending on how much food you typically eat and how far you are going to hike.

Regardless of whether you carry regular or lightweight food, you will most likely want a balance between cold and hot foods. Cold foods are of course more appropriate for lunch, though we meet hikers who go 100 miles without cooking. Some people refuse to face the dawn without hot drinks. Those who dispense with hot foods to save weight and time may suffer mentally on a freezing evening in the North Cascades. Variety is the key. No matter how much time you spend planning your food, however, you are sure to be dissatisfied, somewhere down the trail, with what you brought or with how much of it you brought. You may find that eventually all freeze-dried dinners taste the same to you. You may find that you can never get a full feeling. You may lose 30 pounds. Or you may find that you brought too much. Just be prepared for such things to happen. Fortunately, you are not totally locked into your planned menus. You can mail back—or abandon—what you can't stand, and buy something else at towns and resorts along the way—although it will not be cheap in such places. You can even ask your contact at home to buy some new food items and mail them to you.

In planning menus, remember that at 5000' elevation, cooking time is double what it is at sea level, and at 7,500' it is triple. So don't bring foods that take long to cook at sea level.

Wood won't always be available, and if you are hiking 15+ miles a day, you'll find neither the time nor the energy to gather wood and start a fire. Anyway, wood is getting too scarce to use, due to the large number of backpackers, so we strongly recommend you bring a stove instead. You should know the rate at which your stove consumes fuel, for you will need lots of it if you do the whole PCT. Cartridge stoves, such as the Bleuet, do not burn as hot as white-gas stoves, particularly when the cartridge is low on fuel, but they do have several advantages: they are very easy to start, and virtually foolproof, and you can mail propane cartridges whereas you can't mail white gas. (Unleaded gasoline, purchased at gas stations, works adequately in white-gas stoves, but be ready for more clogging and shorter stove life.)

Water

Usually you can hike most stretches of the PCT carrying no more than a quart of water. But is it safe to drink? Clear lakes and streams may contain *Giardia lamblia,* a microscopic organism that causes giardiasis. While this disease is usually not life-threatening, it can make you feel absolutely rotten, with diarrhea, cramps, gas and the like. You can guard against giardiasis and similar diseases by boiling your water for 3–5 minutes, although this is time-consuming and can use a lot of fuel. Iodine tablets are easier to carry, but may not be 100% effective. Schaffer doesn't like hot water *or* iodine-tasting water, so he uses a water-filtering device, and it has worked—so far.

Clothing

In planning what clothes to take, realize that rain, and sometimes snow, is possible at any time at any point along the Oregon-Washington PCT. Therefore have good protection against wet and cold, whatever it costs. Remember that cotton clothing is useless when wet. Play it safe and assume there will be a storm. Bring along appropriate clothing and *know* how to keep it—and your sleeping bag—dry.

Boots are the most important piece of clothing. They must be broken in before the trip. Otherwise, they may turn out not to fit, and they will surely give you a crop of blisters. For the entire PCT, it's best to have two pairs of boots in the same size and same style. Mail one pair ahead. Schifrin broke his foot because his two pair were of two different styles, and one pair didn't give his feet the support the other pair had accustomed them to. You might go all the way on just one pair, after one or two resolings, but if you try to make the entire PCT through the North Cascades with the boots you started with, you will be sticking your neck out—and maybe your toes. Treat the boots with Snoseal or another effective compound often, to keep them waterproof and to prevent cracking from heat.

It may not occur to you in advance how tough walking will be on your socks too. One PCT trekker said he wore out one pair every 125 miles on the average, though we think that's a little extreme. Still, you will need replacements. You might start out with a three-day supply of socks—three pairs of heavy wool socks and three (or six, if you wear double inners) pairs of inner socks (polypropylene is preferable). Schaffer has gone 1000+ miles with this combination. If you hope to equal that, you must change socks daily and wash them daily. Note also that clean socks are less likely to give you blisters.

Besides boot soles and socks, you are going to wear out some underwear, shirts and, probably, pants. The less often you wash them, the faster they will wear out, due to rotting. In choosing your clothes to start with, remember that as you hike your waist will get smaller and legs bigger.

Light footwear is very nice to have for fording streams and for comfort in camp. It's damn near heaven to take off those 5-pound boots after a 20-mile day. Tennis shoes are traditional, but gymnastic slippers work almost as well around camp (not in streams), and they weigh only a few ounces. SCUBA diving booties may be the best of the three: they wear well, can be worn in bed, don't absorb water, have great traction, are warmer than down booties, can be worn inside your boots, and can even keep your socks dry in stream fords. But they don't breathe, so wear them with clean feet and socks.

Equipment

Spare no expense. Mistakes and shortcuts in equipment mean lost time, lost money, lost sleep and lost health.

Besides your usual summer backpacking equipment, you may need a tent, skis or snowshoes, an ice ax and a rope. You will need a guidebook with maps—this one. And even if you don't normally carry a camera, PCT trekkers say you'll be sorry if you don't take one on the BIG hike.

Almost all PCT hikers carry a *tent,* and are glad they did. A tent is important for warmth in the snowy parts, and for dryness in all the parts. In Oregon, a tent allows you to sleep by keeping the mosquitoes off you. We recommend a quality 2-man mountain tent—on the large side, or you and your companion may become less than friends.

The question of *skis* versus *snowshoes* for early season in the high mountains remains under debate, and some PCT hikers say they'd rather take their chances without either, considering the cost and the weight. The main advantage of skis, of course, is that you can cover a lot of ground downhill in a hurry—if you know how to ski with a pack. We suspect many of the trekkers who chose snowshoes would have used skis if they had been better cross-country-with-pack skiers. The main disadvantage of skis is that you can't mail them; you have to ship them by Greyhound or some other way.

Many PCT through hikers say an *ice ax* is definitely a necessity, and others say it is at least worth its weight for the many different things it will do. We recommend one for any segment where you expect to be in snow. You should take a *rope* for belaying on steep snow or on ice, and for difficult fords at the height of the snowmelt.

Few hikers are satisfied with the pictures from an "instant" *camera.* We recommend a 35 mm single-lens reflex camera, the best you can afford, and a zoom lens, one that ranges from wide-angle (about 28–35 mm) to short-telephoto (about 90–105 mm). With such a lens you'll be able to capture most of your shots. For the far-away shots, use a teleconverter (either 2x or 3x). Make sure both the zoom lens and the lightweight teleconverter are of high quality, or else you won't be pleased with the quality of your photos. Finally, get a polarizing filter, which reduces haziness, darkens the sky and removes unwanted reflections, such as shimmering lake surfaces. Using a telephoto lens, a teleconverter and a filter all require a fairly "fast" film, as do low-light shots, such as those dramatic sunrises and sunsets every trekker hopes to see. Schaffer prefers films in the ASA 200 range. Films of ASA 100 or less can be too slow, and ASA 400 or more, too grainy.

The cost

You can expect to spend several thousand *dollars* for the whole PCT unless you already have almost all the equipment you will need. Take plenty of money in traveler's checks. You won't be able to resist the food when you are in civilization, and you will find yourself with unforeseen needs for equipment. In addition, you will want to be able to correct some original decisions that you have later found unwise or unworkable, and to do so usually takes money.

MAILING TIPS

You can mail yourself almost any food, clothing or equipment. Before you leave home, you won't know whether you are going to run out of, say, molefoam, but you will have a good idea of your rate of consumption of food, clothing, and fuel for your stove. You can arrange for mailings of quantities of these things, purchased at home, where they are probably cheaper than in the towns along the way.

Address your package to:
>Yourself
>General Delivery
>P.O., state ZIP
>HOLD UNTIL (date)

Also, **boldly** write somewhere on the package: Pacific Crest Trail Hiker. Don't mail perishables. Make your packages strong, sturdy and tight. You are *really* depending on their contents. Have your home contact mail packages at least 24 days before you expect to get them, and even then, pay for the postal service called "Special Handling." Do not seal the packages when you pack them, because you are likely to have second thoughts. You can then write your mail contact and ask him to add certain things to (or take certain things out of) the box that goes to X place, or wherever. Before you leave home, phone the post offices you will be sending mail to, to make sure they will hold your mail for your arrival. They are legally required to hold it only 10 days. Also find out what hours they are open. Remember that if you change your plan, you can pick up a package at a post office and mail some or all of its contents to yourself farther along the route—or you can mail it home.

Post Offices Along or Near the Route
South to North

*= recommended for use
Some stations are seasonal, so check in advance if you're not hiking the PCT from mid-June through mid-September. The best pickup time is weekdays 1–4 p.m.; for ranger stations it is weekday evenings. Typical hours for town post offices are 9–12 and 1–5, Monday through Friday. See appropriate hiking sections for location of each.

*Seiad Valley, CA 96086
*Ashland, OR 97520

*Hyatt Lake Resort
   P.O. Box 447
   Ashland, OR 97520

*Fish Lake Resort
   P.O. Box 40
   Medford, OR 97501

Lake of the Woods Resort, OR 97603
*Crater Lake National Park, OR 97604
*Diamond Lake Lodge, OR 97731
*Cascade Summit, OR 97425
Sisters, OR 97759

*Olallie Lake Ranger Station
   c/o Clackamas Ranger District
   61431 East Highway 224
   Estacada, OR 97023
   (Not a post office, but its rangers will
   hold packages from about mid-June
   through late September.)

Government Camp, OR 97028
*Cascade Locks, OR 97014
Stevenson, WA 98648
Carson, WA 98610
*White Pass Rural Branch
   Naches, WA 98937
Crystal Mountain, WA 98022
*Snoqualmie Pass, WA 98068
Skykomish, WA 98288
*Stehekin, WA 98852
Chelan, WA 98816
   (An enjoyable 46-mile ferry-boat ride
   from Stehekin resort to this small city.)
Manning Provincial Park
   British Columbia V0X 1R0
   (Its post office is located at the park's
   East Gate, which is 10 miles northeast
   from the PCT trailhead. Write the park
   for information, if you want to, but don't
   mail parcels to their out-of-the-way post
   office.)

Hypothermia

Every year you can read accounts of hikers freezing to death in the mountains. They die of hypothermia, the #1 killer of outdoor recreationists. You too may be exposed to it, particularly if you start hiking the PCT in April in order to do all three states. Because it is so easy to die from hypothermia, we are including the following information, which is endorsed by the Forest Service and by mountain-rescue groups. Read it. It may save your life.

Hypothermia is subnormal body temperature, which is caused outdoors by exposure to cold, usually aggravated by wetness, wind and exhaustion. The moment your body begins to lose heat faster than it produces it, your body makes involuntary adjustments to preserve the normal temperature in its vital organs. Uncontrolled shivering is one way your body attempts to maintain its vital temperature. *If you've begun uncontrolled shivering, you have hypothermia and must act accordingly: seek shelter, insulation and warmth.* Shivering will eventually consume your energy reserves until they are exhausted. When this happens, cold reaches your brain, depriving you of judgment and reasoning power. You will not realize this is happening. You will lose control of your hands. Your internal body temperature is sliding downward. Without treatment, this slide leads to stupor, collapse and death. Learn the four lines of defense against hypothermia.

Your first line of defense: avoid exposure.

1. *Stay dry.* When clothes get wet, they can lose about 90% of their insulating value. Wool loses less; cotton and down lose more. Synthetics are best.

2. *Beware of the wind.* A slight breeze carries heat away from bare skin much faster than still air does. Wind drives cold air under and through clothing. Wind refrigerates wet clothes by evaporating moisture from the surface.

Hypothermia weather moving in, Glacier Peak Wilderness. Particularly in the North Cascades, you can experience day after day of cold, drizzly rain.

3. *Understand cold.* Most hypothermia cases develop in air temperatures between 30 and 50 degrees. Most outdoorsmen simply can't believe such temperatures can be dangerous. They fatally underestimate the danger of being wet at such temperatures. But just jump in a cold lakelet and you'll agree that 50° water is unbearably cold. The cold that kills is cold water running down neck and legs, cold water held against the body by sopping clothes, cold water flushing body heat from the surfaces of the clothes.

Your second line of defense: terminate exposure.
If you cannot stay dry and warm under existing weather conditions, using the clothes you have with you, *terminate exposure.*

1. *Be brave enough* to give up reaching your destination or whatever you had in mind. That one extra mile might be your last.

2. *Get out of the wind and rain.* Build a fire. Concentrate on making your camp or bivouac as secure and comfortable as possible.

3. *Never ignore shivering.* Persistent or violent shivering is clear warning that you are on the verge of hypothermia. *Make camp.*

4. *Forestall exhaustion.* Make camp while you still have a reserve of energy. Allow for the fact that exposure greatly reduces your normal endurance. You may think you are doing fine when the fact that you are exercising is the only thing preventing your going into hypothermia. If exhaustion forces you to stop, however briefly, your rate of body heat production instantly drops by 50% or more; violent, incapacitating shivering may begin immediately; you may slip into hypothermia *in a matter of minutes.*

5. *Appoint a foul-weather leader.* Make the best-protected member of your party responsible for calling a halt before the least-protected member becomes exhausted or goes into violent shivering.

Your third line of defense: detect hypothermia.
If your party is exposed to wind, cold and wetness, *think hypothermia.* Watch yourself and others for hypothermia's symptoms:
1. Uncontrollable fits of shivering.
2. Vague, slow, slurred speech.
3. Memory lapses; incoherence.
4. Immobile, fumbling hands.
5. Frequent stumbling; lurching gait.
6. Drowsiness—to sleep is to die.
7. Apparent exhaustion, such as inability to get up after a rest.

Your fourth and last line of defense: treatment.
The victim may deny he's in trouble. Believe the symptoms, *not* the patient. Even mild symptoms demand immediate drastic treatment.
1. Get the victim out of the wind and rain.
2. Strip off *all* wet clothes.
3. If the patient is only mildly impaired:
   a. Give him warm drinks.
   b. Get him into dry clothes and a warm sleeping bag. Well-wrapped, warm (not hot) rocks or canteens will hasten recovery.

4. If the patient is semiconscious or worse:
   a. Try to keep him awake. Do not give warm drinks.
   b. Leave him stripped. Put him in a sleeping bag with another person (also stripped). If you have a double bag or can zip two together, put the victim between two warmth donors. *Skin to skin contact* is the most effective treatment. Never leave the victim as long as he is alive. To do so is to kill him—it's just that simple!
5. Build a fire to warm the camp.

Other notes on avoiding hypothermia.
   1. Choose rainclothes that are effective against *wind-driven* rain and cover head, neck, body and legs. Gore-Tex and other PTFE laminates are best, but won't last as long as some other materials.
   2. Take woolen clothing for possible hypothermia weather, such as a two-piece woolen underwear set or long wool pants and sweater or shirt. Include a knit wool cap that can protect neck and chin. Cotton underwear is *worse than useless* when wet, as are cotton shirts and pants. As native Americans long ago discovered, one stays warmer in a cold rain when he is stark naked than when he is bundled up in wet clothes. Some folks in the drippy North Cascade forests carry umbrellas.
   3. Carry a stormproof tent with a good rain fly and set it up *before* you need it.
   4. Carry trail food rich in calories, such as nuts, jerky and candy, and keep nibbling during hypothermia weather.
   5. Take a gas stove or a plumber's candle, flammable paste or other reliable fire starter.
   6. Never abandon survival gear under any circumstances. If you didn't bring along the above items, stay put and make the best of it. An all-too-common fatal mistake is for victims to abandon everything so that, unburdened, they can run for help.
   7. "It never happens to me. I'm Joe Athlete." Not always is it the other guy on the trail. It can be you even if you are in fantastic shape and are carrying the proper equipment. Be alert for hypothermia conditions and hypothermia symptoms.

Outdoor Courtesy

Traveling a wild trail, away from centers of civilization, is a unique experience. It brings intimate association with nature—communion with the earth, the forest, the chaparral, the wildlife, the clear sky. A great responsibility accompanies this experience—the obligation to keep the wilderness as you found it. Being considerate of the wilderness rights of others will make the mountain adventures of those who follow equally rewarding.

As a wilderness visitor, you should become familiar with the rules of wilderness courtesy outlined below.

Trails

Never cut switchbacks. This practice breaks down trails and hastens erosion. Take care not to dislodge rocks that might fall on hikers below you. Improve and preserve trails, as by clearing away loose rocks (carefully) and removing branches. Report any trail damage and broken or misplaced signs to a ranger.

Off trail

Restrain the impulse to blaze trees or to build ducks where not essential. Let the next fellow find his way as you did.

Campgrounds

Spread your gear in an already cleared area, and build your fire in a campground stove. Don't disarrange the camp by making hard-to-eradicate ramparts of rock for fireplaces or windbreaks. Rig tents and tarps with line tied to rocks or trees; never put nails in trees. For your campfire, if you must build one, use fallen wood only; do not cut standing trees nor break off branches. Use the campground latrine. Place litter in the litter can or carry it out. Leave the campground cleaner than you found it.

Fire

Fire is a great danger in the mountains; act accordingly. Smoke only in cleared areas along the trail where a sign authorizes it. Report a mountain fire immediately.

Litter

Along the trail, place candy wrappers, raisin boxes, orange peels, etc. in your pocket or pack for later disposal; throw nothing on the trail. Pick up litter you find along the trail or in camp. More than almost anything else, litter detracts from the wilderness scene. Remember, you *can* take it with you.

Noise

Boisterous conduct is out of harmony in a wilderness experience. Be a considerate hiker and camper. Don't ruin another's enjoyment of the wilderness.

Good Samaritanship

Human life and well-being take precedence over everything else—in the wilderness as elsewhere. If a hiker or camper is in trouble, help in any way you can. Indifference is a moral crime. Give comfort or first aid; then hurry to a ranger station for help.

Land-use Regulations

The Oregon-Washington PCT passes through national parks, national forests, Indian land, land administered by the Bureau of Land Management, state land and private land. All these areas have their own regulations, which you ignore only at your risk—risk of physical difficulty as well as possibility of being cited for violations.

On private land, of course, the regulations are what the owner says they are. The same is true on Indian land. In particular, don't build a fire on private land without the owner's written permission. Regulations on U.S. Bureau of Land Management land are not of major consequence for users of this book, since the route passes through only a few miles of it, in Section B. The same is true of state land, in southernmost Washington.

The Forest Service and the Park Service, for good reason, have more regulations. These are not uniform throughout the states, or between the two services. We list below the Forest Service and Park Service regulations that *are* uniform along the trail, plus some that are peculiar to the Park Service. Special regulations in particular places are mentioned in the trail description when it "arrives" at the place.

1. For about a decade *wilderness permits* were required to enter any official wilderness in either Oregon or Washington, but this requirement was dropped by late 1985. Today the only places you'll need a wilderness permit are in the national parks: Crater Lake (Section C), Mt. Rainier (Section I) and North Cascades (Section K). Permits are needed *only* if you will be camping overnight in the backcountry; they aren't needed for day use. Mt. Rainier National Park requires permits only from June 15 through September 30; the other two parks require permits year-round. Personnel at all three parks would like you to pick up a permit in person, which can be very inconvenient. However, they realize the PCT trekker's predicament, and will accept written requests. For North Cascades National Park don't write to the park headquarters but rather to the Skagit District Office, Marblemount, WA 98267.

2. *Campfire permits* also used to be required, but no longer are. Both the Forest Service and the National Park Service discourage campfires and ask that you carry a stove instead. In Mt. Rainier National Park campfires are prohibited at all but the park's lowest backcountry sites, so plan to bring a stove. Except for emergencies you shouldn't make a campfire anywhere along the PCT, since downed wood hosts organisms on which larger animals feed, and as the wood decays, it adds nutrients to the soil.

3. *A fishing license* is required in Oregon for those 14 or older and in Washington for those 15 and older. Both states have a variety of fishing licenses (and fees), based on your age, state of residency and length of fishing excursion. For further information, contact:

> Oregon Department of Fish and Wildlife
> 506 S.W. Mill Street—P.O. Box 59
> Portland, OR 97207
> (503) 229-5551

> or

> Washington Department of Game
> 600 North Capitol Way
> Olympia, WA 98504
> (206) 753-5700

4. *Destruction,* injury, defacement, removal or disturbance in any manner of any natural feature of public property is prohibited. This includes:
   a. Molesting any animal, picking flowers or other plants;
   b. Cutting, blazing, marking, driving nails in, or otherwise damaging growing trees or standing snags;
   c. Writing, carving or painting of name or other inscription anywhere;
   d. Destruction, defacement or moving of signs.

5. *Collecting specimens* of minerals, plants, animals or historical objects is prohibited without written authorization, obtained in advance, from the Park Service or Forest Service. Permits are not issued for personal collections.

6. *Smoking* is not permitted while traveling through vegetated areas. You may stop and smoke in a safe place.

7. Pack and saddle *animals* have the right-of-way on trails. Hikers should get completely off the trail, on the downhill side if possible, and remain quiet until the stock has passed.

8. It is illegal to cut *switchbacks*.

9. Use *existing campsites* if there are any. If not, camp away from the trail and at least 100 feet from lakes and streams, on mineral soil or unvegetated forest floor—never in meadows or other soft, vegetated spots. Unfortunately, in many popular areas—Jefferson Park, in particular—almost all the good campsites are within 100 feet of water. Until the Forest Service builds or recommends alternate campsites, the hiker will have little choice but to use one of the existing illegal sites.

10. *Construction* of improvements such as rock walls, large fireplaces, bough beds, tables, and rock-and-log stream crossings is prohibited.

11. *Soap* and other pollutants should be kept out of lakes and streams. Use of detergents is not recommended, since they affect the water detrimentally.

12. *Toilets* should be in soft soil away from camps and water. Dig a shallow hole and bury it.

13. You are required to *clean up* your camp before you leave. Tin cans, foil, glass, worn-out or useless gear, and other unburnables must be carried out.

14. *National Parks but not Forests* prohibit dogs and cats on the trail and prohibit carrying or using firearms.

15. *Horses* and other pack or saddle animals should be kept at least 200 feet from any lake, stream or spring, except when watering, loading, unloading, or traveling on established trail routes. Forage may be limited, so you should carry feed. Avoid tying horses to trees at campsites for prolonged periods. Hobble, stake or use a picket line with your stock.

Border Crossing

Most PCT hikers do not cross the U.S./Canada border. In the past, those who did usually crossed it illegally, for dealing with the Customs/Excise and Immigration bureaus of each country was a real quagmire, if not a no-win proposition. Today, legally entering Canada via the PCT is a breeze, but legally entering bureaucratic-minded United States is still a nuisance. Since most trekkers hike north on the PCT (the easier direction of border crossing), we'll first look at that border crossing.

PCT north from U.S. into Canada

If your trek along the PCT will end in Manning Park and you'll then return to the United States by car or other transportation, you're in luck: you won't have to report to Customs. However, if you will be staying in Canada for more than a few days, then you must report to the nearest Canadian Customs office and/or to the Royal Canadian Mounted Police office. For more information about a protracted stay, check at the Manning Park headquarters when you complete your northbound trek along the PCT.

Canadian Customs allows you to bring in personal possessions that you'll need for your brief stay in Canada. Two exceptions are plants and handguns. Rifles and shotguns, other than automatic, are permitted. If you plan to bring any goods to leave in Canada, you'll then have to check with Customs for possible payment of duty and/or tax.

Canadian Immigration requires trekkers to obtain and complete an "Entry to Canada via the Pacific Crest Trail" form. You fill out this simple form *within* two months of the *start* of your trek. Write to:

Canadian Immigration Centre
Huntington, B.C.
Canada V0X 1M0

The Immigration Centre will then stamp and sign the form and return it to you. You must carry this form together with your birth certificate and some other form of identification, such as a driver's license or a passport.

Arriving in Canada on horseback or with a dog compounds your entry problems. If you bring a dog, you must carry a document from a licensed veterinarian which describes the dog and certifies that it has had its shots. Horses crossing the border are subject to inspection.

PCT south from Canada into U.S.

Unlike its Canadian counterpart, U.S. Customs requires all persons entering the United States to report directly to the nearest Customhouse for clearance (Title 19, USC, Section 1459). Customs are at two border towns: Sumas, 68 air miles west of the PCT but 132 road miles west from Rainy Pass; and Oroville, 65 air miles east of the PCT but 121 road miles east from Rainy Pass. The Customs authorities, in their wisdom, perceived that these stations were a bit out of the way for the average PCT hiker, and hence provided a closer site: Marblemount. From Rainy Pass you can now traipse a mere 50 miles west to this settlement, get checked out by a ranger at North Cascades National Park's Skagit District Office, then scurry back to the PCT. This works if you're a U.S. citizen. Trekkers from other countries may still have to report to Sumas. Bon voyage!

And then there's U.S. Immigration. You can be pre-inspected by them. This involves going to a U.S. port of entry (Sumas or Oroville), where you'll get a Form I-94, then head into Canada and start walking south. Upon re-entry into the U.S. on the PCT, you then surrender this form to the office that issued it or else mail it to the office. (No, Immigration hasn't asked the Post Office to install a mail box at Rainy Pass, and no, the Skagit District Office in Marblemount doesn't handle immigration.) All hikers should carry proof of citizenship, such as a birth certificate or passport. Non-U.S. citizens will also need a visa. For them to make a legal entry from Canada, they first must go into the U.S., get pre-inspected, and then head back to the Manning Park trailhead—quite a lot of travel.

For more information on U.S. Customs and/or Immigration, contact:

U.S. Customs Service   North Cascades National Park
Office of District Director   Skagit District Office
Seattle, WA 98174   Marblemount, WA 98267
(206) 442-1598   (206) 873-4590

U.S. Immigration and Naturalization
815 Airport Way, South
Seattle, WA 98134
(206) 442-5956

The information from each agency will probably contradict that from the other two agencies. For more fun and games, contact the U.S. Border Patrol at Oroville and Sumas, then try to maintain your sanity while resolving all the conflicting information you're trying to digest.

Government Administrative Headquarters

General

Regional Forester
  California Region
  630 Sansome Street
  San Francisco, CA 94111
  (415) 556-0122

Regional Forester
  Pacific Northwest Region
  P.O. Box 3623
  Portland, OR 97208
  (503) 221-2971

Bureau of Land Management
  P.O. Box 2965
  Portland, OR 97208
  (503) 231-6274

Specific, South to North

Klamath National Forest
  1312 Fairlane Road
  Yreka, CA 96097
  (916) 842-6131

Rogue River National Forest
  P.O. Box 520
  Medford, OR 97501
  (503) 776-3600

Winema National Forest
  6714 Dahlia
  Klamath Falls, OR 97601
  (503) 883-6714

Crater Lake National Park
  P.O. Box 7
  Crater Lake, OR 97604
  (503) 594-2211

Umpqua National Forest
  P.O. Box 1008
  Roseburg, OR 97470
  (503) 672-6601

Deschutes National Forest
  1645 Highway 20 East
  Bend, OR 97701
  (503) 388-2715

Willamette National Forest
  P.O. Box 10607
  Eugene, OR 97440-2607
  (503) 687-6521

Mt. Hood National Forest
  2955 N.W. Division Street
  Gresham, OR 97030
  (503) 666-0771

Gifford Pinchot National Forest
  6926 E. Fourth Plain Blvd.
  Vancouver, WA 98668-8944
  (206) 696-7500

Mt. Baker-Snoqualmie Nat. Forest
  1022 First Avenue
  Seattle, WA 98104
  (206) 442-0170

Mt. Rainier National Park
  Tahoma Woods, Star Route
  Ashford, WA 98304
  (206) 569-2211

Wenatchee National Forest
  P.O. Box 811
  Wenatchee, WA 98807
  (509) 662-4335

North Cascades National Park
  2105 Highway 20
  Sedro Woolley, WA 98284
  (206) 856-5700

Okanogan National Forest
  P.O. Box 950
  Okanogan, WA 98840
  (509) 422-2704

Manning Provincial Park
  British Columbia, Canada V0X 1R0
  (604) 840-8836

Forgotten Anything?

Here is a checklist of items we feel you should *consider* bringing along. You might prefer to bring other things too.

wallet
keys
watch
travelers checks
wilderness permit
this guidebook
nature guides
pencil and note pad
camera
camera accessories
film
fishing gear
fishing license
mountaineering gear
other special gear
pack
sleeping bag
foam pad or air mattress
ground cloth
tent or tube tent
rain gear (preferably made of Gore-Tex)
down vest or down parka
windbreaker and/or sweatshirt
shirts (preferably wool)

pants (preferably wool)
shorts
swimsuit
towel and/or washcloth
underwear (polypropylene)
socks
gaiters
boots and boot laces
camp shoes
wool cap and/or hat
dark glasses
gloves
sewing kit
toilet paper
personal hygiene items
aspirin
prescription medicine
molefoam
first-aid kit
snakebite kit
insect repellent (lots of it)
suntan lotion
lip balm and/or glacier cream
toothbrush, toothpaste

flashlight
extra batteries
pocket knife
can opener
food and drink
salt and pepper
stove and fuel
matches in waterproof container
pots, bowls and utensils
Sierra cup
soap: leave it home!
water bottles (½ gallon is sufficient)
several trash bags
stuffsacks for sleeping bag and/or bearbagging
50 feet of parachute cord for bearbagging
50 feet of parachute cord for emergencies (tent lines, pack repairs, shoe laces)
100 feet of lightweight nylon rope for stream fords and risky snow-slope traverse

Chapter 3: PCT Natural History

Introduction

The California section of the Pacific Crest Trail is noted for its great diversity of plants and animals, minerals and rocks, climates and landscapes. The Oregon section of the PCT provides quite a contrast, having the most homogeneous vegetation and landscape of this tri-state route. The Washington section falls between these two extremes. Along the route covered by this volume, certain rocks, plants and animals appear time and time again. The most common entities appear to be

rock: andesite, basalt
flower: lupine
shrub: huckleberry
tree: mountain hemlock, subalpine fir, western white pine
invertebrate: mosquito
fish: trout
amphibian: western toad, tree frog
reptile: garter snake
bird: dark-eyed junco
mammal,
    small: chipmunk, golden-mantled ground squirrel
    large: man, deer.

The average elevation of Oregon's section of PCT is about 5120 feet, whereas Washington's section is about 4550 feet—lower in part because the weathering and erosional processes farther north are more intense (contrast Washington's 4550 to California's 6120). Not only is the average trail elevation different between these two northwest states, so too is the typical terrain that the trail traverses. The Oregon section is flatter, drier, more volcanic and less glaciated than Washington's section. In Oregon, a typical hike is through a mountain-hemlock forest while traversing rolling ridges and crossing lake-bound basins. In Washington, a typical hike is through alternating forests of mountain hemlock and subalpine species while climbing over passes and dropping somewhat into glaciated canyons. Both states, of course, have many distinctive features worth investigating.

Geology

We can thank the existence of western America's mountains for the existence of the Pacific Crest Trail. Without these mountains, we'd have instead the Pacific *Coast* Trail. But why should we have mountains in the first place? The answer lies with plate tectonics—the ceaseless movements of the earth's crust and its associated upper mantle. This composite outer layer is made up of a few giant plates plus more abundant, smaller plates, all interacting with one another. Some movements lead to the formation of mountain ranges, others to ocean basins.

Although plate tectonics has been occurring for several billion years, we need concern ourselves only with the last 50 million or so years. Back then, oceanic plates were diving under continental plates, much as they do today. One oceanic plate, the Farallon plate, was diving east under the continental North American plate, and it was being consumed in the process, particularly in its midsection. By 30 million years ago, the midsection had been totally consumed, leaving a southern part and a northern part. It is the northern part we are interested in, now known as the Juan de Fuca plate. Like the larger Farallon plate, the Juan de Fuca plate continued diving under the North American plate. Also like that plate, it continued drifting north with respect to North America (see illustration).

When one plate dives beneath another, it eventually melts, due to increasing temperature. This typically happens at depths of about 60 to 90 miles. The melt doesn't have the same chemical composition as the plate, for overlying oceanic sediments, laden with water, have been dragged down with the descending plate, and these sediments are incorporated into the melt. The resulting melt, or magma, is relatively light in density, and it works its way up toward the earth's surface. If it reaches the surface, a volcanic eruption occurs, such as the devastating eruption of Mt. St. Helens on May 18, 1980. If it doesn't reach the surface, it solidifies at depth as granitic rock. Erosion over millions of years strips off overlying rocks to expose the granitic rock, which is what we see in the North Cascades.

The continual diving of the Juan de Fuca plate insures continual production of magma, thus guaranteeing a future for the Cascade Range. Note, however, that because the plate is drifting north, so too will the zone of active Cascade volcanoes. In the future new volcanoes will erupt in British Columbia, while old ones in southern Oregon and northern California will cease to erupt.

While the foregoing discourse describes the dynamics of the Cascade Range, it does not describe its history. That history is fairly well known from the mid-Tertiary period onward (see Geologic Time Table on page 28). In the late Eocene and early Miocene epochs, deposits from the ancient Cascade Range reached a thickness of six miles in some places. For such an accumulation to occur, the regional crust must have been relatively stable for some time. By the mid-Miocene, the range experienced folding, faulting and, in the north, intrusion by granitic batholiths, plutons, stocks, and dikes. (These intrusive masses are distinguished by their relative size; a batholith may be tens of miles across, whereas a dike may be only a few feet or a few inches across.) During the mid-Miocene, linear vents east of the Cascades opened and poured forth the very fluid Columbia River basalts, which flooded much of the terrain of southern Washington and northern Oregon. The many flows from the fiery episodes are best seen by the hiker as he descends north toward the Columbia River along the lower half of the Eagle Creek Trail.

Plant fossils collected east of the Cascades indicate the environment was considerably more humid than it is today. From this knowledge the paleobotanist infers that the Cascades were lower in elevation, since there was no evidence of a rain shadow that would have been created if they had been as high as today's crests. One need only drive to have been created if they had been as high as today's crests. One need only drive to Sisters or Wenatchee to notice how much drier the east slopes of today's Cascades are compared to their west slopes.

After the partial flooding of the range by the Columbia River basalts, the earth's internal forces, quite likely due to the interaction between the North American and Juan de Fuca plates, uplifted the range and initiated a series of active volcanoes. Uplift and eruptions continued during the Quaternary, but in this epoch, the higher peaks were subjected to repeated glaciations brought on by changes in the world-wide climatic pattern. Some paleoclimatologists have speculated that the moving plates have rearranged the ocean basins, thereby affecting ocean currents and also major weather patterns, but the influences that initiated the Ice Age (the Pleistocene epoch) are still debated.

The same processes at work in the past are at work today. Volcanoes attempt to grow ever upward, but they are checked by the forces of gravity, weathering and erosion. The

Western North America, about 15 million years ago (left) and today (right). The Juan de Fuca plate (gray) is producing new oceanic crust along its western edge, causing sea-floor spreading (large, dark arrows). This plate is bordered by the Pacific plate on its west and south edges, and by the North American plate on its east edge. Note that in the 15-million-year time lapse, the Juan de Fuca plate has changed its orientation with respect to North America, and that it has migrated considerably eastward and northward while diving under the continent (open arrows). Note that the directions of sea-floor spreading and plate diving are very different. In another 15 million years, the Juan de Fuca plate will all but disappear beneath the North American plate. In the map on the right the stars are major Cascade Range volcanoes and the small rectangle is this chapter's geologic map.

higher a peak grows, the more it is attacked by the icy fingers of glaciers. Gravity pulls loose particles downward; the right snow conditions initiate avalanches; minor eruptions and near-surface intrusions melt snowpacks, thereby creating enormous mudflows. Particularly good examples of the destructive power of such mudflows may be seen in the Mt. St. Helens environs.

The major volcanoes we see today are quite young—definitely late Quaternary. Many of them have erupted in geologically recent times, and there is every reason to believe they will erupt again. The Pacific Crest Trail traverses most of these "dormant" volcanoes, including, south to north: Mt. McLoughlin (9495), Crater Lake (11,500-foot-high Mt. Mazama until 6900 years ago), the Three Sisters (10,358, 10,047, 10,085), Mt. Jefferson (10,497), Mt. Hood (11,235), Mt. Adams (12,276), Mt. Rainier (14,410) and Glacier Peak (10,541). Geologic vignettes of these and other summits are included in our trail descriptions.

GEOLOGIC TIME TABLE				
Era	Period	Epoch	Began (years ago)	Duration (years)
	Quaternary	Holocene	10,000	10,000
		Pleistocene	1,800,000	1,800,000
Cenozoic	Tertiary	Pliocene	5,200,000	3,400,000
		Miocene	21,700,000	16,500,000
		Oligocene	35,000,000	13,300,000
		Eocene	49,000,000	14,000,000
		Paleocene	64,000,000	15,000,000
Mesozoic	Cretaceous	*Numerous*	135,000,000	71,000,000
	Jurassic	*epochs*	195,000,000	60,000,000
	Triassic	*recognized*	225,000,000	30,000,000
Paleozoic	Permian		280,000,000	55,000,000
	Carboni-	*Numerous*		
	ferous		345,000,000	65,000,000
	Devonian	*epochs*	400,000,000	55,000,000
	Silurian		435,000,000	35,000,000
	Ordovician	*recognized*	500,000,000	65,000,000
	Cambrian		600,000,000	100,000,000
Precambrian	No widely accepted time units; oldest known rocks are 3.8 billion years old; Earth's crust solidified 4.6 billion years ago.			

Note: In this Geologic Time Table the durations of Cenozoic epochs differ considerably from those of previous time tables. This major discrepancy is due to a reevaluation of these epochs in the light of isotopic dating and new fossil evidence. The Cenozoic era in this table as based on the work of D.H. Tarling and J.G. Mitchell (1976), who made minor changes in the epoch dates set by W.A. Berggren and J.A. Van Couvering (1974).

During the Ice Age, which has *temporarily* abated, an almost continuous mantle of ice covered the Cascades from Mt. McLoughlin north into Canada. From this mantle, huge fingers of glacier ice extended downcanyon, sometimes for tens of miles and some gave rise to enormous lakes, such as Lake Chelan in the North Cascades. Evidence of large southern glaciers can be found near Crater Lake even though Mt. Mazama, their source, was later blown out of existence. When hikers climb east from Diamond Lake on the Howlock Mountain Trail, about 16 miles north of Crater Lake, they climb up a large lateral moraine left by a Mt. Mazama glacier when it retreated about 10,000 years ago, at the time when most of the Cascades' glaciers melted back.

Today we are living in an interglacial period which could come to an end relatively soon. The hiker trekking along the Pacific Crest Trail today thus sees the Cascade Range in its "atypical" form, for in the last million years most of the range lay under an ice sheet about 95% of the time. So, if you experience chilly, wet weather along your PCT hike, be grateful it isn't worse—20,000 years ago, your hike would have resembled a trek across today's icy Greenland.

Biology

One's first guess about the Pacific Crest Trail—a high adventure rich in magnificent alpine scenery and sweeping panoramas—turns out to be incorrect along some parts of the trail. The real-life trail hike will sometimes seem to consist of enduring many repetitious miles through viewless forests, battling hordes of mosquitoes, or even hiking up to a whole day at a time without reaching fresh water. If you get bogged down in such unpleasant impressions, it may be because you haven't developed an appreciation of the natural history of this remarkable route. There is a great variety of plants and animals, rocks and minerals, landscapes and climates along the PCT, and the more you know about each, the more you will enjoy your trek.

FLORA

A backpacker who has just complete the California section of the PCT might conclude that southern Oregon's forests form a more integrated "neighborhood" of species than California's forests did. Passing through different environments of the Sierra Nevada, he may have noticed the segregation of tree species and concluded that as he ascends toward the range's crest, he passes through a sequence of forests: Douglas-fir, white fir, red fir, mountain hemlock. Near the Oregon border, however, he discovers that these four species—and others—reside together. Certainly, this aggregation would never be seen in the Sierra. The great diversity of environments found within that range has allowed each species to adapt to the environment most suitable for it.

In contrast, the southern Oregon environments—and therefore the plant communities—are not as sharply defined. Still, each plant species is found within a certain elevation range and over a certain geographic area. The general elevation and north-south range of 21 Cascade Range conifers are shown on profiles on the following pages. These species make up virtually all the forest cover you'll pass through on your Oregon-Washington trek. Note how the species vary in distribution, both horizontally and vertically.

South-north profiles of the Cascade Range approximately along the Pacific Crest Trail. Each profile shows the altitudinal and latitudinal range of one or two conifers.

Pacific silver fir (*Abies amabilis*)

Red fir (*Abies magnifica*)   Grand fir (*Abies grandis*)

White fir (*Abies concolor*)   Subalpine fir (*Abies lasiocarpa*)

Noble fir (*Abies procera*)

Alaska-cedar *Chamaecyparis nootkatensis*

Western larch (*Larix occidentalis*)   Subalpine larch (*Larix lyallii*)

Incense-cedar (*Libocedrus decurrens*)

Weeping spruce (*Picea breweriana*)   Engelmann spruce (*Picea engelmannii*)

Sugar pine *(Pinus lambertiana)*   Whitebark pine *(Pinus albicaulis)*

Lodgepole pine *(Pinus contorta var. murrayana)*

Western white pine *(Pinus monticola)*

Ponderosa pine *(Pinus ponderosa)*

Douglas-fir *(Pseudotsuga menziesii)*

Western redcedar *(Thuja plicata)*

Mountain hemlock *(Tsuga mertensiana)*

Western hemlock *(Tsuga heterophylla)*

If you've hiked through California's rugged Sierra Nevada, you'll find southern Oregon a much gentler, more uniform landscape. But despite its relatively subdued topography, it still supports a diverse assemblage of plants, and the discerning hiker soon learns what species to expect around the next bend. Ponderosa pines thrive in the drier southern Oregon forests, yet they are nonexistent in the dry pumice soils of the Crater Lake vicinity. Here you'll find lodgepole pines which, ironically, are water-loving trees. These are usually seen growing in boggy soils near lakes, creeks and wet meadows, where they often edge out the mountain hemlocks, which are by far the most common tree you'll see along the PCT in Oregon and Washington. The most suitable habitat for hemlocks appears to be shady north slopes, on which pure stands of tall, straight specimens grow. At lower elevations, mountain hemlocks give way to western hemlocks and Douglas-firs, and, as the environment becomes drier southward and eastward, these two species yield to ponderosa pines. The harder one looks at a forest—even a small piece of it—the more he realizes that this seemingly uniform stand of trees is in fact a complex assemblage of particular plants, animals, soils, rocks and microclimates all influencing each other.

Our trail description commences at Seiad Valley, a man-made ranchland carved from a Douglas-fir forest. Near the end of our odyssey, along Agnes Creek and the Stehekin River, we also encounter a Douglas-fir forest. The two are hardly alike. The Douglas-fir forest of northern California and southern Oregon contains, among other trees, incense-cedar, ponderosa pine, white fir, Oregon oak and madrone. Its counterpart in northern Washington contains, among others, western redcedar, western white pine, grand fir, vine maple and Engelmann spruce.

The two forests vary considerably in the density of their vegetation. Not only does the rain-laden northern forest have a denser stand of taller conifers, but it also has a denser understory. Its huckleberries, thimbleberries, Devil's club and other moisture-loving shrubs are quite a contrast to the stiff, dry manzanita, ceanothus and scrub oaks seen in the southern forest. Wildflowers in the northern forest are more abundant than their counterparts to the south. During rainstorms, they are too abundant, for their thick growth along the trail ensures that you'll be soaked by them from as high as your waist on down. Both forests have quite a number of species in common, but from central Oregon northward, the moisture-oriented species become prominent. Now we find bunchberry dogwood, Oregon grape, Lewis monkey flower and other species growing on the dark, damp forest floor.

In contrast to trees, which are quite specific in their habitat selection, flowers can tolerate a broad range of environments. You'll find, for example, yarrow, a sunflower, at timberline on the slopes of Mt. Hood and also on the Douglas-fir forest floor that borders the southern shore of the Columbia River. Both environments are moist, but the Mt. Hood alpine meadows, at 6000 feet above the bottom of the Columbia River gorge, are a considerably harsher environment.

Some flowers prefer open meadows to shady forests; others prefer dry environments. Thistle, lupine and phlox are found along the sunnier portions of the trail. Growing from crevices among rocks are the aptly named stonecrops, and on the pumice flats too dry for even the lodgepole pines to pioneer, the Newberry knotweed thrives.

In addition to adapting to specific climatic conditions, a plant may also adapt to a specific soil condition. Thus we see on the otherwise barren mica schist slopes of Condrey Mountain, near the southern Oregon border, acre after acre of pink, prostrate pussy paws.

Lastly, a species may have a distribution governed by the presence of other species. Corn lilies thrive in wet meadows, but lodgepoles invade these lands and shade them out. Mountain hemlocks may soon follow and eventually achieve dominance over the lodgepoles. Then the careless camper comes along, lets his campfire escape, and the forest burns. Among the charred stumps of the desolate ruins rises the tall, blazing magenta fireweed, and Nature, once again, strives to transform this landscape back into a mature forest.

From top, left to right: fireweed, paintbrush, tiger lily; Newberry knotweed, corn lily (false hellebore, skunk cabbage), pasqueflower; pearly everlasting, phlox, Sitka valerian

FAUNA

We have seen that plants adapt to a variety of conditions imposed by the environment and by other species. Animals, like plants, are also subject to a variety of conditions, but they have the added advantage of mobility. On a hot summer day, a beetle under a scant forest cover can escape the merciless sun by seeking protection under a loose stone or under a mat of dry needles.

Larger animals, of course, have greater mobility and therefore can better overcome the difficulties of the environment. Amphibians, reptiles, birds and mammals may frequent the trail, but they scamper away when you—the intruder—approach. At popular campsites, however, the animals come out to meet you, or more exactly, to obtain your food. Of course, almost anywhere along the trail you may encounter the ubiquitous mosquito, always looking for a free meal. But in popular campsites you'll meet the robin, the gray jay, the Clark nutcracker, the Townsend and yellow-pine chipmunks, the golden-mantled ground squirrel, and at night, mice and black bears. You may be tempted to feed them, or they may try to help themselves, but please protect them from your food—they will survive better on the "real, organic" food Mother Nature produces. Furthermore, an artificially large population supported by generous summer backpackers may in winter overgraze the vegetation. In the following paragraphs we'll take a closer look at three species.

Mule deer. Two subspecies of this large mammal can be found along much of the Oregon-Washington PCT. Mule deer, like other herbivores, do not eat every type of plant they encounter, but tend to be quite specific in their search for food. Their primary browse is new growth on huckleberry, salal, blackberry, bitterbrush and snowbrush, although they also eat certain grasses and forbs. Together with other herbivores, parasites and saprophytes (organisms feeding on decaying organic matter), they consume a small portion of the 100 billion tons of organic matter produced annually on the earth by plants.

Mule deer face a considerable population problem because some of their predators have disappeared. After the arrival of "civilized" man, the wolves and grizzly bears were exterminated except in some remote areas of northern Washington. In their places, coyotes and black bears have increased in numbers. Coyotes, however, feed principally on rabbits and rodents, and only occasionally attack a fawn or a sick deer. Black bears occasionally kill fawns. The mountain lion, a true specialist in feeding habits, preys mainly on deer and may kill 50 of them a year. This magnificent mammal, unfortunately, has been unjustly persecuted by man, and many deer that are saved from the big cat are lost to starvation and disease. Increasing human population compounds the problem. The expansion of settlements causes the big cats to retreat farther, which leaves them farther from the suburban deer. Forests must be logged to feed this expansion of settlements, and then the logged-over areas sprout an assemblage of shrubs that are a feast for deer. The deer population responds to this new food supply by increasing in number. Then the shrubs mature or the forest grows back, and there is less food for the larger deer population, which is now faced with starvation. Forest fires produce the same feast-followed-by-famine effect.

From top, left to right: Oregon grape, columbine, ligusticum; vanilla-leaf, lupine, eriogonum; yarrow, thistle, beargrass

Golden-mantled ground squirrel. There are two species of these ground squirrels, the Sierra Nevada golden-mantled ground squirrel, which ranges from the southern Sierra north to the Columbia River, and the Cascades golden-mantled ground squirrel, which ranges from the Columbia River north into British Columbia. On the eastern Cascade slopes of Washington, the Cascades golden-mantled ground squirrel lives in the same habitat as the yellow-pine chipmunk, but they have slightly different niches, or roles, to carry out in their pine-and-fir-forest environment. Both have the same food and the same burrowing habits, but the ground squirrel obtains nuts and seeds that have fallen to the forest floor, whereas the chipmunk obtains these morsels by extracting them from their source. The ground squirrel, like its distant cousin the marmot, puts on a thick layer of fat to provide it with enough energy to last through winter hibernation. The chipmunk, like the black bear, only partly hibernates. During the winter, it awakens periodically to feed on the nuts and seeds it has stored in its ground burrow.

Western toad. Every Westerner is familiar with this drab, chunky amphibian. Along the Oregon-Washington PCT, we encounter its subspecies known as the boreal toad. This cold-blooded animal is amazingly adaptable, being found among rock crevices in dry, desolate lava flows as well as in subalpine wildflower gardens in the North Cascades. Its main environmental requirement appears to be the presence of at least one early-summer seasonal pond in which it can breed and lay eggs.

Although you may encounter dozens of boreal toads along a stretch of trail in one day (they occur in clusters), they prefer to actively hop or crawl about at night. Should you bed down near one of their breeding ponds, you may hear the weak chirps (they have no "croaking" vocal sacs) from dozens of males. Moreover, these toads may swarm all over you in their search for meals. Rolling over on one won't give you warts, but later you might feel the puncture, bite or sting of a mosquito, ant or yellow jacket that otherwise would have made a tasty meal for the toad.

mule deer   **ground squirrel**   **western toad**

Chapter 4: Using This Guide

Twelve Hiking Chapters

The bulk of this guide is composed of trail description and accompanying topographic maps of the Pacific Crest Trail. In 12 chapters, Sections A through L, this guide covers the PCT from Highway 96 in northern California to Highway 3 in British Columbia. Readers familiar with this guide's companion volume will note that its Section R is essentially the same as this one's Section A (for an explanation of this duplication, see page 45). We have divided the Oregon-Washington PCT into 12 sections because the vast majority of hikers will be walking only a part of the trail, not all of it. Each section starts and ends at a highway, and often at or near a supply center such as a town, resort or park. All the sections are short enough to make comfortable backpacking trips ranging from about 4 to 12 days for the average backpacker. Each of these sections could be conveniently broken into two or more shorter sections to provide even shorter hikes. However, we've refrained from making a new chapter begin at every road crossing since this would unnecessarily increase the size, weight—and price—of the book. By limiting ourselves to 12 hiking sections, we've kept pre-hike information to a minimum.

Pre-Hike Information

At the beginning of each section you'll find pre-hike information that mentions: 1) the attractions and natural features of that section, 2) the declination setting for your compass, 3) a mileage table between points within that section, 4) supply points on or near the route, 5) wilderness-permit information, if applicable, and 6) special problems. This pre-hike information also includes a map of the entire section.

Features. At the start of each section, an introduction briefly mentions the features— both good and bad—that you'll encounter while hiking through that section. These introductions will help you decide which section or sections are right for you.

Declination. The declination setting for your compass is important if you have to get an accurate reading. Actually, the declination changes very little throughout this whole two-state section, being 17¼°E in northernmost California and increasing to 20°E at trail's end in southernmost British Columbia. Because the magnetic north pole is wandering, the declination is slowly changing. By about the year 2000 A.D., the declinations will have moved only a bit, then giving a range of from about 16½°E to 19¼°E. Since most hikers read their compasses to the nearest 5°, they can set their compasses to the convenient average figure of 18°E and manage fine for this book's two-state stretch.

If your compass does not correct for declination, you'll have to add the appropriate declination to get the true bearing. For example, if your compass indicates that a prominent hill lies along a bearing of 70°, and if the section you're hiking in has a declination of 20°E, then you should add 20°, getting 90° (due east) as the true bearing of that hill. If you can identify that hill on a map, you can find where *you* are on the PCT by adding 180°, getting 270° (due west) in this example. By drawing a line due west from the hill to an intersection of the PCT, you'll determine your position.

Most hikers will agree it's easier to carry a compass with a declination setting than to try and remember if one should add or subtract declination. Regardless of which type of compass you use, you *should not* attempt a major section of the PCT without a thorough understanding of your compass *and* of map interpretation. On a long hike you could be caught in a whiteout and your trail could be buried under snow. Then, your navigation skills, or lack thereof, might determine whether you lived or died. Until you master both map and compass, take only short hikes in good weather.

Mileage Table. Each mileage table lists distances between major points found within its PCT section. Both distances between points and cumulative mileages are given. We list cumulative mileages south to north *and* north to south so that no matter which direction you are hiking the PCT, you can easily determine the mileages you plan to hike. Many of the points listed in the tables are at or near good campsites. If you typically average 17 miles a day—the on-route rate you'll need to complete the tri-state PCT in under 6 months—then you can determine where you should camp to maintain this rate, and you can estimate when you should arrive at certain supply points. Of course, in reality your time schedule may turn out to be quite different from your planned schedule, due to unforeseen circumstances.

At the end of this short chapter we've included a mileage table for the entire Oregon-Washington PCT. By scanning this table's *distances between points,* you can tell at a glance just how long each section is. You can then select one or more of appropriate length, turn to that section's **Introduction,** and see if it sounds appealing. Then read its **Problems** (if any) and see if it still sounds appealing. Of course, you need not start at the beginning of any section, since *every* PCT section is cut by one or more access roads.

Supplies. If you're going to be on the trail for more than two weeks, you'll probably want to stop somewhere to resupply. This pre-trail section mentions the resorts, stores, post offices and towns that are readily accessible to the hiker. In most cases the supply point is just a resort or small store with minimal food supplies and perhaps with a post office. By "minimal" we mean a few odds and ends that typically cater to passing motorists, e.g., beer and potato chips. Therefore, it is best to make your own "CARE" packages and mail them to appropriate post offices. See page 15 for a list of these, their ZIP codes and mailing tips.

Wilderness Permits. In sections C, I and K, you'll pass through a national park. In these you'll need a permit if you camp in their backcountry, and their pre-trail paragraphs tell you where you can write for one or pick one up. Also see page 20 for general information about wilderness permits and page 23 for addresses.

Problems. In every section but B, you can expect early-season snow patches to hinder your progress, while later you can expect pursuing mosquitoes to speed it up. This pre-trail paragraph, not found in every section, mentions these two problems when they are found in superabundance. It also mentions extensive waterless stretches, which are amazingly frequent for such a wet mountain range. After reading about a section's special problems you may decide to reschedule the time you plan to hike through it, or perhaps you may choose a more appealing section.

Section Map. Early editions of the two-volume *Pacific Crest Trail* guides contained only a long sequence of narrow topographic maps. Hikers using them reasonably complained of these maps' "tunnel vision": without a Forest Service map, you couldn't tell what lay more than a few miles east or west of the PCT; you could only look ahead or behind. In response to this problem, we've widened the maps so they are up to 46% wider than in the early editions, thus permitting you to take compass readings on more-distant topographic features. With this expanded lateral coverage you can locate yourself faster and better.

Still, there are instances when you'd like to see miles of lateral coverage, particularly when your trek has gone afoul due to bad weather, injury or other disaster. Then you'll want to know the quickest way out to civilization. Hence we've included section maps to show you the trails, roads, towns and other features you should know about if you must abort your hike. Because we've included these large-area section maps, you should be able to get along entirely without Forest Service maps or any other aids.

Route Description

When you start reading the text of a PCT section, you will notice that a pair of numbers follows each of the more important trail points. For example, at Russell Creek in the Mt. Jefferson Wilderness, this pair is (5520-2.8), which means that you cross this creek at an elevation of 5520 *feet* and at a distance of 2.8 *miles* from your last given point, which in this example is at a junction with the Woodpecker Trail. By studying these figures along the section you are hiking, you can easily determine the distance you'll have to hike from point A to point B, and by noting the elevation changes you get a good idea of how much climbing and descending you'll have to do. Along this guide's *alternate* routes, which are set aside by rows of asterisks, there are occasional second mileage figures, each of which represents the cumulative mileage along the alternate route to that point.

In addition to giving accurate directions, the route description tells you where you can camp, where you can get water, what hazards you should be aware of, how streams and trail condition may change with season, and other useful hiking information. In addition, the description also tells you something about the country you are walking through—the scenery, the geology, the biology, and sometimes a bit of history. We hope this added information will increase your outdoor perception and add to your enjoyment of your trek.

The Topographic Maps

Each hiking section contains all the topographic maps you'll need to hike that part of the Pacific Crest Trail. All these maps are at a scale of 1:50,000, or about 0.8 mile per inch (1 mile per 1¼ inches). Most hikers are acquainted with 7.5′ maps (1:24,000) and 15′ maps (1:62,500). Since our topos are based on these two map sizes, we chose an intermediate scale of 1:50,000 because if 7.5′ maps are reduced any farther, say to 1:62,500, the names and numbers on them become too difficult to read. Yet, if we were to enlarge the 15′ maps to 1:24,000, the size, weight and price of the book would increase by about 25% and the lateral extent of each map would be cut in half. We think the 1:50,000 scale has the best cost:benefit ratio.

Many of this guide's topos show township-and-range sections, which are *usually* square and *usually* measure one mile on a side. Topos with these sections thus have a one-mile grid pattern, which aids in judging distances.

On the topos, the PCT route appears as a solid black line where it exists as trail or a *closed* road and as a dashed black line where it exists as a temporary route along a road. Any alternate route that is set apart in the text by asterisks is also shown on the maps, and it is indicated by an alternating dot-dash black line. Proposed PCT (not yet built or still under construction) has the same symbol as a cross-country route, that is, a dotted black line. A map legend at the end of this chapter lists most of the symbols you'll find on this guide's topographic maps.

Text and Map Cross References

To make this guide as functional as possible, we've tried to place the maps as close as possible to the appropriate columns of trail description, and we've included four reference systems. Perhaps the most obvious system is the one composed of a set of large, bold letters and numbers (**A1, A2,** etc.), which are found at the bottom of each column of route description. These sets identify the appropriate map (Map A1, Map A2, etc.) that shows the section of PCT being described in the column of route description. In most cases, that map is no more than a page or two away.

But what if you see a feature on a map and you want to find where it is mentioned in the text? In that case, turn to the index, which lists entries for both text and maps.

The last two reference systems deal with maps only. Since the Pacific Crest Trail is not an arrow-straight north-south path, neither is the sequence of topo maps that show it. Therefore, along the border of each map we list the maps that touch it. For example, turn to map C3 on page 91. Note that three maps border this map: C1, C2 and C4. The blue tick mark between "see MAP C1" and "see MAP C2" tells you where map C1 ends and map C2 begins. The blue tick mark to the right of "see MAP C4" tells you where the right border of map C4 is. (Its left border is off the page, hence the tick mark lies flat, indicating that the map continues in that direction.) By learning the significance of the topos' tick marks, you should be able to go from map to map with a minimum of orientation problems.

But if you still have problems in determining the location of one map with respect to another, then use our fourth reference system, the large-area section map at the beginning of each hiking chapter. On it all the topo map borders for that chapter are printed in light blue. In like manner, the Oregon-Washington map on page vi shows all the large-area maps for this book's hiking sections, A through L. Thus if you want to hike, say, Sections E through G, you can easily visualize how much of the entire Oregon-Washington stretch you're going to be doing.

Following the Trail

The "Pacific Crest Trail" is usually a trail, though in a few places—notably Goat Rocks' Packwood Glacier and Glacier Peak's Red and Fire Creek passes—it is usually a snowfield. On a clear midsummer's day, the PCT is easy to follow, even if it is a snowfield. However, in early season or in a storm, the trail could be buried under snow. If the snow is a foot or more deep, then the trail's course may become obscure. When this happens, you may have to watch for other visual clues: PCT emblems, posts, blazes and ducks. (A blaze is a place on a tree trunk where someone has carved away a patch or two of bark to leave a conspicuous man-made scar; a duck is an obviously man-made pile of rocks.) Since all these markers can be ephemeral, our route descriptions usually do not emphasize them.

In fact, we're even reluctant to state that a trail junction is "signed," since the sign may disappear in a year or two. Where we mention trail junctions (or road junctions, for that matter), we give the trail's official name and number, if it has both (for example, Jefferson Park Trail 3429). Some trails have only official names or official numbers. Others have neither, and for these we say "trail" instead of "Trail." If a trail once had a trail number but no longer does, we still prefer to state it, since we can fit numbers onto the book's topo maps far easier than lengthy trail names. When the Pacific Crest Trail came into prominence in the early 1970s, it received a lot more hiker use, and consequently it has been kept up very well. With all the signs and markers along it, the PCT can almost be followed without map or guide through Oregon and Washington—if you have good weather and no emergencies.

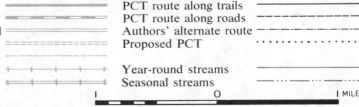

LEGEND

Heavy-duty road		PCT route along trails	
Medium-duty road		PCT route along roads	
Improved light-duty road		Authors' alternate route	
Unimproved dirt road		Proposed PCT	
Jeep road or trail			
Railroad: single track		Year-round streams	
Railroad: multiple track		Seasonal streams	

Scale of maps, 1:50,000   1   0   1 MILE

Oregon-Washington PCT Mileage Table

Mileages:	South to North	Distances between Points	North to South
Highway 96 in Seiad Valley....................	0.0		1006.2
Section A		64.5	
Interstate 5 near Siskiyou Pass.................	64.5		941.7
Section B		54.0	
Highway 140 near Fish Lake	118.5		887.7
Section C		76.0	
Highway 138 near the Cascade crest............	194.5		811.7
Section D		61.3	
Highway 58 near Willamette Pass	255.8		750.4
Section E		75.8	
Highway 242 at McKenzie Pass.................	331.6		674.6
Section F		112.5	
Highway 35 near Barlow Pass..................	444.1		562.1
Section G		54.4	
Interstate 84 at Bridge of the Gods	498.5		507.7
Walk across Bridge of the Gods		0.5	
Highway 14 at Bridge of the Gods..............	499.0		507.2
Section H		147.5	
Highway 12 near White Pass	646.5		359.7
Section I		98.6	
Interstate 90 at Snoqualmie Pass	745.1		261.1
Section J		74.5	
Highway 2 at Stevens Pass	819.6		186.6
Section K		117.5	
Highway 20 at Rainy Pass.....................	937.1		69.1
Section L		69.1	
Highway 3 in Manning Provincial Park..........	1006.2		0.0

Old and new PCT diamonds plus a duck with post and plastic streamer

12 Trail Chapters

North Sister, from South Matthieu Lake

The Pacific Crest Trail in Section A

This section's PCT
Other trails
Hwys and major rds
Other roads
Campgrounds

0 1 2 3 4 5 miles

RED BUTTES
WILDERNESS

Section A: Highway 96 in Seiad Valley to Interstate 5 near Siskiyou Pass

Introduction: Pacific Crest Trail hikers who have used the *Volume 1: California* guide will note that its Section R is essentially the same as this volume's Section A. The reason for this duplication is that the Pacific Crest Trail crosses the California-Oregon border in the middle of nowhere, roughly midway between Seiad Valley, on Highway 96, and Ashland, on Interstate 5. Hence hikers wanting to do every foot of California will logicaly continue northeast toward Ashland (or at least to Interstate 5) while those wanting to hike north along every foot of Oregon will logically start near Seiad Valley.

Actually, you can drive to within a short walk of the point where the Pacific Crest Trail enters Oregon. To do this, drive west from Medford, Oregon, on Highway 238, passing through Jacksonville in about 5 miles. The route then goes 7 miles southwest to the tiny community of Ruch, where you leave 238 and head south on a road up the Applegate River. In 6½ miles you'll pass the Star Work Center, then in an additional 2½ miles you'll cross to the east bank of the Applegate River and immediately branch left on Road 20. This road climbs 14½ miles to Silver Fork Gap, located at the east end of Yellowjacket Ridge. From here, Road 20 climbs east to Jackson Gap, but you descend southeast on Road 2025, which winds 4¼ miles to a gap just east of Donomore Peak. Just 40 yards south of this gap the Pacific Crest Trail crosses your road, and if you follow the trail about 200 yards southwest, to where it turns abruptly northeast, you'll be a few feet inside California. By starting north here, you'll save 2–3 days of hiking.

In this guide's Section A, the hiker makes a long traverse east to get over to the Cascade Range. The long traverse west in California, from Burney Falls to Marble Mountain, was quite necessary, though inconveniently long, since a route going north from Burney Falls past Mt. Shasta would be a dry, hot one indeed. Before the Pacific Crest Trail route became final, this sun-drenched corridor was the one most hikers followed to the Oregon Skyline Trail—Oregon's section of the Pacific Crest Trail. Section A's route, almost completely built by late 1978 and due to be completed in 1987, stays remarkably high for most of its length, dropping significantly only at each end. Although high, it has been only mildly glaciated, and because glaciers haven't scoured away the soil, thick forests abound. These, unfortunately, are rampant with logging roads. From Reeves Ranch eastward you are always paralleling one road or another, so you certainly lose the wilderness feeling this high-crest hike is supposed to offer. Views, however, are pleasing enough, and surprisingly few logging operations are seen from the trail. Before early July these roads are an advantage, for signficant stretches of trail are still snowbound. The roads, being more open, are quite easy to follow, though they still have enough snow patches on them to stop motor vehicles. As you progress east on trail or road, you walk across increasingly younger rocks, first late-Paleozoic/early-Mesozoic metamorphic rocks, then mid-Mesozoic granite rocks of the Mt. Ashland area and finally mid-to-late Cenozoic volcanic rocks of the Interstate 5 area.

Declination: 17¼°E

Mileages:	South to North	Distances between Points	North to South
Highway 96 at Seiad Valley....................	0.0		64.5
Lower Devils Peak saddle....................	6.5	6.5	58.0
Cook and Green Pass.......................	15.1	8.6	49.4
Lowdens Cabin site spur trail	20.4	5.3	44.1
Alex Hole Camp entrance	27.9	7.5	36.6
Mud Springs spur road.......................	30.2	2.3	34.3
Bearground Spring..........................	32.6	2.4	31.9
Wards Fork Gap	33.9	1.3	30.6
California-Oregon border.....................	36.7	2.8	27.8
Sheep Camp Spring.........................	41.1	4.4	23.4
Wrangle Gap	43.4	2.3	21.1
Long John Saddle	48.8	5.4	15.7
Grouse Gap	53.8	5.0	10.7
Road 2080	57.6	3.8	6.9
Interstate 5 near Mt. Ashland Road 20...........	64.5	6.9	0.0

Supplies: No supplies are available once you leave Seiad Valley. Along this crest route virtually all roads south will get you down to Highway 96, which has a smattering of hamlets, and virtually all roads north will ultimately channel you down to the Ashland-Medford area. However, we don't think you should descend either direction since you would then be way off route. Even in an emergency situation, you're likely to get help from people driving along the near-crest roads long before you could reach any settlement. If you're continuing through Oregon, you'll want to end Section A in Ashland, and 3 routes to it are described in this chapter. You won't find any more sizable towns within an easy day's walk of the PCT until you reach the Oregon-Washington border area, more than 400 miles beyond this section's end. If you think you'll need a new pack, a camera or a pair of boots, certainly stop in Ashland.

We begin this section at the Seiad Store and post office (1371' elevation, 46 miles west of Interstate 5 via Highway 96). Walking west along the highway, we immediately cross Seiad Valley Road, which heads northeast up to Horse Tail Falls and beyond to Cook and Green Pass. Not much farther on, we reach School House Gulch (1380-0.5), from where the PCT route once started. Following the road as it curves west, we quickly reach a newer trailhead for Lower Devils Peak Lookout Trail 12W04 (1380-0.3). Since it is an exhausting 4400' ascent to potential campsites by the Kangaroo Mountain meadows, one is prudent to start this strenuous trek in the cool shade of the morning.

Under a cover of madrone, Douglas-fir, in-cense-cedar and Oregon oak, our trail curves west and climbs moderately to reach a junction

(1600-0.2) with a trail that parallels Highway 96 west for 1.4 miles before ending close to a stream-gaging cable that spans the mighty Klamath River. The PCT was supposed to cross there, rather than on the Highway 96 bridge east of Seiad Valley, but this plan was abandoned.

From the junction with the trail paralleling Highway 96, where we cross under some minor powerlines, our trail heads north into a shaded gully with its poison oak, and we soon reach a junction with the original Devils Peak Lookout Trail, now abandoned. About ¼ mile beyond this junction we reach Fern Spring (1900-0.7), a small seep trickling from a pipe into a concrete cistern. You may find a trail register here.

Our well-engineered trail switchbacks up shady, though fly-infested, south-facing slopes, then follows a ridge system northeast up toward

A1   **A1**

A1

BUTTES WILDERNESS

COOK AND GREEN PASS 8 MI.

see MAP A3

see MAP A1

Lower Devils Peak. Along this stretch you'll see some trees scorched in a widespread fire started by lightning in the summer of 1987. The damage here is minor compared to that north of Lower Devils Peak. Where the ridge fuses with the peak's flank, we climb up some short switch-backs, then traverse north across west-facing slopes to a junction. From here a 40-yard-long trail goes over to Lookout Spring. This trickling spring is *usually* reliable, though one has to marvel at how any water flows at all, since the spring is so close to the Devils Peaks crest. From

A1   **A1**

the junction we climb about 300 yards in a final push up to Lower Devils Peak saddle (5020-4.8), on the Devils Peaks crest. From the saddle you can follow a faint, rocky trail ¼ mile over to the remains of Lower Devils Peak Lookout, which was dismantled in 1976. The views you obtain from it are fine, but the many views ahead equal those from the lookout site. The lower room of the lookout still remains, albeit roofless, and it does offer a flat, fairly wind-free campsite.

From the crest saddle we start across the first of several major burns we'll traverse before Lily Pad Lake. Note the charred remains of knobcone pines here. These pines need a major fire, whose heat opens their cones, to release the seeds. These short-lived pines die in the process, but new pines soon sprout. Without periodic fires, the population would die out. On the east ridge of Middle Devils Peak we meet the Darkey Creek Trail (5170-0.6), starting down the burned-over ridge. As we traverse the northeast-facing slopes of Middle Devils Peak, we pass the first of several small groves of weeping spruce, spared from the conflagration. Note the trees' drooping "Douglas-fir" branches, their oversize "hemlock" cones and their scaly "lodgepole" bark.

North of the peak we reach a saddle, and from here, as well as from short switchbacks above it, we can pause for views of snow-capped Mt. Shasta (14,162') to the east and the Marble

Schaffer at sinkhole

A1

Weeping spruce and Red Butte

Mountain Wilderness to the south. Beyond the switchbacks we reach Upper Devils Peak's western arm (5820-1.0), from where a spur trail once descended 330 steep yards past western white pines to a seeping spring amid a cluster of alders. The pines and the trail are largely gone, but if you bear about 330° downslope, you should have very little trouble finding the spring.

Our trail now makes a traverse north, and along it we pass the charred remains of a forest before we come to a small grove of weeping spruce. Just past it we descend briefly to a saddle, which has a junction with faint Portuguese Creek Trail 12W03 (5760-1.2). If you need water, you can drop west about 300 vertical feet along it to the seasonal headwaters of Portuguese Creek and then follow the creek down another 300–600' in elevation to find flowing water. The PCT next climbs north up to a quickly reached junction with Boundary Trail 12W47 (5940-0.3). Before the creation of Red Buttes Wilderness in 1984, this was known as the Rattlesnake Mountain Trail. As you can see

A1

To ROAD 46N50 and HIGHWAY 96

on this section's first map, the trail stays quite close to the south boundary of Red Buttes Wilderness. You'll likely have noted by now a high, often snowy peak along the western skyline, 7309′ Preston Peak.

Now we head 100 yards southeast to a minor saddle on nearby Devils Peaks crest, which also happens to be the south ridge of rusty Kangaroo Mountain. The mountain's glaciated, broad-floored basin greets us as we start a short, switchbacking descent, and along it you may see two tiny ponds, each having a nearby campsite. Heading north from the switchbacks, we discover a creek that disappears into a sinkhole dissolved from a layer of light-gray marble that contrasts strongly with the ancient, orange ultramafic intrusives of this area. These rocks are likely the northern extension of the rock types one sees along the PCT in the Marble Mountain Wilderness, on the distant southern skyline.

Likely because of the often damp nature of the basin's floor, the basin was largely spared from the 1987 fire. The basin's western lands are drier, and if you need to camp, look for a site there. Heading east, we reach a spring (5760-0.8) in spongy ground. From this spring—the easternmost of the Kangaroo Springs—the trail soon reaches a southeast slope. This the trail traverses, and soon you reach Kangaroo Mountain's east ridge (5900-0.5) and leave burned, *trailside* vegetation behind, although you'll see burned slopes on lands south of you all the way to Cook and Green Pass.

From the east ridge we can gaze down at Lily Pad Lake, with its small, poor, adjacent camp-sites and its multitude of frogs. Our trail stays high above this lake and arcs northwest over to a narrow ridge, which is a small part of the Red Buttes Wilderness boundary. Along this ridge you may find a trail register, and just past it is a junction with a spur trail (5900-0.2). This goes 115 yards north along the boundary ridge to a jeep road, on which you could pitch a tent. Westward, within the wilderness, the jeep road is closed, but eastward it is still open and is definitely used. The PCT will parallel it at a distance down to Cook and Green Pass.

With that goal in mind, we go but 200 yards northeast on the PCT before intersecting an old trail that starts from the jeep road just above us and drops to Lily Pad Lake. Now we descend gently east to a ridge that provides views down into the lake's glaciated canyon. From the ridge we circle a shallower, mildly glaciated canyon

and cross the jeep road (5710-1.0), which has been staying just above us. The trail has kept below the road to avoid the Chrome King Mine, which lies just southwest of the road crossing. Next we traverse through a stand of timber, then climb past more brush to a junction on a crest saddle (5900-0.5). From it Horse Camp Trail 958 descends northeast toward nearby Echo Lake, whose environs provide camping superior to that at Lily Pad Lake.

Leaving the saddle and the last outcrop of marble we'll encounter on our northbound trek, we make a long, mostly brushy descent, first east and then north, down to Cook and Green Pass (4770-2.5). There is room for at least several hiking parties on the forested, nearly flat crest immediately west of the road that crosses the pass. Get water by going along a trail that leads northwest from the pass. You'll reach a spring in 150 yards; if it's dry, continue another 225 yards to a creeklet. Here, along the crest border between Klamath National Forest to the south and Rogue River National Forest to the north, a major USFS road crosses the pass and then descends about 10½ miles to the start of this section's route, Seiad Store. The PCT route is about 4½ miles longer. Northbound from Cook and Green Pass, the USFS road snakes its way about 10 miles down to Hutton Campground, which is situated about a mile from a large reservoir, Applegate Lake.

From this pass we follow an obvious trail east up the ridge toward Copper Butte. On it we pass scattered knobcone pines in a vegetative cover that includes manzanita, western serviceberry, tobacco brush and Sadler's oak. Like tombstones, slabs of greenish-gray, foliated mica schist stand erect along the trail and, in the proper light, reflect the sun's rays as glacially polished rocks do. Our trail makes a long switchback up to the crest, passing a clearcut in the process. There are other clearcuts to the south, on slopes east of Seiad Creek, and this patchwork landscape of forest and clearing contrasts with the burned slopes, which are mostly west of the creek. We must remember that this section is logging country, and one may run into ongoing logging operations along the route east.

Once back on the crest, the PCT enters a stand of white fir, red fir, mountain hemlock, Douglas-fir, ponderosa pine and knobcone pine—a combination we'd never see in the Sierra Nevada, where these trees are altitudinally zoned to a much greater extent. On the north slopes just below the crest, you'll also find

A1   **A1, A2**

Deer on crest near Mud Springs

weeping spruce. Rather than struggle to the top of Copper Butte, as early PCT hikers did on the old trail, we make a slight ascent to its south ridge, on which we meet Trail 11W02 (6080-2.8), which descends south to Low Gap, Salt Gulch and Seiad Valley. Our course now becomes a northeast one and we keep close to the crest, crossing several forested crest saddles before arriving at an open one (6040-2.2), from which Horse Creek Trail 11W01 begins a brushy descent south to Middle Creek Road 46N50. This road descends southeast to the hamlet of Horse Creek on Highway 96. We continue northeast to another saddle (6040-0.3), where you'll intersect the faint Tin Cup Trail. South-southeast, it heads 230 vague yards to a small spring with an equally small campsite at the Lowdens Cabin site. It is better to camp at the saddle, where there is a bit more room. Leaving it, we start a contour east around a brushy bowl, and after ¼ mile—just before leaving it—we pass Beardog Spring, a few yards below the trail.

Our brushy contour becomes a forested one of Douglas-fir, Jeffrey pine and incense-cedar before we reach a deep crest saddle. Along the south slope of White Mountain we cross somewhat open slopes again, reach its spur ridge, and then arc east across the upper limits of a meadowy hollow. At its east end is a junction (5950-2.0) with the old PCT, which will lead you to a seasonal seep near the hollow's west edge. Just beyond this junction we reach another saddle and from it we climb east up to a higher crest. We stay close to it on a path that glitters with mica flakes before we eventually curve southeast and descend an open slope. On it we cross, then parallel, a crest road that takes us

across a long saddle, then almost touching the hairpin turn of Road 47N81 (6310-2.4). You can take the lower road branch south about ¼ mile to one of the Reeves Ranch Springs, located near the top of an alder grove just below

A2, A3

see MAP A5

the road. Note that this is the *second* alder grove you'll pass. The first one has a seasonal spring. More springs lie along the next ½ mile of road.

The Pacific Crest Trail parallels the east side of the road's upper branch, climbing first south, then east, and eventually traversing the south slopes of Condrey Mountain before descending ¾ mile to a saddle (6630-3.1). On it, a spur road leaves Road 47N81 to descend west-southwest 0.3 mile to Buckhorn Camp, a poor campsite beside a trickling spring a few yards farther east. Another spur road leaves the saddle, this one de-

scending north ¼ mile to delightful Alex Hole Camp, located near a willow-lined spring. Here, where your far-reaching view north is framed by cliffs of mica schist, your only neighbors may be deer, chipmunks and mountain bluebirds.

Back on the PCT, we start to parallel ascending Road 47N81, then veer north away from it to climb the main Siskiyou crest. We almost top Peak 7043 before descending into a mountain-hemlock forest. Long-lasting snow patches can make the next mile to the Mud Springs spur road difficult to follow, but if so you can take the crest

A3, A4   A4, A5

Wrangle Campground shelter

road, just east of us, to the same destination. Just yards away from Road 40S01, the PCT crosses the Mud Springs spur road (6730-2.3), and you can continue northwest 0.2 mile down this road to its end, where there are several very refreshing clear-water springs and a couple of small campsites on sloping ground. You may prefer to camp on level ground up by the PCT.

Past the spur road we have a wonderful, open, near-crest traverse that passes a prominent rock midway in our approach to less imposing, misnamed Big Rock. We descend northeast across its open, gravelly east slope of glistening mica, briefly enter a patch of firs, leave it, and head south back into forest as we descend to a crossing of Road 40S01 (6250-1.6). Our trail now enters an old logging area as it first continues southward, then turns northeast and descends to cross a road (5930-0.8), which lies immediately north of Bearground Spring. As you'll see, this is an area of several springs. This vicinity, which in former days was heavily used by car campers, is now favored by equestrians.

From the Bearground Spring road you start among shady Shasta red firs and make a steady descent northeast, crossing an abandoned logging road midway to a saddle. Nearing this saddle, you cross narrow Road 40S01 at its hairpin turn, immediately recross the road, and in a couple of minutes reach a 6-way road junction on the saddle, Wards Fork Gap (5317-1.3). Southbound Road 47N01 traverses over to

Road 47N44, and from that junction both descend to Beaver Creek. Along the creek, Road 48N01 descends to Highway 96, reaching it just 0.7 mile northeast of Klamath River, a small community with store and post office. Road 48N15, descending east from the saddle, also will get you to Beaver Creek. Road 1065 traverses west from the saddle, but later drops to Road 1050, which makes a long, leisurely descent west to Hutton Campground and the nearby Applegate Lake area.

Between north-climbing Road 48N16 and east-climbing 40S01, the PCT starts to climb northeast from Wards Fork Gap. This short stretch is usually overgrown and hard to follow. If you can't, then from the saddle head north briefly up Road 48N16 to a bend, from which a logging spur continues north. You'll see the PCT just above it, paralleling it first north, then west. Walk south up Road 48N16 midway to its second bend, and you should be able to find the northbound PCT without much trouble.

On it we make a short climb north before embarking on a long traverse that circles clockwise around a knoll to Donomore Creek. This you parallel east to within 100 yards of the Donomore Meadows road, then bridge the creek (5600-1.5) and wind northward up an amorphous ridge that may be crisscrossed with misleading cow paths. In ½ mile we cross this road at a point about 80 yards east of a cabin, then parallel a jeep road, immediately below us,

A5   **A5**

Here we cross wide Road 2025, then climb east up a clearcut crest, and leave it to make a long, curving traverse northward to the west ridge (6750-1.6) of twin-topped Observation Peak. Kettle Lake, below us, immediately comes into view as we start an uphill traverse east; if you want to camp at it, then descend directly to it. We climb east to Kettle Creek, then climb north from it high above Kettle Lake before rounding the large northwest ridge of Observation Peak. A southeast traverse through stands of mountain hemlocks—snowbound until mid-July—gets us to Observation Gap (7030-1.2), a shallow saddle just west of and above 40S01.1. From the gap we go ½ mile on our crest trail, cross Road 40S01.1, traverse around the east slopes of Peak 7273, and then parallel the crest north to Jackson Gap (7040-1.2). Before reaching this gap you'll certainly notice landscape terracing in the Jackson Gap area, done to prevent erosion on the burned-over slopes. Crossing this gap just a few feet above us is broad Road 20, which we'll parallel all the way to the end of Section A. Before mid-July, snow drifts will probably force you to take this road rather than the PCT.

Leaving the cover of hemlocks and firs, we arc clockwise across the upper slopes of a huge open bowl, soon reaching a spur road (6920-0.3) to Sheep Camp Spring, located 10 yards south on it. Camp space is very limited, and since it lacks tree cover, you would probably greet next morning's sunrise from a very wet sleeping bag. Departing east from the spur road, we gradually descend, with unobstructed views, to a spur ridge, then arc northeast to Wrangle Gap (6496-2.3), reaching it ¼ mile after we cross to the north side of Road 20. From here a spur road descends steeply west to Wrangle Campground—the answer to an exhausted hiker's prayer. This little-used recreation site, nestled among Shasta red firs, has a large stone shelter complete with fireplace, two stoves and tables. In the '70s it also had tap water. Unless the USFS decides to reinstate piped-in water, you'll have to get some at the upper end of a small bowl, where you'll find a spring that is about 150 yards south-southwest from the shelter.

From Wrangle Gap the PCT route could have gone east, but instead it makes a long climb north to the end of Red Mountain ridge and starts to wind southeast up it. The route does have the advantage of giving you sweeping panoramas of southern Oregon and its pointed landmark, Mt. McLoughlin—an Ice Age vol-

which follows the meadow's edge north. At the meadow's upper end, our trail curves east above it, then switchbacks west for a short, partly steep ascent northwest into Oregon, and soon veers north up to a logging-road saddle (6210-1.4).

cano. After crossing the ridge we contour south and then east, leaving Red Mountain's slopes for a winding, moderate descent to the west end of open Siskiyou Gap (5890-3.8), where we cross Road 20. The northeast quarter of Section 34 lies in private land, and for many years the owner resisted attempts at building a direct trail, paralleling Road 20, over to nearby Long John Saddle. Finally in desperation, the USFS built a trail twice as long to that goal. It first parallels Road 20 briefly over to its junction with Road 40S12, then parallels that road briefly over to a crossing (5800-0.3). Then it makes a long swing around a hill, offering us some Mt. Shasta views in partial compensation for our added hiking effort before finally reaching a 5-way road junction (5880-1.3) on forested Long John Saddle.

Road 20 traverses north across the level saddle and a minor logging road descends northeast. Between the two the Pacific Crest Trail starts to parallel Road 20 north, then climbs northeast through an old logging area. After a mile of progress, we come to a spur ridge and exchange this scarred landscape for a shady forest climb north. From a gully our gradient eases to give us a pleasant stroll northeast to an open crest saddle (6710-2.1). On it, our tread almost disappears as it parallels Road 20 for a few yards, then it becomes prominent again and climbs a short ½ mile up to a saddle just north of

Siskiyou Peak. From this saddle you'll see chunky Pilot Peak on the eastern skyline—a guiding beacon for early pioneers and for us. If you're continuing through Oregon, you should pass by it in a few days. Our road now winds ⅓ mile northeast toward a saddle on the main crest, crossing a spur road (6900-0.8) that is just 25 yards below its departure from crest-hugging Road 20. The saddle is signed as the Meridian Overlook, since it is a viewpoint close to the Willamette Meridian.

We parallel Road 20 northeast, sometimes below it and sometimes above it, to another saddle (7030-1.1) south of the main crest. Here the road bends north to descend, but we first go south briefly before switchbacking to descend northeast to reach Road 40S30 (6630-1.0) at its junction with Road 20 on expansive Grouse Gap. This road takes you 0.2 mile south to a fork, from where you branch left on Road 40S30A for a minute's walk to Grouse Gap Shelter, built in the mid-70s. The shelter provides protection from the elements and it offers dramatic sunrise views of Mt. Shasta. You can usually get water from the creeklet just northeast of and below the shelter, but late-season trekkers will likely have to backtrack on 40S30A to 40S30, and then take that road ⅓ mile southwest down to an obvious gully with a spring-fed creeklet.

A7, A8   A8, A9

Mt. Shasta, from Mt. Ashland Campground

A8

Wagner Gap

33 Water 34 35 36 31

2250

4

Greely Creek 3 2 Cold Spring Wagner Butte 1 6

Lookout 7140

5535 6870

2040 Sheep Cr

9 10 McDonald 11 22 12 Wagner Glade Gap 7

4278 Jim Cr 6754

Freezeout Cabin Rock

R I V E R Split Split Rock

16 15 14 13 Creek 18

4159 Center

F O R E S T McDonald Pk

7226

21 22 23 24 19

Bear Gl 20

Meridian Overlook KNF

2040 T A I N S 6838

22 ROAD 6862

27 26 25

20 6400 Siskiyou Pk

28 7147 30

6424 MERIDIAN

M O U WILLAMETTE

Long John Saddle

BM 5879

33 Siskiyou Gap 34 35 36 31

20 LOOP 40S16

40S12 BM 5079

see MAP A7

see MAP A9

Pilot Rock and distant Mt. Shasta, from PCT above Mt. Ashland Road

From Grouse Gap the PCT parallels Road 20 and passes several seeping springs before it gradually drops away from it down to a crossing of Road 40S15 (6480-1.9), which climbs ½ mile northeast up to this crest road. From their junction, Road 20 contours ½ mile northeast to the Mt. Ashland Ski Area, and eastward the road is paved. An alternative to camping at Grouse Gap Shelter is to camp at Mt. Ashland Campground, which straddles both sides of Road 20. To reach it, leave the PCT and follow Road 40S15 about 250 yards up to its bend left, from where you'll see an abandoned logging road that climbs directly upslope to the campground. The piped water isn't always flowing, and when it's not, get water in a little gully just above the campground's upper (north) sites. From Road 40S15 the PCT contours southeast to the bend and then traverses northeast to an open bowl below the ski area. From this it traverses southeast to a saddle, where we cross Road 20 (6160-1.5). Continuing southeast down-ridge, we follow the PCT down to Road 2080 (6060-0.4).

*   *   *   *

From our ridge you can take a supply route by following Road 2080 north down to Bull Gap (5500-2.8), where you meet Road 200, which

climbs southwest up to the Mt. Ashland Ski Area. Continuing north, take Road 200, which in 3 miles rejoins Road 2080, all the way down to Glenview Drive (2200-8.5) in Ashland. Descend this road north, then descend Fork Street. You quickly reach Pioneer Street and follow it two blocks to C Street. The Ashland Post Office is one block southeast on it, at the corner of First and C streets (1920-1.1). To get back to the PCT, head southwest one block to East Main and walk southeast. It quickly becomes two-way Siskiyou Boulevard (1950-0.3), and you continue southeast on it to Highway 66 (Ashland Street) (2010-1.1). Take this east past the Ashland Shopping Center to Washington Street, which has the Ashland Ranger Station at its end. Just east of this short street you reach Interstate 5 (1980-1.3-15.1). Since hitchhiking on freeways is legal in Oregon, you can hitchhike up it 9 miles to the Mt. Ashland exit. Alternately, you can continue on Highway 66, then go south up Highway 273 to that exit, about a 12-mile route. This route is described in the opposite direction at the end of this chapter.

*   *   *   *

If you decide against the supply route, then continue east down the forested trail. The PCT

A9   **A9**

see MAP A8

see MAP A10

stays on or north of the crest, but after 0.7 mile it crosses to its south side and in ¼ mile crosses a jeep road that climbs northeast back to the nearby crest. Not until 1987 was the next stretch—through sections 23, 24 and 26—completed. Rights of way across private property held up PCT construction for more than a decade.

The PCT continues its eastern descent, first past grass and bracken ferns, and then mostly past brush. Soon the trail switchbacks and then quickly reaches the shady grounds of Mt. Ashland Inn, a bed-and-breakfast establishment opened Christmas 1987. The rates are very reasonable, as such establishments go, but they are nevertheless far too high for the average long-distance hiker. However, the owners,

Elaine and Jerry Shanafelt, do freely offer water to passing hikers.

A minute's walk below the inn we cross a saddle (5490-1.5), and then parallel Road 20 for a generally brushy traverse over to another saddle (5110-0.8). Next we make a similar traverse, this one to a saddle with 4 roads radiating from it (4990-0.8). Eastbound, the PCT is confined between an old crest road and Road 20 for the first ⅓ mile, then it parallels the latter as both descend east around ridges and across gullies. Three closely spaced gullies near the end of this descent provide spring-fed water before they coalesce to flow into East Fork Cotton Creek.

Because we are on private land, we aren't allowed to deviate from the trail's tread and aren't allowed to camp. Thick brush prevents us

A9

A10

Ashland's Emigrant Lake, along alternate route

from doing either, anyway. About 0.4 mile past our last spring-fed gully, we cross a road (4610-2.5) that descends steeply southeast to nearby Road 20, which here turns southeast to cross a broad saddle. Then, after a short, steep descent of our own, we cross a road (4470-0.1) that climbs gently west up to a union with the first road at paved Road 20. Both dirt roads are private—off limits—as is a third road that we parallel east before we momentarily turn south to cross (4360-0.1). Now we parallel this road, staying just above it, dip in and out of a gully with a sometimes flowing freshet, and soon curve away from the road as we glimpse busy, nearby Interstate 5. Our path ends (4250-0.8) at an abandoned segment of old Highway 99, which we take for 140 yards around a hollow to a fork. Here we go left and descend an old, closed road 150 yards to trail's end on Highway 99. This trailhead is 250 yards north of where Mt. Ashland Road 20 ends at Highway 99 (4240-0.3), and that junction in turn is immediately north of where Interstate 5 crosses over the highway. Here, at the junction of Road 20 and Highway 99, our section ends. The Mesozoic granitic rocks we've traversed along the eastern crest of the Siskiyou Mountains are here overlaid by mid-Tertiary, thick, basaltic andesite flows; and the Shasta red firs and mountain hemlocks have yielded to Douglas-firs and orange-barked madrones.

If you've hiked the PCT through much or all of California, you may want to celebrate your entry into Oregon by visiting Callahan's Restaurant. Go north on Highway 99 for ⅔ mile to Highway 273 and on it cross under Interstate 5 at its Mt. Ashland exit. The restaurant is just east of it. This ever-popular place, closed on Mondays, serves only dinners, and though Callahan's is expensive by backpackers' standards, it is one of the better dining places along or near the entire Pacific Crest Trail. If you've been starving these last few miles, you'll be glad to know that each of their dinners includes all the salad, soup and spaghetti you can eat.

To resupply for another stretch of the PCT in southern Oregon, you can hitchhike 9 miles down Interstate 5 to the Highway 66 interchange and take the highway west into downtown Ashland.

*   *   *   *

An old, temporary PCT route offers you another way down to Ashland. From Callahan's (3950-0.9 mile from end of Road 20), you can go down tree-lined Highway 273 to a junction with Highway 66 (2290-6.7). Just east of it is the shallow upper end of Emigrant Lake, a popular fishing area; the deeper parts are relegated to water skiers, boaters and swimmers. Northwest, Highway 66 leads you to the main entrance to the Emigrant Lake Recreation Area (2150-1.8). Here a paved road heads southeast 0.4 mile up to a lateral dam, then curves north 0.6 mile to a public campground. Past the recreation area's entrance you'll come to fairly expensive but well-equipped Glenyan KOA campground (2140-0.2) with showers and a store. It caters to backpackers as well as to car campers, and the larger your hiking group, the cheaper your per-person camp fee will be.

Continuing northwest on Highway 66, you meet Dead Indian Road (1920-2.6) before your highway turns west and climbs to cross Interstate 5 (1980-0.7-12.9) at the outskirts of Ashland. Some backpackers prefer to celebrate in Ashland rather than at Callahan's, for there is quite a selection of good-to-excellent cafes and restaurants. In addition, more cultured backpackers take in one or more performances of Ashland's Oregon Shakespearean Festival, which runs most of the year. If the weather has been dreary or snow patches abundant, then perhaps a Shakespearean comedy will lift your spirits. Just north of the festival's grounds is the Ashland Hostel (150 N. Main), which welcomes PCT hikers and even has a PCT register.

A10   **A10**

The Pacific Crest Trail
in Section B

0 1 2 3 4 5   10 mi

This section's PCT
Other trails
Hwys and major rds
Other roads
Campgrounds

Section B: Interstate 5 near Siskiyou Pass to Highway 140 near Fish Lake

Introduction: Sections A and C are among the highest stretches of Pacific Crest Trail to be found in either Oregon or Washington. In contrast, Section B, between them, is one of the lowest, and it is certainly the driest, least scenic section to be found in either state. This section abounds with past and present logging projects which the PCT often passes through or skirts around. And if these eyesores don't detract from this section's appeal, the lack of wilderness sensation will: often you are closely paralleling logging roads or jeep roads. Furthermore, although two sizable lakes are approached—Hyatt and Howard Prairie—both are dammed and both lack any alpine or subalpine character. And there is a *notable* lack of drinking water. With such a list of detractions, Section B will certainly be shunned by the masses and its trail will likely be taken only by long-distance hikers passing through to a more scenic section.

Declination: 17¼°E

Mileages:	**South to North**	**Distances between Points**	**North to South**
Interstate 5 near Mt. Ashland Road 20.............	0.0		54.0
		4.6	
Cross upper Pilot Rock Jeep Road.................	4.6		49.4
		5.0	
Fenced-in spring	9.6		44.4
		4.3	
Hobart Bluff spur trail	13.9		40.1
		3.4	
Highway 66 at Green Springs Summit	17.3		36.7
		4.8	
Little Hyatt Reservoir	22.1		31.9
		1.5	
Hyatt Lake Campground spur trail.................	23.6		30.4
		7.9	
Road to Klum Landing Campground...............	31.5		22.5
		1.9	
Keno Access Road..............................	33.4		20.6
		9.1	
Dead Indian Road	42.5		11.5
		11.5	
Highway 140 near Fish Lake	54.0		0.0

Supplies: If you need major supplies, get them in Ashland before you start hiking this section. Directions to this city are given at the end of the previous section. Since this section is short, the need for supplies will be minimal, and minimal supplies is all you'll find at Hyatt Lake, Howard Prairie Lake, Lake of the Woods and Fish Lake resorts. All but Hyatt Lake Resort are somewhat out of your way, especially Lake of the Woods Resort. Hyatt Lake, Fish Lake and Lake of the Woods resorts conveniently hold packages (see page 15), so the long-distance trekker who is racing against time doesn't have to take a day or two out of his schedule to make a side trip to Ashland.

Problems: In this section you'll have to hike up to 22 miles between on-route water sources. If you intend to do this unattractive hiking section, then try to do it in June, when snow problems are minimal, yet seasonal creeks are flowing.

PCT striking east toward Pilot Rock

Section B's southern starting point is at the junction of Mt. Ashland Road 20 and Highway 99 (4240), this point being immediately north of Interstate 5. To reach it by car, start in Ashland at the Highway 66 exit and drive 9 miles south on I5 up to the Mt. Ashland exit. If you're driving north, note that this exit is 16½ miles past the Highway 96 exit in northern California. From the exit proceed ⅔ mile south on Highway 99 to the Road 20 junction.

From this junction start hiking south up the highway, immediately crossing under noisy Interstate 5. You hike straight for ⅓ mile, then start to curve right. In about 250 more yards you

should see the resumption of PCT tread (0.5–4380), which crosses a gully that runs down the highway's east side. Note that there isn't a large trailhead sign, since this would attract bikers, something the landowners don't want. If you reach a road branching east, you've gone about 120 yards too far.

On the PCT we cross the gully, then momentarily cross the road. On private land we traverse eastward about ¾ mile across Section 28, and then our winding path angles north at a spring (4490–0.9), but quickly switchbacks. On a southward track, we climb moderately up toward a ridge, passing close to another spring,

B1   **B1**

see MAP A10

B1

see MAP B3

see MAP A10

Buck Rock
4203

Airway
Beacon
Steinman

Carter

17
BM
3920

16
BM
3091

15

14
4090

4286

INTERSTATE 5

PACIFIC

273

BM 3259

22

23

20
Siskiyou
4129

21

Callahans

4507

29

28

27

26

4458
Airway Beacon

Siskiyou
Pass
4466

40·2E·33

233

34

35
5306
Porcupine Mtn

see MAP B2

32

Gravel Pit

4400

HIGHWAY 99

M
O
U
N
T
A
I
N
S

PILOT
ROCK
JEEP ROAD

4800

5
3665

4
4562

3

2
Pilot Rock
VABM 5910

5405

5200

5317

INTERSTATE 5

TRAIL

229

9

JEEP

4151

4000

10
4656

11

Hutton

4800

99

17

OREGON
CALIFORNIA
3600

16

15

14
JACKSON
SISKIYOU

18

17

16

YREKA 23 MI.   HIGHWAY 96 9 MI.

almost a half mile after the first, just before leaving Section 28. In Section 33 we wind gently ⅓ mile south up to a crest and, after a moment's walk down a spur ridge, reach a road junction. One of the roads descends to a broad saddle, and we do the same, keeping east of the road as our path, an abandoned jeep road, winds 0.2 mile down to a major intersection (4420–1.3). Here, roads go in all directions, two of them leading south along the east side of a crest. In this general vicinity you'll see evidence of intensive logging operations.

Starting on lumber-company land, the Pacific Crest Trail begins beside the western southbound road. In 0.2 mile, however, it almost touches the wider, eastern one, then climbs ⅓ mile through a cool forest of Douglas-fir and white fir. As our trail emerges onto public land and southwest-facing slopes, the forest thins rapidly, junipers appear and temperatures rise. We hike southeast across a long, open crest, and past its low point our trail, mixing with old jeep tracks, can become rather vague. However, head toward a cluster of trees, through which our faint trail passes, bearing toward steep-sided Pilot Rock. In a few minutes we cross a secondary crest, bend southwest and traverse to a minor road, which we cross and then parallel as it curves east to a prominent intersection atop a broad saddle (5080–1.7).

The Pilot Rock Jeep Road starts east from this saddle, soon climbing steeply toward the base of Pilot Rock. Our trail makes an obscure start along this road's south edge and after 270 yards (5120–0.2) crosses it for a northeast climb to a nearby volcanic point. If you have the time, you might first make an excursion to the summit of Pilot Rock. The jeep road ends at the rock's base, from which you'll see an obvious chute up to the top. This route is relatively safe and no rope is required. However, acrophobics or careless climbers could get in trouble.

From the volcanic point beyond the Pilot Rock Jeep Road, the PCT goes briefly east along an abandoned road, then descends northeast 180 yards to a trailside outcrop with a summit that provides fair views across the northern landscape. Continuing our northeast descent, we round a ridge in ¼ mile and momentarily reach a crest. This we parallel northeast for a few minutes before turning east across it at a gate (5160–0.9)—the first of many. Immediately, a dramatic volcanic landscape unfolds before us, with a huge blocky pinnacle in the foreground and towering Pilot Rock to the south.

The trailside pinnacle is easier to climb than it looks, but due to its exposure, it should be climbed *only* by experienced climbers.

Beyond the pinnacle our trail quickly angles north, then makes a pleasant, winding descent through a Douglas-fir forest to a large gate only a few yards south of a crest saddle (4990–0.7). A road from the southeast climbs up to our saddle, crosses it, and swings west, eventually joining the Pilot Rock Road, which climbs east from Highway 99. Also at this crest is a reappearance of the Pilot Rock Jeep Road, which seems to be quite abandoned west of the saddle. East of it, however, it is in good shape, as we'll see, for we will cross it again and again. On our next stretch, as on most of Section B, our route alternates between private land—usually lumber companies—and Bureau of Land Management (BLM) land.

From the crest saddle, our trail first descends southeast, then curves northeast over to a gully. The PCT is now routed on an abandoned, overgrown roadbed, which we follow east for a few minutes, then climb north to a crest (5020–1.2).

B1, B2

Pilot Rock and trailside pinnacle

B1

A short segment of trail leads us east across north-facing slopes to a road, up which we walk 65 yards to a minor crest saddle and the trail's resumption, on our left (5040-0.2). This trail segment goes but 110 yards, and then we cross the jeep road and parallel it east. Twice more we cross this road, the second time where a minor road (5270-0.8) starts a descent southeast.

Our trail now parallels the jeep road northeast, and after ¼ mile it provides us with a half mile of almost continuous views of Mt. Shasta. Pilot Rock, our former guiding beacon, is now

B2

B2

see MAP B1

see MAP B2

hidden. Beyond the views our trail enters forest and descends gently east, crossing a broad saddle just before it turns northeast to enter a fenced-in compound with a dilapidated hut beside a very refreshing spring (5290–1.2). This spring, complete with cistern and water faucet, is a full 7.7 miles from the upper spring near the southeast corner of Section 28 (Map B1). Happily, the water situation ahead starts out much better. Since this fenced-in spring is your first reliable water in many miles, you might plan to camp here. The fence keeps out cows—a definite plus—but all the enclosed area is gently sloping—a definite minus.

Still following the jeep road, the PCT descends northeast to a saddle (5140–0.3). The last faint 15 yards of this trail stretch is along the west side of an abandoned, overgrown road—not always apparent to southbound hikers. From the saddle the Baldy Creek Road descends north, another descends east, a third contours northeast, and just above it our jeep road climbs

northeast. The PCT parallels this road's north-west side, twice crosses it, skirts past the south slope (5550–0.9) of unassuming Little Pilot Peak, then dips to the north side of a saddle (5550–0.1). On this saddle you could make a small camp by or on the jeep road. Here you'll see a tiny, man-made pond on an open slope 90 yards north below the PCT. The pond's water should be treated if you drink it.

We continue northeast for a ¼-mile traverse, then bend east for a continuing traverse, passing a seeping spring found between two open slopes. Past the second slope the trail curves northeast and you quickly see a pond and an adjacent spring-fed tub, 80 yards northwest down from the trail (5550–0.8). Before leaving here, tank up, for your next reliable water will be at a spring north of Green Springs Mountain, a dry 8.8 miles away.

Continuing our traverse, we meet an old trail (5560–0.2) that climbs 300 yards to a saddle junction with the Soda Mountain Road. Our companion, the Pilot Rock Jeep Road, ends at this road about 0.3 mile south of the saddle. The PCT stays below the saddle, traversing open slopes that give you views west to Mt. Ashland and all the countryside below you. Beyond the views the trail drops to a shaded saddle (5420–0.6), traverses north along a crest, then drops past powerlines to a crossing of Soda Springs Road (5300–0.5).

Just east of an open saddle, we start north-northeast through a meadow with vegetation that sometimes obscures the trail, but in 100 yards we re-enter forest cover for a shady traverse around Hobart Peak to a long saddle. One-third mile past it we will meet the Hobart Bluff spur trail (5220–0.9), which climbs ⅓ mile to the juniper-capped summit. From it you'll see distant Mt. Shasta to the south-southeast, Soda Mountain to the near south, Pilot Rock behind Hobart Peak to the southwest, Mt. Ashland to the west, the spacious Ashland-Medford Valley to the northwest, and pyramidal Mt. McLoughlin, which we'll see close-up at the start of Section C, to the north-northeast.

From the Hobart Bluff spur trail the PCT traverses through a woodland of pygmy Oregon oaks before emerging on more-open slopes and then curving northwest down into forest cover. This temporarily gives way to a dry-grassland slope, then the PCT descends north-northeast, giving us our last view of the Ashland environs. We climb again and almost top Peak 4755, then descend north-northwest, spying Keene Creek reservoir before we cross Highway 66 at Green Springs Summit (4551–3.4). You can reach the tempting reservoir by hiking ¼ mile northeast along Highway 66, then dropping to the nearby shore. Spots of ground are level enough for camping (no campfires, please).

Immediately east of north-climbing Hyatt Lake Recreation Road 100-90, the PCT climbs gently northeast from Green Springs Summit, then rolls northwest across private land, crossing a one-lane road about 90 yards past a small powerline. If you need water, head 0.2 mile north down the road to private cattleland, leave the road and, staying west of a fence, drop to nearby grass-bordered Keene Creek. Just 0.2 mile past the road crossing on private land, we cross Road 100-90 (4700–1.4) and then climb south-southwest up to a crossing of the Greensprings Mountain Road (4840–0.5). The PCT then continues briefly to the meadow's head, curves north around it, then closely follows the road almost to a saddle. By the

saddle we cross a spur road (4940–0.7) that climbs briefly west from the main road. We then cross immediately north of the actual saddle and descend gently northwest to open slopes with views west. The trail quickly turns northeast and through a shady forest it contours over to a water faucet (4800–0.6) fed by an uphill spring. (Southbound hikers take note: this spring is your last on-route, reliable water until a spring-fed tub of water, 8.8 miles away.)

Beyond the faucet the PCT drops 300 yards to the Greensprings Mountain Road, which we follow northeast for 150 yards, then leave it immediately before this road curves northwest for a moderate descent. Back on trail we descend briefly northeast to jeep tracks beside the Ashland lateral canal (4600–0.5), now a dry gully. It once diverted water from Keene Creek west down to Ashland and thence to the Rogue River, but today Keene Creek flows as it used to, ultimately down to the Klamath River.

The PCT has made a westward diversion of its own—to avoid private property—and it now climbs east to a ridge, drops into a gully, crosses a second ridge, and in a second gully meets a trail (4670–0.9) that climbs northward ¼ mile to Little Hyatt Reservoir. We head east down to the nearby canal, cross it, then follow it momentarily up to the reservoir's dam and adjacent Hyatt Lake Recreation Road 100-90 (4610–0.2). Under ponderosa pines along the reservoir's east shore, you can fish or just stretch out and relax. Swimming is best near the dam, from which you can dive into the tranquil water. It is a great place for a layover day, for it lacks the noise and congestion found at larger Hyatt and Howard Prairie lakes. At Little Hyatt Reservoir you can camp in the *de facto* campground (with toilet) above the east shore.

Moving along, we find the PCT's resumption 25 yards south of where it ended at Road 100-90. The trail first climbs southeast and barely pokes into Section 28's private land—a totally unnecessary intrusion—then it climbs generally northeast past old roads to a road fork (5090–1.5), at which the northbound Hyatt Lake Road branches northwest as Road 100-85 and northeast as Road 100-80. From this fork you can follow steps *over* a fence and then follow a trail north ¼ mile to a campsite that is 80 yards west-southwest of Hyatt Lake Campground's shower rooms. The campsite was specifically established for PCT hikers, but because the trail to it is vague, the authors prefer to take the automobile approach; from the road fork, walk 170

B2, B3, B5, B4   **B4, B5**

Little Hyatt Reservoir

see MAP B5

see MAP B3

yards northeast down to the entrance road, descend another 170 yards to a sign-in, *pay* for a shower, then take the camp's west-climbing road over to the nearby shower rooms. If you don't camp at Little Hyatt Reservoir, you'll almost certainly want to do so at Hyatt Lake Campground. From the campground's north end, a shoreline trail heads west over to the lake's nearby dam, and from its far side, you can walk over to Hyatt Lake Resort, which has a cafe and a limited supply of groceries plus showers and a laundry room. By this route, the resort is a ¾-mile side trip from the road fork.

Back at the road fork, the PCT crosses the Hyatt Lake Road and curves east around the south side of the recreation area's administration building. After 280 trail yards, we reach a spur trail that heads north 140 yards to a drinking fountain—installed for PCT hikers—then continues 100 yards along the building's access road to Road 100-80. The campground entrance road is found 100 yards west on this road. The drinking fountain is your last reliable source of water until Grizzly Creek and its adjacent canal, about 8.5 miles farther.

Beyond the spur trail the PCT climbs east to a usually dry gully, then traverses northeast, crossing gullies and rounding ridges. Our tread stays above usually visible Road 100-80 and snag-tarnished Hyatt Lake. We cross southeast climbing Road 39-3E-15 (5100-2.1), down which one could walk 160 yards to the main, paved road and then follow it 220 yards west to the entrance road of the Hyatt Lake Overflow Camping Area. Next we wind over to east-climbing Wildcat Glades Road 39-3E-11 (5090-0.9). You could briefly descend this road to the main, paved road and then follow it (or the shoreline) westward to Hyatt Lake North Overflow Camping Area, on the lake's peninsula. Heading east on the PCT, we soon cross an older road (5100–0.2) to Wildcat Glades and immediately reach a seeping creek that drains the nearby glades.

Along the seeping creek's north bank, our trail starts upstream but quickly veers north and passes two sets of jeep tracks as it climbs up a ridge. After a switchback our trail swings to the east side of a secondary summit, then in 200 yards approaches the main one (5540–1.0). The scramble up to it (5610) gives you a disappointing view. Now halfway through this book's Section B, we descend northeast along a crest, almost touch a saddle (5310–0.5), then turn east for a long descent. Midway along it a jeep road climbs south across our trail up to a nearby saddle. Just past this road we get a fair view of Mt. McLoughlin and Howard Prairie Lake. Our descent ends when we cross a road (4620–2.0) that climbs southwest to a nearby rock quarry.

At this crossing we are only a few yards south of a major forest road. You can take it 1.6 miles northwest to a spur road that descends ¼ mile to Howard Prairie Lake and the Willow Point Campground. Just off this spur road you'll also find a ranger station. From the spur-road junction you can hike 0.7 mile west up to a paved road, follow it north 1.0 mile, then branch right 0.4 mile down to bustling Howard Prairie Lake Resort, which logically caters more to boating enthusiasts than to backpackers. However, meals and limited supplies can be bought. Howard Prairie Lake, though shallower than Hyatt Lake, is considerably better in appearance, since all the trees were removed before its basin was flooded.

From the quarry-road crossing, the PCT parallels the major forest road east to a quick junction (4620–0.1) with a road that descends an easy ½ mile to Soda Creek before climbing ¾ mile to the Wildcat Glades Road. Water obtained from Soda Creek is certainly better than what you'll find in Grizzly Creek—your next on-route source. Beyond the Soda Creek road, the PCT more or less dies out along a broad, open saddle. At its far end (4620–0.2), where a secondary road starts a climb east, the PCT starts a climb northeast and quickly you'll leave the company of the major forest road.

On the ascent, we get a couple of views down the length of Howard Prairie Lake, but these

Snag in Hyatt Lake

disappear before our trail's high point, the views being blocked by Douglas-firs, grand firs, sugar pines and incense-cedars. Our easy ascent is

B5, B6

see MAP B6

see MAP B4

see MAP B3

mirrored by an equally easy drop to a crossing of a little-used road (4670–0.9). You can follow this road 250 yards southwest down to the major forest road, then go an equal distance north on that road to the Klum Landing Campground entrance. Like the Little Hyatt Reservoir *de facto* campground, this campground is a good place to

spend a layover day. Relax, fish, or perhaps swim out to Howard Prairie Lake's interesting island.

Past the little-used road, the PCT drops northeast to a well-maintained road (4610–0.2) that traverses southwest to the start of the little-used road. Southbound hikers may want to take

B6

B6

this well-maintained road to the major forest road and thence to Klum Landing Campground. The PCT now heads north through a meadow whose seasonally tall grasses and herbs can hide the tread. Quickly, however, the trail enters forest cover, the tread becomes obvious, and we wind down to a canal, cross it and its maintenance road, then drop in 90 yards to a long bridge over Grizzly Creek (4440–0.5). You *could* camp in this area, which is within BLM boundaries, but all too often you would smell the water in both the canal and the creek. Klum Landing Campground is certainly more desirable, even if it is ⅓ mile off route. You are now 8.5 miles past your last on-route water, near Hyatt Lake, and your next reliable on-route water, northeast below Devils Peak, is a ludicrous 48½ miles away. Fortunately, a near-trail source, with plenty of room for camping, lies only 4.0 miles distant.

B6   **B6**

see MAP B6

Mt. McLoughlin rising above Howard Prairie Lake

Distant Mt. Shasta, from slopes of Old Baldy

Working toward that goal, we climb east, cross a forgotten road in 160 yards, then continue up to a crossing of the Moon Prairie Road (4580–0.4). The trail now turns northeast and climbs gently to a crossing of paved Keno Access Road (4720–0.8), a major trans-Cascade route for logging trucks bound for Klamath Falls. The PCT continues northeast and climbs to an old road (4790–0.2) whose traffic was pre-empted by the newer logging road. From it we round the northwest corner of a clearcut, pass a minor spur road, then curve east to a bend in the Brush Mountain Road (4960–0.6). Westbound hikers: please note that the last few yards of trail can be hidden by mulleins, thistles and other "weeds" that characteristically spring up in logging areas; therefore, just plow west from the bend.

We initially climb southeast from the bend but gradually curve northeast up through a shady forest of Douglas-fir and grand fir, cross a broad gully, climb to an adjacent ridge and just beyond it reach an old logging road (5480–1.5). This descends 0.3 mile to Griffin Pass Road 2520, which is also our immediate objective. So we continue our moderate climb northeast and soon approach it (5640–0.5). The PCT bends north beside this road, but you should seriously con-

sider walking 25 yards over to the road and down it 75 yards to an eastbound spur road. This spur road immediately crosses a creeklet that has been dammed, thus providing the hiker with a pond of fresh water—his last reliable source until the off-route Fish Lake Resort, a long 19.4 miles ahead. Since most long-distance backpackers average 15–20 miles a day, they should plan to camp here one night, then at Fish Lake the following night.

Where the PCT turns north, it parallels Road 2520 up to a crossing (5670–0.2) that is 250 yards short of ill-defined Griffin Pass. Still on BLM land, we parallel the Rogue River National Forest boundary east, immediately crossing the seasonal Big Springs creeklet. Don't bother looking for water upstream, since selective logging in that area apparently causes a considerable reduction in the springs' output. In ⅓ mile our trail bends southeast for a brief climb to a broad, shady saddle, then it angles northeast for a brief moderate climb to Old Baldy's clearcut slopes. Our ascent east around this conical landmark is an easy one, and its brushy terrain lets us have plenty of views south across miles of forest to majestic Mt. Shasta.

Chinquapin, tobacco brush and greenleaf manzanita yield to noble fir as our curving trail

B6, B7   **B7**

see MAP B10

see MAP B7

climbs to a northeast spur ridge, from which we traverse 140 yards northwest to the Rogue River National Forest boundary (6190–1.7). Before 1972 the Pacific Crest Trail route followed the old Oregon Skyline Trail route—mostly roads in southern Oregon—and it came up a now-abandoned trail to the boundary. In pre-'72 days the "PCT" headed north directly from Shasta rather than making the giant swing west to the Marble Mountains as it does today.

You can scramble south to Old Baldy's nearby summit (6340') for 360° views. Abandoned by fire lookouts, it is now under the watchful eye of turkey vultures. From it you can see Mt. Shasta (bearing 176°), Yreka (185°), Soda Mountain (217°), Pilot Rock (223°),

B7   **B7**

Hyatt Reservoir and Mt. Ashland (242°) and Mt. McLoughlin (354°). With these landmarks identified, a careful observer should be able to trace the PCT route over miles of country.

Now within Forest Service land, as we will be almost continually to the Washington border, we start northwest and quickly bend north to descend a pleasant, forested ridge. As we approach a ridge saddle, we come upon a faint spur trail (5880–1.0), which heads 140 yards west to Road 650. Beyond the spur trail, the PCT touches upon the saddle, then switchbacks down the northwest slopes of our ridge, swings east almost to Road 3802, turns north, and quickly crosses a closed road (5390–1.2). We parallel Road 3802, soon cross it (5390–0.3) and then wind north to a trailhead parking area by a crossing of Dead Indian Road (5360-1.9). The parking area is about 300 yards east of the road's junction with Road 3802. If you are covering hundreds of miles of PCT rather than just Section B, you may want to follow Dead Indian Road over to Lake of the Woods Resort. This alternate route is described at the end of this section.

Northbound, the PCT climbs away from Dead Indian Road, cuts northeast across a broad ridgecrest and then descends through an old logging area to a crossing of Road 740 (5270–1.9). This crossing is about 100 yards south of the road's junction with Road 500, which makes a loop—as our trail does—round the headwaters of South Fork Little Butte Creek. If you've been experiencing water-shortage problems, you'd be better off making a 3¼-mile trek—first north, then west—along Road 500. On it, you're likely to find water at two creek crossings and certainly will find it at a third, where the road crosses the Brown Mountain Trail branch of South Fork Little Butte Creek. From this creek the road climbs ¼ mile north to a broad saddle. Leave the road here and head northeast toward Brown Mountain. You should rejoin the PCT in less than ¼ mile. Here, you'll be about 3.6 trail miles beyond Road 740 and 5.8 trail miles from a junction with Trail 1014 to Fish Lake.

From Road 740 the PCT first contours northeast, then north, paralleling Road 500, which you sometimes see below as you cross an old logging area. Some gullies that you cross may contain water, particularly if you are hiking through in the mosquito-plagued month of June. Finally the trail drops to cross the Brown Mountain Trail branch of South Fork Little

Butte Creek (5180–2.2). The trail was abandoned with the construction of Road 500.

The PCT follows the seasonal creek westward until the stream angles south, then the trail traverses west for ½ mile before turning northwest and dropping 20 feet to a hollow. A 60-foot gain northwest from it takes us to a minor ridge (5210–1.4) to which those taking Road 500 will have climbed. From the ridge our trail continues its long, irregular arc around the lower slopes of Brown Mountain. Although the trail on the map superficially appears to be an easy traverse, careful study of it reveals that it has plenty of ups and downs—some of them steep—as you'll find out. As we traverse the northwest slopes of Brown Mountain, views of Mt. McLoughlin—a dormant volcano—appear and disappear. Nearing Highway 140, we reach a junction with Fish Lake Trail 1014 (4940–5.8).

Unless you are ending your hike at Highway 140, you'll want to visit the Fish Lake environs both for water and for supplies. A layover day wouldn't hurt. Trail 1014 winds ⅓ mile down to a seasonal pond, soon crosses the equally seasonal Cascade Canal, rambles across varied slopes, then treads a stringer separating a youthful upper lava flow from an equally youthful lower one. Next, it descends more or less alongside the lower flow and intersects Road 900 just before that road starts a traverse across the flow. With 1.5 miles between us and the PCT, we wind 100 yards west almost to Fish Lake, turn northeast, and momentarily end at the south tip of Fish Lake Resort's campground. Note the trail's end, for it may not be too obvious, and you'll want to find it later when you return to the PCT. But first, head over to the resort's office and cafe, located just above the boat dock. Food and supplies cater to the beer-drinking fishing crowd, though a beer (or two) will probably sound very tempting after your long, dry haul. Pick up your parcel if you've mailed one to the resort. Get a hot meal and a shower, do some laundry and then perhaps head ⅓ mile west over to the USFS Doe Point Campground.

After your stay at Fish Lake, return via Trail 1014 to the PCT. In 85 yards along the PCT you cross an old, abandoned highway bed, then soon reach broad, straight Highway 140 (4980–0.2). Cascade Canal crosses under Highway 140 about 40 yards west of your crossing. You'll meet the canal just beyond the highway. Don't expect any water flowing in it after midsummer.

B8　　　　　　　　　　　　**B8, B9**

B9

Your first near-trail water will be at Freye Lake, ¼ mile off the PCT and 4¾ miles from the highway.

*   *   *   *

Those who take the Lake of the Woods alternate route will reach Highway 140 about 4½ miles east of the PCT's highway crossing. However, rather than traverse west to it, they will climb north to meet it in the popular Sky Lakes Wilderness. By climbing north you pass more than a dozen lakes worth camping at, plus about two dozen trailside ponds—quite a contrast with the virtually waterless Pacific Crest Trail segment to which this is an alternate.

B9, B8   **B8**

The alternate route begins where the PCT crosses Dead Indian Road. It climbs east ¼ mile from the PCT to the Cascade crest, then descends down to a junction with Lake of the Woods' West Shore Road 3601 (4974–4.7). You could take this road north 3.5 miles to a junction with State Highway 140, from which Mt. McLoughlin Trail 3716 climbs 3.0 miles up a ridge to a crossing of Road 3650, then 1.0 mile up slopes to the PCT. But if you would prefer to take the PCT, rather than Mt. McLoughlin Trail 3716, north from Highway 140, then follow the highway west 3.6 miles. At the junction of the West Shore Road with 140, you can also head east, quickly passing the Lake of the Woods Work Center/Visitor Center, then Billie Creek, and in 250 yards reach a road to the Rye Spur trailhead—see end of chapter.

Disregarding these hiking possibilities, the hungry PCT trekker bears east from the West Shore Road junction, then curves north and passes the Winema National Forest East Side Recreation Residences, along the shore, before reaching the entrance to Sunset Campground (4990–2.2). In summer this is crowded with water skiers, swimmers, campers and fisher-

B8, B10   B10

Mt. McLoughlin and Lake of the Woods early in the morning

men. You'll find the lake's waters are stocked with Kokanee salmon, rainbow and eastern brook trout, and brown bullhead.

Continuing north, you reach a junction with Road 3704 (4954–1.0), along which you trek northwest to a spur road (5000–0.3) that heads ¼ mile southwest down to the lakeshore and the Lake of the Woods Resort. Here you can restock with enough supplies to last you until Crater Lake Post Office, 52 miles away by this alternate route. The resort also serves good meals and its store has a small post office at which you can pick up goodies you've mailed to yourself.

Back on Road 3704, continue northwest past the entrance to Aspen Point Campground

(4970–0.4), which is also the entrance to a picnic area and a safe swimming area. If you haven't yet taken a dip, do so here. Onward, you reach Highway 140 (4980–0.7), which you then take 0.2 mile west to a pole-line road. Start north, but in 5 yards branch right from it, making a hairpin turn onto a minor road. Follow it 100 yards to the start of Rye Spur Trail 3771 (4990–0.3). Measuring 9.6 miles from the PCT crossing at Dead Indian Road, this alternate route to a Highway 140 trailhead is about 2 miles shorter than the PCT route. A continuation of this alternate route, which is also shorter than the continued PCT route, is described in the early part of Section C.

B10

B10

The Pacific Crest Trail in Section C

N

0 1 2 3 4 5   10 mi

This section's PCT ————————
Other trails   ------------------
Hwys and major rds — — —
Other roads
Campgrounds   ▲

Section C: Highway 140 near Fish Lake to Highway 138 near the Cascade crest

Introduction: Both Sections A and B have a paucity of lakes and a surplus of roads, but in Section C the scenery changes and at last the hiker feels he is in a mountain wilderness. In fact, before the mid-1970s the scenery south of Highway 140 was deemed too poor to have a crest trail, and in those days anyone who hiked from northern California to southern Oregon had to follow a route that was almost entirely along roads.

The bulk of Section C is composed of two attractive areas: Sky Lakes Wilderness and inspiring Crater Lake National Park. The number of lakes in the wilderness rivals that in any other mountain area to be found anywhere along the PCT, while the beauty and depth of Crater Lake make it a worldwide attraction.

Unfortunately, the Pacific Crest Trail avoids Crater Lake entirely, and it takes a route the authors find very undesirable. Only equestrians and day hikers take part or all of this essentially viewless route. It is a good stretch to take if one wants to avoid crowds. We have yet to meet any long-distance PCT hiker who has bypassed Crater Lake and preferred the PCT. All have hiked up to the Rim Drive, and most have taken it clockwise for an ever-changing panorama of the lake. This alternate route, plus others in Sky Lakes Wilderness, is described along with the official PCT route.

Declination: 17½°E

Mileages:

	South to North	Distances between Points	North to South
Highway 140 near Fish Lake	0.0		76.0
		4.7	
Mt. McLoughlin Trail, westbound	4.7		71.3
		9.2	
Red Lake Trail (cross the alternate route)	13.9		62.1
		9.6	
Snow Lakes Trail (end of alternate route)	23.5		52.5
		2.4	
Devils Peak/Lee Peak saddle	25.9		50.1
		5.9	
Middle Fork Basin Trail to Ranger Springs	31.8		44.2
		4.6	
Jack Spring spur trail	36.4		39.8
		7.3	
Stuart Falls Trail, northeast end..................	43.7		32.3
		5.2	
Highway 62	48.9		27.1
		6.5	
Lightning Springs Trail..........................	55.4		20.6
		7.9	
Red Cone Spring.................................	63.3		12.7
		3.9	
North-rim access road	67.2		8.8
		8.8	
Highway 138 near the Cascade crest...............	76.0		0.0

Supplies: There are no on-route supply points, but an alternate route is described that takes you past the Crater Lake Post Office, which is found in the same building as the park headquarters. This building is about 55½ trail miles north of Fish Lake Resort, in northern Section B, and about 29 miles (via Rim Drive and North Crater Trail) south of Diamond Lake Resort, in southern Section D. Be aware that the post office doesn't like to hold packages longer than one week. Up on the lake's rim you can get meals and limited supplies at the "Rim Village," and meals at Crater Lake Lodge.

Wilderness Permits and Special Restrictions: To camp in the Crater Lake National Park backcountry, you'll need a wilderness permit. It doesn't matter whether you are on foot, horseback or skis, or whether you are entering on a popular summer weekend or in the dead of winter—they are still required. In person, you can get a permit either at the Park Headquarters or at the Rim Village Visitor Center. You can also get a permit in advance by writing to Superintendent, P.O. Box 7, Crater Lake National Park, Crater Lake, OR 97604, or you can phone park personnel at (503) 594-2211.

There are specific camping restrictions at the park. No camping is allowed within one mile of any paved road, nature trail or developed area, and none is allowed within 1½ miles of Sphagnum Bog or Boundary Springs. As in any wilderness area, no camping is allowed in meadows or within 100 feet of any water source. Size of each backcountry party is limited to a maximum of 12 persons and 8 stock.

Problems: Sky Lakes Wilderness is an area of abundant precipitation and abundant lakelets. Both combine to ensure a tremendous mosquito population that will ruin your hike if you're caught without a tent. However, by mid-July the mosquito population begins to drop, and by early August a tent may not be necessary.

Since Crater Lake National Park lacks ponds and lakelets and also has a paucity of flowing streams, you would expect it to also be mosquito-free, right? Sorry, it isn't. This is because the lake's rim receives a yearly average of 48 feet of snowfall and the resulting snowpack provides moist, mosquito-bearing ground through most of July. This same snowpack also can make hiking difficult before mid-July, but in early August, after it has disappeared, drinking water may become scarce. From midsummer onward, the stretch from Red Cone Spring to Section D's Thielsen Creek, a 21-mile stretch, may be dry.

A large trailhead parking lot is provided for those hikers who plan to leave their vehicles along Highway 140. There is a signed road to this lot that begins 0.4 mile east of the PCT's highway crossing. From the sign you go 15 yards north on Fourmile Lake Road 3650, turn left, and parallel the highway west to the nearby lot. From the lot's northwest corner a trail goes 0.2 mile north to the PCT. Don't park at the small space where the PCT crosses the highway, since long-distance backpackers may want to camp there when water is available in the adjacent Cascade Canal.

Our description begins where the PCT starts north from Highway 140 (4980). This point is just 0.2 mile west of the Jackson/Klamath county line and 40 yards east of the Cascade Canal. Just after we start up this trail we cross this seasonally flowing canal, then parallel it northeast to a junction (5100–0.3) with the short trail back to the large trailhead parking lot. Just past this junction the trail almost touches the canal before it angles away and ascends open slopes that provide a view south toward Brown Mountain and its basalt flows. As the PCT climbs, it enters Sky Lakes Wilderness, where it too crosses lava flows, and then it enters a white-fir forest and continues up to a junction with Mt. McLoughlin Trail 3716 (6110–4.0), in a forest of red firs and mountain hemlocks. Southeast, this heavily used trail descends 1.0 mile to a trailhead at Road 3650, and then its lightly used continuation descends 3.0 miles to the Highway 140/Road 3601 intersection near the Lake of the Woods Work Center/Visitor Center. If you've been hiking the last part of Section B along the lake's west shore, you'll take this trail to regain the PCT.

On the PCT, which briefly doubles as the Mt. McLoughlin Trail, we climb shortly west on an easier grade to the Freye Lake spur trail (6190–0.2), which is just 50 yards past a gully. This ill-defined trail goes ¼ mile over to the shallow, semistagnant lake and its camps.

After an equally short distance west on the PCT (6240–0.2), the Mt. McLoughlin Trail takes its leave, climbing 3½ miles up to the summit of this dormant stratovolcano. The views you get from it are among the best obtained from any peak situated near the tri-

C1   **C1**

state PCT. If you have good weather, don't pass up the opportunity to climb it. Drop your heavy backpack nearby and take 2 or 3 hours to reach the often snowy summit. On your return you can sometimes use tempting snowfields to speed your descent, but be forewarned that these can lead you astray, as they diverge south-southeast from the east-descending trail.

Leaving the west-climbing Mt. McLoughlin Trail, the PCT quickly tops a ridge, then winds slowly down through the forest, not once offering us a view, and comes to a junction with the Twin Ponds Trail (5840–3.7). This junction lies between two shallow ponds that by late summer are no more than dry, grassy meadows. Small campsites can be found at Summit Lake, 0.4 mile northwest down this trail, but beyond the lake the trail, which is numbered 993, becomes very brushy. To the southeast the trail is numbered 3715, and it winds 2.5 miles to a trailhead at the west end of Fourmile Lake Campground. From the junction our trail starts northeast, quickly veers north past a stagnant pond, climbs steadily up a ridge, and then descends slightly to a junction with Cat Hill Way Trail 992 (6100–1.6). This path climbs 3.6 miles north to a popular trailhead, which also serves more-popular Blue Canyon Trail 982. Southward from our junction you may note the abandoned tread of deteriorating Blue Rock Trail 3737, which can still be followed 2.0 miles, passing Fourmile Lake before ending at the Twin Ponds Trail, along the south shore of Squaw Lake.

Our trail heads north to a gully that is snowbound until late June, then veers east up to a gentle slope before curving northeast and climbing to a broad saddle (6300–1.6). Our route now contours across a slope forested with mountain hemlock, red fir and western white pine. We round a north ridge, descend southeast to another saddle (6240–1.2), then bear northeast down toward a saddle and meet Red Lake Trail 987 (6020–1.1).

*   *   *   *

Some hikers may have taken Section B's alternate route that guides them first to Lake of the Woods Resort for supplies and then north to Highway 140. The following description takes them on an 11.2-mile route north back to the Red Lake Trail junction with the PCT. This stretch, 2.7 miles shorter than the comparable stretch of PCT, provides you with a lower, lake-dotted alternate route from Highway 140.

To reach the trailhead start from the north end of Lake of the Woods' east-shore Road 3704, which ends at Highway 140. Walk 0.2 mile west on the highway, then branch north onto a pole-line road. (If you're eastbound on the highway, you'll find this road about 250 yards east of Billie Creek.) You go but 5 yards north on the road and then branch right, making a hairpin turn onto a minor road. Follow it 100 yards to the trailhead, located just before the pole line. Our mileage begins from here (4990).

Rye Spur Trail 3771 starts west and quickly meets the Billie Creek Nature Trail (5000–0.2), which continues west for a loop around a part of Billie Creek. Our Rye Spur Trail switchbacks steeply northward, then climbs at an easier pace to Road 3633 (5290–0.5). We walk 160 yards northwest up it to the Cascade Canal (5701–0.8). In early summer the canal flows swiftly, but by August it can be bone-dry. The Rye Spur Trail continues climbing northward until it reaches the first of three clustered outcrops (6230–1.2). Here you get some fine views of the scenery from Pelican Butte, to the northeast, across to Mountain Lakes Wilderness, to the southeast. Beyond the outcrops your views disappear, and you hike at a leisurely pace to a recrossing of the Cascade Canal (5730–3.3). This point is but 30 yards down the canal's road from a parking area by Fourmile Lake's dam. Had you hiked north along the canal road to this point, rather than taking the Rye Spur Trail, you'd have saved yourself 0.2 mile distance and about 500 feet of climbing effort. If evening is fast approaching, you can mosey west a short ½ mile to the lake's campground, then on the next day either continue along the alternate route or take Twin Ponds Trail 3715 a rolling 2.5 miles over to the PCT.

Keeping to the alternate route, one walks but 30 yards east down the canal's road to the start of Badger Lake Trail 3759. Just 35 yards up this trail you meet Fourmile Creek Trail 3714, forking right. The Badger Lake Trail visits two of Fourmile Lake's lodgepole-snag bays, presenting us with views of Mt. McLoughlin and its avalanche-prone lower slopes. Now entering Sky Lakes Wilderness, we climb ½ mile to Woodpecker Lake, which is mostly less than chest deep. In ¼ mile we reach more appealing Badger Lake (5910–1.6), with better fishing and swimming than its neighbor. Look for a fairly nice campsite by the lake's northeast edge. Next we pass knee-deep Lilly Pond, then pass a marshy meadow, both of interest to wildflower enthusiasts. Northward, we have a seasonally

C1, C3, C4, B10   B10, C2, C3

see MAP C2

see MAP B10

boggy terrain to traverse, and then we climb ½ mile northeast to a junction with Long Lake Trail 3713 (6050–1.7). This winds 0.3 mile east to a junction near the south shore of Long Lake. From it, misnamed Horse Creek Trail 3741 departs south down Long Creek, while a spur trail shoots east to a good south-shore campsite. The lake is quite shallow, though deep enough to support trout and to offer some fair swimming.

Our alternate route, part of the defunct Oregon Skyline Trail, immediately begins a ½-mile easy descent northeast to the west shore of Long Lake, then continues north along it to a junction (6050–0.8) by the lake's north shore. Eastward, a spur trail goes over to Long Lake Camp, spacious enough for group camping. Be aware that mosquitoes can plague the site as late as early August. North of Long Lake our fault-line trail crosses an unnoticeable gentle divide, then descends past a marshy meadow on its way down to a junction with Lost Creek Trail 3712 (6000–1.0). This trail quickly rounds Center Lake, which is knee-deep in its prime but only a grassy meadow in late summer, and then the trail descends 1⅓ easy miles to a switchback in Road 3659 (just off Map C4). Eastward, this road goes 1.3 miles to a main road, 3659, which northward ends in 1.7 miles at Cold Springs Campground. From the Lost Creek Trail junc-

tion Badger Lake Trail 3759 ends and Red Lake Trail 987 begins. We climb over an adjacent ridge and immediately intersect the PCT (6020–0.1–11.2).

*   *   *   *

After the PCT intersects the Red Lake Trail, it makes a quite level, easy traverse north, staying close to a fault-line crest. In about an hour you should reach a junction with the short No Name Trail (6070–2.7).

*   *   *   *

A more rewarding alternate to this essentially viewless traverse is to continue along the Red Lake Trail, then head up the No Name Trail. Along this route you first make a short, moderate descent to the east end of Blue Canyon Trail 982 (5900–0.2). Westward, you can follow it 0.4 mile to a good spur trail that goes 130 yards north to Island Lake's most abundant campsites. Secluded ones lie above the lake's west shore. Onward, the Red Lake Trail directs us through huckleberry bogs to a junction by the northeast corner of Island Lake (5910–0.5). From an adjacent campsite a *de facto* trail goes 0.4 mile west to very pleasing Dee Lake. You'll find an improved horse camp on the low ridge separating Dee and Island lakes. Dee is an excellent lake for swimming—shallow enough to have warm water, yet deep enough that it isn't an oversized swamp (like the north half of Island Lake, which is mostly less than waist deep).

Beyond Island Lake your boggy, huckleberry-laden route north passes several ponds that are more suited to mosquitoes than to humans, then arrives at large but grassy and extremely shallow Red Lake, with possible camping and fishing. After another ½ mile walk north past the lake, we reach a junction (5870–1.4). Ahead, the Red Lake Trail is abandoned, so we climb east moderately up the No Name Trail to rejoin the PCT (6070–0.7–2.8).

*   *   *   *

From this junction the PCT makes an easy, viewless, uneventful climb northeast to the start of another lake-studded route, the southwest end of Sky Lakes Trail 3762 (6140–1.0).

*   *   *   *

Several optional routes are possible, and they'll add 2–3 miles to your hiking distance as

C3, C4

see MAP C3

see MAP C1

see MAP B10

C4, C5

Mt. McLoughlin beyond Island Lake

compared to the PCT. We start northeast on the Sky Lakes Trail, which was once part of the now defunct Oregon Skyline Trail. Soon we crest a broad divide, then make a moderate ¼-mile diagonal down a fault escarpment before leveling off near mostly shallow Deer Lake (6070–0.5). Some folks camp here, but far better camping, fishing and swimming lie ahead. Eastward, you arc past a pond to a junction with Cold Springs Trail 3710 (6050–0.4), which winds 2.6 miles over to Cold Springs Campground. Next our trail winds northeast to a junction with Isherwood Trail 3729 (6030–0.3).

The 1.5-mile Isherwood Trail is 0.8 mile longer than the Sky Lakes Trail counterpart, but it passes five lakes and a greater number of campsites. Just a stone's throw over a low ridge the Isherwood Trail comes to Lake Notasha. This lake, with a camp above its east shore, is the deepest of the five lakes, and it is the only one stocked with both rainbow and brook trout. Another low ridge separates Notasha from Elizabeth, which is shallow enough for warm swimming, yet deep enough to sustain trout. Next, you drop to the brink of a fault escarp-

ment along the west shore of Isherwood Lake, one of the few lakes in the wilderness you can dive directly into; for most lakes, you have to wade out to deep water. From a horse camp midway along the escarpment you can walk due west to adjacent, chest-deep Lake Liza, with marginal appeal. Beyond Isherwood the trail winds north to a meadow, then veers east to the north tip of north Heavenly Twin Lake. For isolated camps, look for sites above its west shore. After passing a northeast-shore camp, the Isherwood Trail ends at the Sky Lakes Trail just southwest of shallow Deep Lake.

If you shun the Isherwood Trail, your Sky Lakes Trail soon passes between the Heavenly Twin Lakes, the smaller, deeper southern one being far less attractive than the northern one. Look for secluded camps along the latter's west shore. By these two lakes you reach a junction with misnamed South Rock Creek Trail 3709 (5980–0.3), which traverses 3.1 miles over to Cold Springs Campground.

The Sky Lakes Trail turns north, skirts along the east shore of northern Heavenly Twin Lake, and then meets the northeast end of the Isher-

see MAP C5

C4

Smith
Rock
12   6640

e Rock
5588
ookout

North Blue Lake
Group

Round
Lake
13

Beal
Lake

SKY

Mud Lake

Blue Lake
6308

South Blue Lake
Group

Meadow Lake

Red
Lake

5938

987

LAKES

Dee
Lake

Island L

982

WILDERNESS

Bert L

LOST   CR   TR
3712

Center Lake

Lost Pe
6761

19

Pear
Lake

20

Carey
Lake

20

21

3759

MDW LAKE TR

992

Blue Canyon
Lake

6540

Horseshoe
Lake

6210

25

30   6200

29   29

28

6449

6200

6400

see MAP C3

see MAP C4

C3

992

30

29

28
6348

3759

Long Lake
Camp

Long Lake

6200

SKY

Swan   Cr

6000

LAKES

TRAIL

3713

WILDERNESS

31

3737

32

33

Horse   Lake

6000

Long   Cr

6400

6589

JACKSON CO
KLAMATH CO

5800

Cr

t Lake

993

Squaw
Lake

Fourmile   Lake

5744

5

Lilly
Pond

Badger
Lake

6049

Woodpecker
Lake

TRAIL

CREEK

3741

Creek

3

6

Norris Pond

3745

5

BADGER

4

HORSE

3

Orris Pond

6200

see MAP C1 | see MAP C2

see MAP C4

COLD|SPR. C.G. and ROAD 3651 ¼ MI.

wood Trail (5980–0.4). From it you continue north past chest-deep "Deep" Lake and its seasonal satellites and reach Wickiup Trail 3728 (6004–0.9). For those who have had their fill of lakes, this trail—2.0 pond-speckled miles through appropriately named Dwarf Lakes Area—provides the first of four routes back to the PCT. Shallow, uninviting Lake Land lies just below the Wickiup Trail's east end. The lake at best provides some warm swimming; however, you'd be better off visiting Wizzard Lake, a fairly deep lake just 200 yards northeast below Lake Land's outlet. Next we soon pass a knee-deep pond, on the right, then, past a low ridge, two waist-deep lakelets. The south shore of Trapper Lake lies just ahead, and from where you see it you could go 250 yards cross-country southeast to 38-foot-deep Lake Sonya, easily

C5   C5

the basin's deepest lake. More likely, you'll want to camp at the east-shore sites of scenic Trapper Lake. By this lake's outlet we meet Cherry Creek Trail 3708 (5940–1.2), which descends 5.2 miles to a trailhead at Road 3450. This road in turn descends 1.9 miles to heavily traveled County Route 531, should you need to vacate the wilderness.

From the upper end of the Cherry Creek Trail, you walk but a minute north along Trapper Lake to its northeast corner, where you'll meet Donna Lake Trail 3734. This 0.9-mile trail makes an initial ascent northeast before curving past Donna and Deep lakes, then climbing back to the Sky Lakes Trail. You can camp at either lake. Donna, being shallow, is a good one for swimming, particularly in early summer, when snow patches still hang around Deep Lake.

The Sky Lakes Trail next climbs briefly west to a ridge junction just above Margurette Lake (6010–0.3). You'll find a couple of camps both north and south of this junction. Starting southwest, Divide Trail 3717 is your second route back to the PCT. It is well-graded, but at 2.6 miles is unnecessarily long. It ends on a saddle immediately west of Luther Mountain. That peak, which is the throat of an old volcano, is well worth climbing. Scramble east up to the summit to get a commanding view of the entire Sky Lakes Area plus an aerial view down Cherry Creek canyon.

Beyond the Divide Trail the Sky Lakes Trail skirts past attractive Margurette Lake. With a prominent cliff for a tapestry and Luther Mountain for a crown, this deep lake reigns as queen of the Sky Lakes. In quick time we pass two lakelets, then meet the northwest end of Donna Lake Trail 3734 (6010–0.4). Ahead, we top out near chilly, unseen Tsuga Lake, just west of the trail, then descend past a lower pair of Snow Lakes, which have a scenic but chilly backdrop. About 200 yards beyond them one could initiate a westward slog through huckleberries to shallow Wind Lake, though only the most determined fisherman will put up with its usual horde of mosquitoes. Our descent ends at nearby, waist-deep Martin Lake, and then we traverse 0.4 mile to a junction with Nannie Creek Trail 3707 (6060–1.3), a 4.2-mile trail that is popular on summer weekends.

Northeastward, we're climbing on Snow Lakes Trail 3739, which makes an exhausting start that abates where it turns southwest (6320–0.4). Ahead, an abandoned but still used segment of the defunct Oregon Skyline Trail climbs rather steeply 1.5 miles to the Devils

Peak/Lee Peak saddle—your third route (and the most direct one) back to the PCT. The Snow Lakes Trail switchbacks up a ridge before switchbacking up to the top of a cliff. On it lie the upper Snow Lakes, which offer scenic, relatively mosquito-free camps. Just 0.2 mile past the southwest lake we end our lake-blessed alternate route as we rejoin the PCT (6670–1.4–7.8).

*   *   *   *

Back where the Sky Lakes Trail departs from the PCT toward the escarpment above Deer Lake, our Pacific Crest Trail heads north-northwest in a forest of lodgepole pines and mountain hemlocks, ascends a gentle slope past several nearby ponds, then reaches an open forest as it approaches a cliff above the Dwarf Lakes Area. Glaciated Pelican Butte (8036) is the prominent summit in the southeast; the more subdued Cherry Peak (6623) is directly east. We can't see the lakes below us, because the area is so forested. Our trail switchbacks slightly up to avoid the cliff, switchbacks slightly down the west side, and soon encounters a 100-yard spur trail (6600–2.5), which takes us to an overlook with a view that encompasses most of the rolling hills to the west. We now switchback several times up to a small summit before descending the ridgeline to a saddle and an intersection of Wickiup Trail 986/3728 (6585–1.0). East, Trail 3728 descends 2.0 miles past more than a dozen stagnant ponds before reaching the Sky Lakes Trail 70 yards south of Lake Land. West, Trail 986 is abandoned. It used to take one through perhaps the best huckleberry fields in all of Sky Lakes Wilderness.

The PCT now takes us northeast up to a ridge where the views east of the Sky Lakes Basin really begin to open up. Along the trail segment that crosses a barren slope of volcanic blocks, you are likely to find, sprouting in the thin volcanic soil, numerous creamy-white western pasqueflowers (also called anemones), which are readily identified by their finely dissected leaves, hairy stems and dozens of stamens. By August their flowers are transformed into balls of silky plumes. Our trail contours north-northeast to the west edge of a saddle and reaches Divide Trail 3717 (6840–1.2). The 2.6-mile Divide Trail strikes due east across the rocky slopes of this peak (7153), makes ten switchbacks down to three presentable ponds, and then winds gradually down to the Sky Lakes Trail junction at Margurette Lake (6010), but

C6

SKY

LAKES

WILDERNESS

not before passing virtually every body of water in the vicinity. This is quite a lovely side trip to take if you are not in a hurry. Also, if you have the time, climb nearby Luther Mountain for stupendous views of the Sky Lakes Area.

From the Divide Trail saddle we descend moderately to a ridge and follow it north as it gradually levels off to a junction with Hemlock Lake Trail 985 (6600–1.0). This trail is abandoned but followable. Still, most hikers won't want to make the 0.8-mile excursion down to the lake, for the 500-foot-elevation climb back to the PCT is quite a struggle with a heavy pack. After starting up the crest we quickly meet Snow Lakes Trail 3739 (6670–0.2), this junction being the end of the highly recommended alternate route. A 0.2-mile traverse on it takes you over to the first of a pair of Snow Lakes, the environs offering scenic, relatively mosquito-free camps.

C5

Mt. McLoughlin, from PCT on Shale Butte

C5, C6

We climb again, snaking up a ridge, then we obtain views of Mt. McLoughlin, to the south, as we round the west slopes of Shale Butte (7367). Not shale or even slate, it is really a highly fractured andesite-lava flow. Next we traverse the east slope of Lucifer (7481) to a long saddle, on which we meet Devils Peak Trail 984 (7210–1.7). This traverses 1.5 miles northwest to Seven Lakes Trail 981, on which you can go 2.7 miles, first descending past South, Cliff, Middle and Grass lakes, then climbing briefly back to the PCT. On summer weekends the Seven Lakes Basin receives heavy use, and it should be avoided then.

Just 100 yards after you leave the saddle's northeast end you'll spot an abandoned segment of the Devils Peak Trail (7190–0.2). Like Luther Mountain, Devils Peak is the remnants of an old volcano, and its summit views are well worth the effort. The abandoned trail segment makes a ½-mile, no-nonsense climb to the summit, from which you can make an even steeper 300-yard descent to the Devils Peak/ Lee Peak saddle. To the north, summit views include some of the Seven Lakes plus a good chunk of the Middle Fork canyon, including Boston Bluff. On the northern horizon is pointed Union Peak, which like our summit and Luther Mountain (2½ miles south of us) is the resistant plug of an eroded volcano. Immediately west of Union Peak you see Mt. Bailey (8363), which like pointed Mt. Thielsen (9182), is a hefty 36 miles away. Mt. Scott (8926) is the easternmost and highest of the Crater Lake environs peaks. On most days you also see Mt. Shasta (14,162), 85 miles due south. Mt. McLoughlin (9495) is the dominating stratovolcano 15 miles to the south-southwest. Try to imagine this landscape, say, 20,000 years ago, when all but the major summits and ridges lay buried under glacier ice, and the glaciers extended east down canyons to the edge of the Klamath Lake basin.

Those who don't visit the summit have a leisurely climb up to the Devils Peak/Lee Peak saddle (7320–0.5). The descent from the saddle is often a snowy one, and it can be impassable to pack and saddle stock even as late as August. Early-summer backpackers generally slide or run down the snowpack until they locate the trail in the mountain-hemlock forest below. Those ascending this north slope on foot will find the climb strenuous but safe. The PCT northbound switchbacks down this slope, crosses a cascading, bubbling creek, and then in ¼ mile passes by a meadow. We cross its outlet creek, switchback downward, recross that creek plus the earlier, cascading creek, and soon arrive at a junction (6250–2.4). Southwest, a trail traverses 0.3 mile over to Seven Lakes Trail 981, along which you can walk 0.1 mile to Cliff Lake. A trail along the lake's east shore leads to a group of very popular campsites (the lake should be avoided on weekends). At the west end of this camping zone, by the edge of a large talus slope, you'll find a small, bedrock cliff that makes a perfect platform for high diving into the lake. No other lake in the wilderness can boast of such a feature.

Beyond the Cliff Lake lateral we head northeast, quickly cross a creek, then make a steepening descent to a junction with Sevenmile Trail 3703 (6130–0.7). Southwest, this trail drops to overused Grass Lake, with its multitude of campsites. If you feel compelled to camp near this lake, try sites along its south shore. Northeast the PCT (a.k.a. Sevenmile Trail) rambles down to a couple of inferior campsites by usually flowing Honeymoon Creek (5980–0.5). Past it we rollercoaster across generally viewless slopes and hear Ranger Springs, unseen below us, as we approach a junction where we leave the Sevenmile Trail (5760–2.1). This trail goes an easy 1.8 miles northeast down to diminutive Sevenmile Marsh Campground, at the end of Road 3334. On weekends the trailhead can be packed.

The PCT descends quickly to a flat, broad saddle, where you'll meet the Middle Fork Basin Trail (5750–0.2), which winds southwest 0.9 mile gradually down to the sonorous, tumultuous Ranger Springs. Northbound, water is scarce, so tank up at these pristine springs unless you plan to visit out-of-the-way Stuart Falls. Bound for Crater Lake we first cross a dry flat and then make an ascent up to a junction with Big Bunchgrass Trail 1089A (6020–1.0). You may not see this trail, since it is officially abandoned. In the past it wound 2.0 miles around Big Bunchgrass—a relatively youthful volcano—to a junction with Trail 1089. On the PCT we reach McKie Camp Trail 1089 (6380–0.9) as we approach a meadowy saddle. This trail goes 3.1 miles down to a junction with Halifax Trail 1088. Solace Cow Camp lies about 90 yards down that trail. Just north from the Halifax Trail junction is a usually flowing creek with an adjacent hikers' camp. Northbound on the McKie Camp Trail one reaches the McKie Camp environs in 1.6 miles, and it too has a usually flowing creek. One can then take the trail 1.9 miles northeast up to the Stuart Falls Trail, reaching it just under ½ mile northwest of

C6

see MAP C6

the PCT. Hikers would take this described route only if they really needed water, for it is quite a bit out of the way. However, the route may appeal to equestrians, since Solace and McKie camps are popular horse camps.

From the saddle between Big Bunchgrass and Maude Mountain the PCT climbs to the latter's west spur, from where it traverses north along west slopes past Ethel and Ruth mountains to a saddle just east of Lone Wolf. We now start east but quickly switchback northwest and descend ½ mile through a snow-harboring fir-and-hemlock forest before curving north to a flat. Here, where others have camped, we spy the Jack Spring spur trail (6190–2.7). It heads west to a low saddle, then from it drops steeply ½ mile northwest to Jack Spring. Due to the steepness of this descent, plus the difficulty some folks

C7   **C7**

have finding bucket-size Jack Spring, you should take this trail only if you *really* need water.

Your route now winds gently down to the Oregon Desert, which holds a reservoir of water, all of it underground. The landscape has been buried in pumice and ash deposited from the final eruptions of Mt. Mazama about 4900 B.C., eruptions that led to the stratovolcano's collapse and the subsequent formation of Crater Lake in the resulting depression. Most of the area's streams were buried under ash and pumice, and the trekker faces water-shortage problems all the way to Thielsen Creek, in Section D, some 47 trail miles away. We traverse the west edge of the "desert," which in reality is an open lodgepole-forest flat, and we pass a wisp of a trail, heading east, about ⅓ mile before we meet abandoned Dry Creek Trail 3701 (6040–2.4), striking southeast. Leaving the "desert" behind, we top a low, adjacent saddle and then meet the south end of Stuart Falls Trail 1078 (6050–0.2).

*　　　*　　　*　　　*

Once the snow melts you won't find any water on or near the PCT all the way north to Highway 62, some 10.8 miles away. And from there you'll have to walk almost a mile east to Annie Spring or ½ mile farther to Mazama Campground. Unless you've got enough water to make this stretch, you are going to have to take the Stuart Falls Trail. In just under ½ mile this trail meets the north end of McKie Camp Trail 1089, which was briefly described earlier. Next we walk an easy 1¼ miles north, then descend moderately northwest to a junction with Lucky Camp Trail 1083 (5420–2.3). Westward this trail passes at least a half dozen springs as it rolls in and out of gullies 1.0 mile over to Red Blanket Falls Trail. That trail, in turn, drops 0.6 mile to Upper Red Blanket Trail 1090, reaching it just above the brink of two-tiered Red Blanket Falls. Trail 1090 then guides the hydrophilic adventurer 0.8 mile back up to the Stuart Falls Trail.

From the Lucky Camp Trail junction the Stuart Falls Trail passes three creeks of various staying power before it crosses always reliable Red Blanket Creek to reach the upper end of the Upper Red Blanket Trail (5360–0.7). (This trail is called *Upper* because it is now just the upper 3.8-mile part of the formerly much longer Red Blanket Trail. A first-rate road, 6205, has supplanted the trail, whisking wilderness travelers to the popular trailhead.)

We now stroll up along Red Blanket Creek to a spur trail which takes us momentarily to Stuart Falls Camp (5450–0.4). This large, flat area near the base of Stuart Falls is for humans only. If you've got stock animals, you must picket them immediately north of the Stuart Falls Trail, not down at the camp. Stuart Falls provides rhapsodic music for campers, a feature that few other southern Cascade campsites have. Next day, tank up on water and start up the Stuart Falls Trail. In about ⅓ mile you enter Crater Lake National Park near a gully with a seasonal creek. From it your route is an old, abandoned road, which faithfully guides you back to the PCT (6290–2.5–5.9).

*　　　*　　　*　　　*

Meanwhile, from the south end of the Stuart Falls Trail, PCT devotees start northeast from the fork. The PCT heads toward the crest, once again thwarting your hopes for water. It climbs north across the lower slopes of the Goose Egg, reaches the crest just beyond it, and then stays very close to it as it descends to a crossing of an old, closed road only a few yards before the trail tread ends at a second old, closed road (6290–5.6). Southwest, the first road descends 2.5 miles to Stuart Falls Camp; northeast, it traverses, as the Pumice Flat Trail, 2.8 monotonous miles to Highway 62.

Already a solid mile within Crater Lake National Park, we head deeper inland, progressing along the second old, closed road. In one mile you may see an abandoned road branching west from ours, but only those with keen orienting abilities will notice it. We ramble onward, gaining slightly in elevation, enter an oval, open flat, then top out at the south end of a long but narrow, open flat (6550–2.4). From this end another closed road—the Union Peak Trail—meanders 1⅔ miles west over to the start of a steep summit trail. Weather permitting, you should not pass up the opportunity to scale this prominent landmark. Drop your heavy pack at the end of the old road and scramble, sometimes using your hands, up to Union Peak's tiny summit.

Onward, the PCT traverses the narrow, open flat, then takes you down through a dense, viewless forest that contains some of the finest specimens of mountain hemlocks you'll find anywhere. Before mid-July this shady stretch can be quite snowbound. Finally we come to a small trailhead parking area along the south side of Highway 62 (6108–2.8). Ahead, your next

C7, C8　　　　　**C8, C9**

on-trail water will be from the Castle Creek headwaters tributaries, at least 1¾ miles away.

The PCT route, which begins as a trail on the other side of the highway, makes a long arc around the lake's west rim, generally staying 2 to 3 miles away from it and 1000 to 2500 feet below it. The route avoids the lake's rim because one of the criteria for the PCT is that it bypass heavily traveled routes—and the Rim Drive surely is one of them. But since we know that you're not going to hike past the lake without seeing it, we'll now describe a road route that takes you up and along the rim before it descends to a reunion with the PCT.

*   *   *   *

From where the PCT crosses Highway 62 at a level stretch 0.8 mile west of the highway's junction with the park's south-rim access road, we start east. In ⅓ mile the highway bends southeast, and we leave it, descending ¼ mile northeast on the old highway's abandoned roadbed. This ends at the base of a gully, up which the Annie Spring Cutoff Trail climbs ½ mile north back to the PCT. Our route heads south-southeast about 300 yards over to the Crater Lake south-rim access road (6010–0.7). This spot is opposite a ranger residence, and it is about midway between Annie Spring and the entrance to Mazama Campground. Since you won't have a legal camping opportunity anywhere along the park's roads, you might as well head 250 yards south to the campground's entrance road, then 0.4 mile on it to the camp-

ground proper. If you've started your day's hike from Stuart Falls by 7 a.m., you'll reach the campground by 3 p.m., even if you've taken in the side trip to Union Peak. By 5 p.m. the campground is often full, though on weekends it can fill much earlier.

Next morning, retrace your steps to where you first met the south-rim access road, and curve 0.1 mile over to a bridge that spans Annie Creek (6010–1.1). You'll see copious Annie Spring—the source of the creek—just upstream from the bridge. Eastbound, we pass Goodbye Creek Picnic Area (6010–0.8), with water, then soon reach a curve north (6040–0.4). From it the Godfrey Glen Trail makes a one-mile loop out to vertical-walled Annie Creek canyon and back. North, we have almost an hour's trek up Munson Valley along the viewless access road, and we pass ranger residences and a gas station just before reaching Crater Lake's Rim Drive (6460–2.2). Still well below the rim we start north, only to meet park headquarters and its post office (6479–0.1). Pick up whatever packages you've mailed to yourself. You can also get information on weather, naturalist programs, wildflower conditions and the like. Here too, you can get a wilderness permit, should you wish to camp in the park's backcountry (such as at Lightning Springs or Red Cone Spring). And you can buy books and pamphlets about the park or the Cascade Range.

From the park headquarters you head north up the Rim Drive, which in ⅔ mile bends south. You wind in and out of a couple gullies and, upon

C9   C9, C10

Wizard Island in Crater Lake, from Rim Village

C9

Bybee

Creek

Lightning
Spring
Spring

Overlook

7172

RIM

DRIVE

2500

Disco

6750

6250

6000

6000

6000

6750

6250

6500

6500

6235

BM 5929 ×

Castle   Creek

6000

Little

Castle

5750

6250

Trapper Cr.

Creek

Dutton

BM 6086

Castle

Whitehorse

Llaos
Hallway

BM
5720

Creek

BM 5662

HIGHWAY

62

Cr.

6100

MEDFORD 65 MI.

5750

Whitehorse   Bluff

Whitehorse
Pond

6000

BM 6125 ×

Watershed
Divide

6250

6500

BM 6108

Annie S

Mazama
C G

Castle Pt

5750

6000

C   A   D

6250

Arant
Point

58/5

6000

5750

6000

6250

Rogue
Klamath

C

Quillwort
Pond

Wizard Island
C R A
BM 6940
C10

Governors Bay

very Pt

Eagle Cove

BM 6179

Sinnott Memorial

Rim Village
Crater Lake Lodge

BM 7076
Munson Sprs

Castle Crest

Garfield Pk
VAE
800

Dya

Park Headquarters
Crater Lake PO

BM 6479

Munson Ridge

Creek

Munson Creek Valley

7020

7009

Munson Pt

6250

Munson

BM 6217

pring

Goodbye Picnic Area

Middle Fork

Duwee Falls

Annie

Creek

6250

6000

6500

5750

see MAP C9

reaching the westernmost one, you have the option of hiking ⅓ mile due north up it to Crater Lake Lodge. Otherwise, head southwest on the Rim Drive up to Munson Ridge, then north ¾ mile to the Rim Village junction (7090–2.7). Just 60 yards before this junction you'll see the top end of the Dutton Creek Trail, which descends rather steeply 2.4 viewless miles to the PCT. If you want to adhere to the PCT as much as possible, take a quick look at Crater Lake and then head down this trail.

Your first view of this 1932-foot-deep lake, like one's first view down into the Grand Canyon, may be one of disbelief—your memory tries to recollect a similar feature. As the deepest lake in the United States and the seventh deepest in the world, Crater Lake is a pristine ultramarine blue on a sunny day, and the 900-foot height of our Rim Village vantage point deepens the color. The lake is also one of the world's youngest, having begun to fill just after the demise of Mt. Mazama and reaching its present level by around 4000 B.C.

Mt. Mazama was a large volcano that was born about ½ million years ago. Over several hundred thousand years it grew, via periodic eruptions, to a large Cascade Range stratovolcano. Fairly late in the Ice Age, perhaps 100,000 years ago, it may have reached an elevation of 11,000–12,000 feet. In size it was larger than Mt. Hood, and perhaps close to the size of Mt. Adams. During glacial times, glaciers extended as far as 17 miles from the mountain's summit. But we know how rapidly a volcano can be destroyed in a cataclysmic eruption, such as the one that decapitated Mt. St. Helens in minutes on May 18, 1980. Mt. Mazama self-destructed about 4900 B.C., only its eruption was about 40 times more voluminous than that of St. Helens. The immediate landscape was buried under tens of feet of ash and pumice; Mt. Rainier, 280 miles to the north, was mantled with 3 inches of it, while southern British Columbia and Alberta received trace amounts.

The eruption took place at night, according to an ancient Klamath Indian legend, and morning's light revealed a huge gaping hole—a caldera—where the mountain had stood. The mountain had died, but there was still enough magma in the bowels of the earth to construct a small volcano—Wizard Island—within perhaps months or years after the catastrophe. A smaller volcano, known as Merriam Cone, also formed, but 500 to 1000 years of precipitation filled the caldera to its present volume, about 4 cubic

C10

Oasis Butte
5685

Watershed
Divide

6128

Red Cone Spr
BM 6265

VABM Red
7372

6085

6250

6000

um

North

5593

5750

Fork

6000

6250

BM 5920

Middle Fk

South Fk

6000

6500

6750

7000

7250

Hillman Pk
8156

VABM

The Watchman

8056

Overlook

8056

Skell

miles, and in doing so it buried the top of Merriam Cone under 500 feet of water.

From the Rim Village junction one can walk east through the "village," which has a complex with a gift shop, a small grocery store, a cafeteria and a restaurant. Behind this complex are rustic cabins for rent, usually on a daily basis. Just past

the complex is a small Visitor Center, from which stairs drop to the Sinnott Memorial, which provides one of the best views of the lake. Crater Lake Lodge, open only during summer, looms above the end of the Rim Village road, and from it the Garfield Peak Trail climbs 1.7 miles to what Schaffer thinks is the most scenic view of Crater Lake.

To resume your journey, hike northwest from the Rim Village junction, taking either the crest-hugging Discovery Point Trail or the saddle-hopping Rim Drive. On the road you reach Discovery Point at your second saddle, and then the Lightning Springs Trail (7172–2.2) at the third. (Here, at the south end of this saddle, the Discovery Point Trail dies out.) Here too you have a second opportunity to return to the PCT. About ¾ mile down the 4.1-mile Lightning Springs Trail you'll find a short spur trail heading south to campsites among the two Lightning Springs. You'll have more access to water farther down, where the trail—an old road—approaches Bybee Creek.

C10, C9   **C9**

Lake gazers continue north on the Rim Drive, circling around The Watchman, which is a lava flow that formed on Mt. Mazama's flank about 50,000 years ago. From Wizard Island overlook (7600–1.5), a saddle just north of The Watchman, an often snowbound closed road climbs to that peak's summit. If you like the views at the overlook, you'll love the views from the summit. Onward, we leave the lake views for a couple miles, but do get a glimpse of Diamond Lake, to the north. At times past, glaciers flowing north from Mt. Mazama advanced as far as the lake's north end. Indeed, the lake is dammed behind some of these glacial deposits. Mt. Bailey rises above the lake's west side, while Mt. Thielsen— a day's hike away—rises above its east side. As you descend northeast, you're almost certain to pass roadside snowfields. These will be your last sources of water until Thielsen Creek, though most hikers first head over to closer Diamond Lake. Crater Lake views return as we march down to a junction with the north-rim access road (7253–2.1). Bidding farewell to one of the world's greatest natural wonders, we wind north down the access road, which offers lakeless views until about ¼ mile before we intersect the PCT (6510–2.6–16.4).

*   *   *   *

The Pacific Crest Trail from Highway 62 over to the north-rim access road is about 2 miles longer than the highly scenic alternate route. This entirely viewless section begins by climbing, part of it up a fault-line gully. Then it descends momentarily east to the head of a second fault-line gully (6310–0.8). Southward, the Annie Spring Cutoff Trail heads down it, ending in a flat just west of Annie Spring. The PCT now descends to a closed road (6130–0.6), on which we'll hike 16.9 miles over to the park's north-rim access road. Westward, the road is abandoned but followable; we start northeast. Soon we pass three seasonal tributaries of Castle Creek before we turn west and pass a fourth, which is permanent in some years. About 2 minutes past it we reach very reliable Dutton Creek (6080–0.7), with a spur trail southwest down to some close-by campsites. Here too you'll find the Dutton Creek Trail, which climbs 2.4 fairly hard miles to Crater Lake's Rim Village junction. To take in a bit of Crater Lake scenery, you can hike up this trail, head northwest on either the Discovery Point Trail or Rim Drive, and then descend back to the PCT via the Lightning Springs Trail.

The PCT descends 1¼ miles to two-forked Trapper Creek, passing two seasonal creeks on the way. Trapper Creek flows most of the summer, but later on you'll have to go downstream to find it flowing. Ahead, you ramble about 1¼ miles over to a divide, then make a noticeable descent north to four forks of South Fork Bybee Creek. The first two flow most of the summer and have potential camps; the third flows just as long but is campless; the fourth is vernal. Past the fourth the road briefly rises, then descends ½ mile to lasting Bybee Creek (5860–4.4). Immediately beyond it, an old road, the Lightning Springs Trail, begins a 4.1-mile climb to the Rim Drive. You can camp just north of the trail junction, or you can wind on down to another junction (5610–1.1), from which an old, closed spur road descends ⅓ mile west to camps along a tributary of Bybee Creek. If the tributary is dry, look for water just downstream.

Beyond the spur road the PCT soon turns west and then descends ½ mile to a very abandoned road, which starts west in a small, grassy area. Our route turns north and soon crosses the fairly reliable South (5470–0.9) and Middle (5470–0.2) forks of Copeland Creek. Open, lodgepole-punctuated meadows stretch ¼ mile beyond the Middle Fork, and these, like the meadows north of them, are favorite browsing spots for elk. From the second set of meadows and an adjacent, westbound, abandoned road, you climb 2⅔ miles to a ridge, follow it briefly east, then continue one mile east up gentle slopes to a junction with another abandoned road (6085–4.7). This is now the Crater Springs Trail, which descends moderately a full 3 miles west to the springs, which are at the head of Sphagnum Bog. That area is an interesting one for naturalists, but it is too far off the beaten track for most PCT hikers. No camping is permitted within ½ mile of the bog.

Next, we climb to a very important junction (6240–1.0), from which a spur trail heads 150 yards east-southeast to Red Cone Spring and several adjacent camps. If you plan to avoid any side trips to the Diamond Lake Recreation Area, your next on-trail water will be at Thielsen Creek, about 21 miles away. And if you plan to visit the recreation area, you will have similar water problems. Obviously, one doesn't drop to Diamond Lake to get water, since he could reach Thielsen Creek just as fast. Rather you visit it to resupply and/or enjoy its amenities. Prepare yourself for a long, dry day, unless you are hiking before mid-July, in which case you're likely to encounter trailside snow patches.

C11, C12, C9   C9, C11

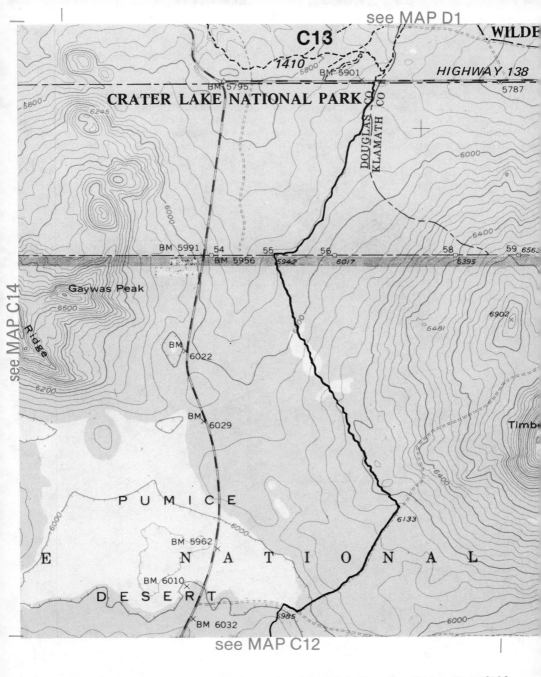

see MAP D1

see MAP C14

see MAP C12

If you find the thought of a long, waterless stretch too distressing, you do have a water-blessed option. And you have to hike a total of only about 14 miles to reach Broken Arrow Campground, above the south shore of Diamond Lake. To take this route, first continue north on the PCT, like other trekkers, down to a

junction with the Boundary Springs Trail (6128–0.6).

* * * *

On the alternate route you leave the eastbound PCT adherents as you descend a dry, viewless, monotonous trail north to a junction with the westbound Oasis Butte Trail (5635–4.1). Continue north, then northwest, down to Boundary Springs (5250–1.9), which are so voluminous that you could start, immediately below them, a raft trip down the Rogue River (though fallen trees make such a trip impractical). For many years Crater Lake National Park's north boundary crossed this vicin-

ity. No camping is allowed within ½ mile of the springs, so continue north down the Rogue River canyon, leaving the park in about ¾ mile, then presently reach a junction (5080–1.2). From it your Boundary Springs Trail 1057 heads 100 yards north to Road 760, while Rogue River Trail 1034 heads northeast along the river to the road (5070–0.2). If you want to do some

C14 | see MAP C15   **C14**

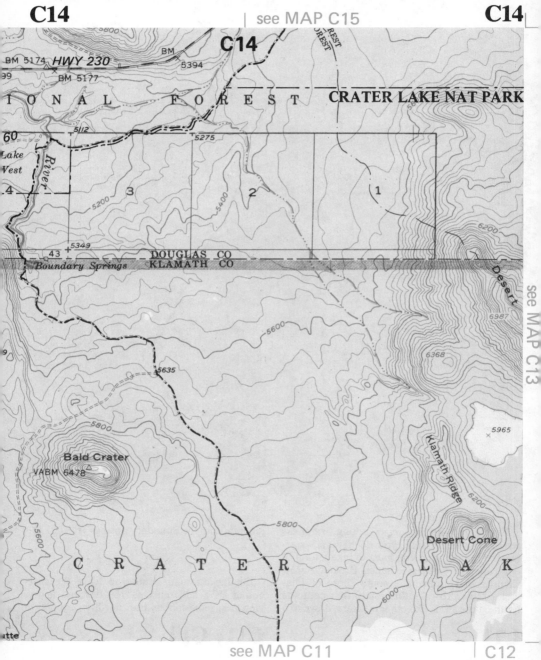

see MAP C11 | C12

Road 4795, you walk briefly north to a day-use parking area, to the west, and the old Mt. Thielsen Trail, to the east (5190–0.1–14.1). For further instructions see Section D's first alternate route, which also heads north on Road 4795.

*   *   *   *

Hikers hell-bent for punishment ignore the Boundary Springs alternate route and make a generally uphill, usually easy traverse. Most of it is through an open lodgepole-pine forest, and you'll round avalanche-prone Red Cone about 1½ miles before you reach a small trailhead parking area alongside the north-rim access road (6510–3.3). Here, those taking the recommended Rim Drive alternate route rejoin us for a northbound trek.

You begin your viewless, waterless trek by walking east over to the nearby base of Grouse Hill, a huge mass of rhyodacite lava that congealed just before Mt. Mazama erupted and collapsed to create the Crater Lake caldera. Its eruptions, occurring about 6900 years ago, "sandblasted" the top of Grouse Hill, and it is unfortunate that the PCT doesn't traverse that interesting surface.

But it doesn't, so you trod north between road and flow, the two gradually diverging before you reach the Timber Crater Trail. On this closed road you walk 260 yards east to a road fork (5985–2.9) and there branch northeast. We climb gently up toward Timber Crater, and where the road becomes steeper, we branch left, back onto trail tread again (6150–1.3). We climb but ¼ mile northwest before continuing in that direction on a long, viewless, snaking descent to the pre-1980 north boundary of Crater Lake National Park (5942–2.7). From here an old trail heads west ⅓ mile along that boundary line to an abandoned road that goes 1½ miles north to Highway 138, then just beyond that to the North Crater Trail. Short-cutters, take note.

Heading toward Highway 138, the PCT takes a longer way, first striking west along the old boundary, then traversing north-northeast to reach the new boundary immediately before Highway 138 (5920–1.9). This it crosses just 70 yards west of a broad, low crest pass of the Cascade Range. You won't find any parking here, so continue 230 yards from the highway to a junction, from which North Crater Trail 1410 descends ¼ mile northwest to a well-developed trailhead parking area.

camping, take the former trail to Road 760 and follow it west 0.4 mile over to Lake West, which caters to car campers. If you're bound for Diamond Lake, take the latter trail, reach Road 760, and immediately bridge the Rogue River. On 760 you head east, then northeast, to a junction (5390–2.9), from which a short road winds 0.3 mile northwest to busy Highway 230. Northeast, you continue on an abandoned road, whose end is blocked off by a newer section of Highway 230 (5240–2.3). Cross the highway, relocate the abandoned road, and follow it north to the old Highway 230 section (5210–0.3). Southbound hikers: note that this road begins about 100 yards east of Horse Lake. If you reach that lake, you've walked a bit too far. On the unused Highway 230 section you proceed northeast, spying in ⅓ mile the southernmost loop of sprawling Broken Arrow Campground. From here onward you can leave the road at any point and walk over to any of the campground's loops. The old highway section ends in under a mile; then you turn left on old Highway 138 (a.k.a. 4795) and head ¼ mile north to a junction with Road 271 (5205–1.1), which loops around Diamond Lake. Keeping to east-shore

The Pacific Crest Trail in Section D

-N-

0 1 2 3 4 5 miles

This section's PCT
Other trails
Hwys and major rds
Other roads
Campgrounds ▲

OAKRIDGE 17 MI.
HIGHWAY 58
5897
D13
500
Maiden Pk
Willamette Pass
5899
5810
PCT
ODELL LAKE
4666
Creek
Odell
D11
Mt Yoran
D12
DIAMOND PEAK
Lakeview Mtn
Diamond Peak
Crescent Lake
p.o.
Royce Mtn
WILDERNESS
Crescent
D9
D10
60
Emigrant Pass
6010
Summit Lake
CRESCENT LAKE
700
60
6020
2154
5825
HIGHWAY 58
Deschutes
River
2154
Cowhorn Mtn
D8
5526
5825
251
2605
2615
Windigo Pass
60
5830
Little
1445
2587
268
Tenas Pk
Tolo Mtn
D6
D7
Lemolo North Lake
Umpqua
60
MT. THIELSEN
1446
Miller Mtn
5840
5835
9774
9774
Cinnamon Butte
D4
3725A
5840
9772
9772
Chemult
ROSEBURG 74 MI.
HIGHWAY 138
Thielsen
1472
Tipsoo Pk
D5
3725
Tilt Lake
9772
Red Cone
1448
Howlock Mtn
D2
D3
9711
4795
1448
1468
1449
9776
Diamond Lake
1456
1456
Mount Thielsen
WILDERNESS
9776
HIGHWAY 97
4624
230
9777
9777
9770
86
D1
PCT
9775
Summit Rock
HIGHWAY 138
Cottonwood
Creek
9770
Creek

Section D: Highway 138 near the Cascade crest to Highway 58 near Willamette Pass

Introduction: Needle-pointed Mt. Thielsen, approached early on this hike, is this section's star attraction; its terrain is even more spectacular than that seen along the PCT through this section's Diamond Peak Wilderness. Unfortunately, when the Pacific Crest Trail was finally completed through this section around 1977, its route proved to be inferior in esthetics compared with its predecessor, the Oregon Skyline Trail. That trail touched on enjoyable Diamond Lake, which most long-distance PCT hikers visit anyway. It also took you past Maidu Lake, which was one of this section's best camping areas (when mosquitoes weren't biting), and it was an important water source. Now it is almost one mile out of the way. Furthermore, the old trail went past a series of lakes, but this route has been replaced with a nearly lakeless route that remains more faithful to the crest. This new route tends to be snowbound about a month longer than the older route. Finally, whereas the Oregon Skyline Trail came to within ½ mile of the Cascade Summit store and post office at Odell Lake, the Pacific Crest Trail comes only to within 1½ miles of it. Consequently, we will describe the old route as well as the new one.

Despite the foregoing criticisms lodged against this section's Pacific Crest Trail, it is still a good experience. The trail is well-graded and it has interesting, if not dramatic, views of Mt. Thielsen, Sawtooth Ridge, Cowhorn Mountain, Diamond Peak and Mt. Yoran. All are easily accessible to peak baggers, but Mt. Yoran should be left for experienced mountaineers. The only *significant* lake along the official PCT route, Summit Lake, is, like Diamond Lake, a worthy place to spend a layover day.

Declination: 18°E

Mileages:	South to North	Distances between Points	North to South
Highway 138 near the Cascade crest..............	0.0		61.3
		6.2	
Mt. Thielsen Trail......................	6.2		55.1
		2.2	
Thielsen Creek Trail...........................	8.4		52.9
		3.1	
Howlock Mountain Trail	11.5		49.8
		6.8	
Maidu Lake Trail	18.3		43.0
		6.2	
Tolo Camp.......................	24.5		36.8
		5.9	
Windigo Pass........................	30.4		30.9
		7.0	
Stagnant pond (6380').......................	37.4		23.9
		5.7	
Road 6010 near Summit Lake Campground	43.1		18.2
		12.0	
Unnamed lake (6030')........................	55.1		6.2
		3.1	
Midnight Lake................................	58.2		3.1
		1.5	
Pengra Pass..................................	59.7		1.6
		1.6	
Highway 58 near Willamette Pass................	61.3		0.0

Supplies: Since there are no on-route supply points, most long-distance PCT hikers take one of our alternate routes down to a walk north along Diamond Lake. The store at Diamond Lake Lodge is one of the best to be found anywhere near the PCT. This spacious resort also has a post office, and it serves good meals at reasonable prices.

Near Section D's north end you can leave the PCT at Pengra Pass and descend 1.5 miles to Shelter Cove Resort, which houses the Cascade Summit Post Office. The resort's small store caters to fishermen.

Our section's hike begins at Highway 138 (5920) just 70 yards west of the almost flat watershed divide in this locale of the Cascade Range. Trailhead parking is available just north of Highway 138 and west of the PCT. The short road that goes northeast to the trailhead starts from Highway 138 just 0.5 mile west of the Cascade divide and 0.8 mile east of Crater Lake's north-rim access road.

From Highway 138 the PCT heads northeast 230 yards to a junction with the south end of North Crater Trail 1410 (5910–0.1). Just 3 minutes into our hike, we're faced with a decision—the first of several routes leaving the PCT for the Diamond Lake environs. The North Crater Trail doesn't go to any crater; rather it descends toward Diamond Lake, runs north

above its east shore, then in 9.3 miles ends at the Diamond Lake Corrals, which are situated about ½ mile northeast of Diamond Lake Resort. If you want the quickest, easiest route to Diamond Lake, start along this trail.

*   *   *   *

North Crater Trail 1410 reaches the trailhead parking area in ¼ mile, then continues onward. In 60 yards it reaches an old southwest-descending road that dies out in both directions. Go just 200 yards down this road, then fork right onto a broad path that descends to a gully. From here a snowmobile route climbs northeast, leading eastbound hikers astray. Westward, you cross, in 0.5 mile, an old road, which was

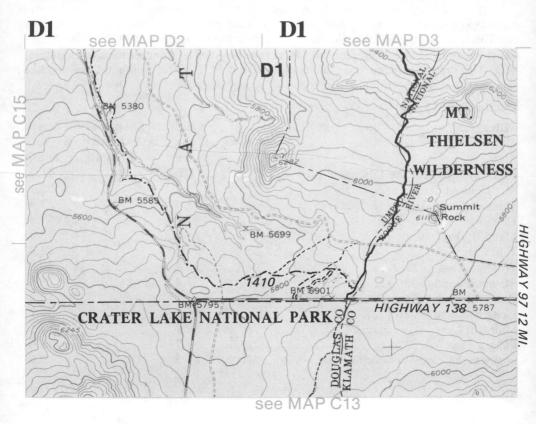

referred to at the end of Section C. Just 0.6 mile later our trail tread joins that road again, where it loops into a gully (5640–1.9). We follow the road ¾ mile down to where it curves west and flattens out. Leave the road and take a trail that starts north along a crest between two gullies. Your route ahead should now be obvious, and you parallel Highway 138 until it diagonals across your path (5275–2.5). Dash across the busy highway and follow a short trail segment over to Highway 230 (5245–0.2). You could continue north along the North Crater Trail, but since that route is largely viewless, you might miss a number of lakeside attractions. Therefore, walk 100 yards west on Highway 230 to a junction with east-shore Road 4795. Just under ½ mile north on it you meet a straight, southeast-heading road—the old Highway 230—along which Section C's Boundary Springs Trail alternate route joins our route (5220–0.5). As in that route we head ¼ mile north to a junction with Diamond Lake's loop Road 271. Anywhere along this last stretch you could have walked west to the east side of nearby Broken Arrow Campground.

In another ¼ mile we pass a day-use parking area, on our left, and the *old* Mt. Thielsen Trail and a private campground on our right, then arrive at South Store (5190–0.5). If you've been living for days out of your pack, you'll certainly welcome this store and its cafe. Just north of the store is the south end of 2-mile-long Diamond Lake Campground, which is sandwiched between the lake and Road 4795. You can drop to it any time you desire. Midway along the lake's east side we reach an intersection (5236–1.4), with the campground's entrance to the west and the Diamond Lake Information Center to the east. From that center a spur trail goes 0.1 mile north to the North Crater Trail, while another goes ¼ mile south to it. Onward, you pass more of the campground, then from its north end you can hop onto a trail that parallels your road and the lakeshore over to Diamond Lake Resort's entrance road (5200–1.2). Head over to the complex (5200–0.3), resupply at its well-stocked general store, pick up your mailed parcels at the post office, and/or enjoy a hearty meal at the restaurant. If you're well-funded, rent a fishing boat and catch a rainbow trout or two, which grow considerably larger here than in the lakes of Sky Lakes Wilderness. Some long-distance hikers may even be desperate enough for civilization's amenities to stay at the resort's lodge.

D1, D2

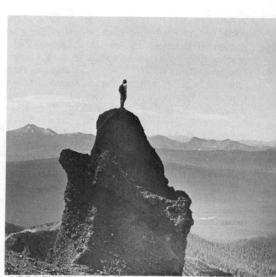

A Mt. Thielsen pinnacle and distant rim of Crater Lake

View south-southeast from Thielsen's summit

After your stay, however brief or long, start north up the road immediately east of the gas station. This road climbs up to Road 271, reaching it only a minute's walk west of a junction with Road 4795 (5340–0.5). Also at this junction is the entrance road to Diamond Lake Corrals. Walk east to the road's far end, and beside it you'll find a tread (5340–0.1–9.1). Northward, Howlock Mountain Trail 1448 swings east, spinning off Spruce Ridge Trail 1458 (which goes over to Mt. Thielsen Trail 1456) and Thielsen Creek Trail 1449. All take you back to the PCT and will be described in the pages to come. Southward, North Crater Trail 1410 snakes 9.3 miles to the PCT, ending just north of Section D's start, Highway 138.

*   *   *   *

Back at that junction, those taking the mostly viewless, waterless PCT route have an easy climb up to the old, abandoned Summit Rock Road (5935–0.5). This road, which is a ski route in winter, also provides one with a route—albeit inferior—to Diamond Lake. The road curves 4.2 miles over to the new Highway 138, on which one walks 0.4 mile along its shoulder, then follows the defunct Mt. Thielsen Trail 0.5 mile west over to Road 4795, at the lake's southeast corner.

Onward, the PCT climbs gently north for a mile, then the gradient steepens and the trail makes a few open switchbacks up a ridge before it curves northwest around it. We now make a long but comfortable ascent, rounding Mt. Thielsen's southwest ridge before traversing across a glaciated bowl to a trail junction on the peak's west flank. Here we meet the top part of the Mt. Thielsen Trail (7260–5.3), which will now be described east up to the summit. Westward, the still followable but abandoned trail descends 2.8 miles to the new Highway 138, then continues 0.5 mile west to the old highway—Road 4795—meeting it at the lake's southeast corner.

*   *   *   *

The summit of Mt. Thielsen (9182), sometimes called the "Lightning Rod" of the Cascades, is easily accessible and should not be bypassed. When you ascend it, however, leave your pack behind; it has probably one of the steepest trails in existence—more of a climb than a hike. The trail quickly exits above treeline

and then climbs up increasingly loose pumice slopes toward a cleaver, where it seems to veer right (south) around it. This scree slope is the *descent* route. Rather than fight your way up this unstable slope, climb up solid rock along the left

D3
ROSEBURG 77 MI.

see MAP D1

(north) side of the cleaver and continue up toward the 80-foot-high summit pinnacle, which can be climbed unroped only from its southeast ridge. The near-vertical north and east faces make this last few feet off limits to those with acrophobia.

The view from the summit area is both spectacular and didactic. You can see north 107 miles to Mt. Jefferson (10,497), and south 120 miles to Mt. Shasta (14,162). We can see from the dips, or inclinations, of the strata that Mt.

D3

D3

see MAP D4

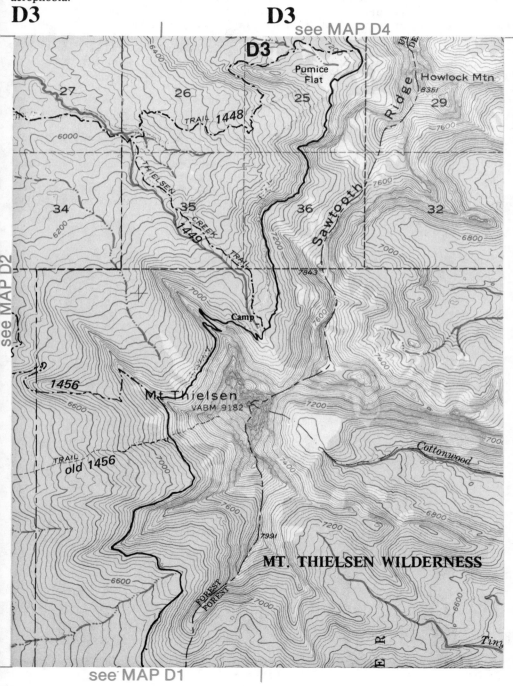

Thielsen's summit once lay to the east, and about 1000 feet higher, above what is now a deeply glaciated canyon. Here is a vulcanologist's natural observatory, for the mountain's anatomy is stripped bare. After downclimbing the summit pinnacle, we head south a short way along the ridge and pass some enormous pinnacles clinging to the east wall. Soon we come to an obvious spot, not too far from an isolated scrubby whitebark pine, where nearly everyone begins to descend the scree slope to the trail.

*   *   *   *

From Mt. Thielsen's summit trail the PCT traverses north to the peak's west ridge, on which it meets the new Mt. Thielsen Trail 1456 (7330–0.3).

*   *   *   *

If you want to drop to Diamond Lake for recreation or supplies, but don't want to miss a

foot of the PCT, start down the Mt. Thielsen Trail. This descends at an average gradient of 9¼%, versus 13% for the old Mt. Thielsen Trail. Since the PCT is not supposed to exceed 15%, the old Mt. Thielsen Trail fell within acceptable limits of steepness, and it is unfortunate that the newer, 1¼-mile-longer trail was built. But the new trail's gradient does make for an easy descent, and in under an hour you arrive at a junction with Spruce Ridge Trail 1458 (6240–2.3). You can take either route down to Diamond Lake, but to maximize scenery, why not make a loop?

On the waterless Mt. Thielsen Trail, descend to a trailhead on Highway 138 (5360–1.7). Unfortunately, the trail doesn't continue west to the lakeshore road, as the old trail did, so hike ½ mile north on 138, to where it begins to curve northeast. Drop west about 200 yards cross-country to North Crater Trail 1410. Walk ¼ mile north on it to where it splits, Trail 1410 branching northeast to circle behind a USFS

D3

D3, D2

see MAP D6

see MAP D3

Cloud-capped Mt. Thielsen, from near Tipsoo Trail junction with PCT

information center. You branch northwest and in ¼ mile reach, along east-shore Road 4795, the entrance to the information center, which is opposite the entrance to Diamond Lake Campground (5236–1.1). Now follow the previous alternate route 1.2 miles north to Diamond Lake

Resort's entrance road, 0.3 mile over to the resort, 0.5 mile up a minor road to Road 271 and momentarily east to nearby Road 4795, then 0.1 mile east through Diamond Lake Corrals to the Howlock Mountain trailhead (5340–2.1–7.2).

Howlock Mountain Trail 1448 heads northeast, joining another trail from the corrals immediately before passing through a horse tunnel under Highway 138 (5360–0.2). From the far side of the tunnel a minor trail heads northward, but you climb southeast up the slopes of a lateral moraine. The glacier that carried this morainal debris originated on the north slopes of Mt. Mazama, a towering volcano that collapsed about 6900 years ago at the site now occupied by Crater Lake. Immediately beyond the crest of the moraine you meet a second minor trail, which heads north down a gully. You then switchback to the crest of a higher moraine and on it meet Spruce Ridge Trail 1458 (5680–1.0), which is the first of three options back to the PCT:

1) The waterless Spruce Ridge Trail 1458 starts along a minor ridge and makes an easy, spruce-free, generally viewless ascent south to the Mt. Thielsen Trail (6240–2.6). Up it, retrace your steps to where you left the PCT, on the west ridge of Mt. Thielsen (7330–2.3–6.1 miles from Diamond Lake Corrals).

2) Continue east on the Howlock Mountain Trail, passing in ⅓ mile the seasonal west fork of Thielsen Creek, later skirting Timothy Meadow, and then ½ mile beyond it reaching Thielsen Creek and adjacent Thielsen Creek Trail 1449 (6040–2.4). Take this moderately climbing trail, which parallels its namesake, back up to the PCT (6960–2.3–5.9). You'll pass a short spur trail over to Thielsen Creek Camp just 100 yards before this junction.

D2, D3

3) From the lower end of the Thielsen Creek Trail, continue east up Howlock Mountain Trail 1448, which can have snow patches in mid-July, but can be waterless by early August. You'll see Howlock Mountain, rising 1000 feet above you, just before you reach the PCT (7320–3.6–7.2).

If you began your alternate route from the southern end of North Crater Trail 1410, your total mileages for these three return routes will be 15.2, 15.0 and 16.3 miles. If you began your alternate route from the upper end of Mt. Thielsen Trail 1456, your total mileages will be 13.3, 13.1 and 14.4 miles.

*   *   *   *

From the Mt. Thielsen Trail 1456 junction the Pacific Crest Trail crosses the open, view-packed northwest slopes to the northwest ridge (7370–1.0). From it we see our next major peak—bulky, snowy Diamond Peak. Our trail now makes long switchbacks down from the ridge, then it descends southeast to Thielsen Creek (6930–1.1). Over this last mile of trail, snow sometimes lingers through late July. Thielsen Creek is your first source of permanent water since Red Cone Spring, 21 miles back. Your next on-route *pure* water is at Summit Lake, a whopping 33 miles ahead, so many hikers stop at out-of-the-way Maidu Lake, a good camping area, only 10.8 miles ahead. Just past the Thielsen Creek crossing you reach Thielsen Creek Trail 1449 (6960–0.1), on which you can descend about 100 yards to a spur trail that leads 100 yards west down to Thielsen Creek Camp. Since this is the first PCT campsite with water since Red Cone Spring, it can be overcrowded.

From the Thielsen Creek area the PCT makes a winding contour 2.7 miles north to an open bowl, Pumice Flat, through which the Oregon Skyline Trail once traversed northeast. The Pacific Crest Trail heads east just above it into a stand of mountain hemlocks. If you are hiking through this area in early season, you might want to camp under a cluster of hemlocks and lodgepoles near the low summit ¼ mile west of you. Early-season water is obtained from the seasonal creek just north of it or from nearby snow patches.

After the PCT heads east into the hemlocks, it quickly starts an ascending, counterclockwise traverse around the bowl. Just past a meadow where the trail turns from north to northwest,

you'll reach a junction (7320–3.1) with well-used Howlock Mountain Trail 1448. The last Diamond Lake alternate route, described earlier, ends here.

The PCT, which can be vague in spots over the last half mile, now makes an obvious climb to a crest saddle (7435–0.4), which lies on a western spur of the ragged, severely glaciated Sawtooth Ridge. Leaving the crest saddle, you may encounter lingering snow banks before you reach your first meadow. The meadows usually have posts through them to help PCT hikers keep on track. Nevertheless, some hikers may be led astray by old Oregon Skyline paths, and as the hiker approaches Tipsoo Peak, he may be confronted with two sets of posts. The correct set is along the upper (northern) tread, and along it you may still see the Cinnamon Butte Trail sign, even though that trail hasn't existed for years. About 50 yards past the abandoned trail, the two treads reunite and in about a minute you reach the high point—in elevation—of the Oregon-Washington PCT (7560–1.3). Tipsoo Peak, due north, is an easy 20-minute climb for peak baggers, and its summit views are second only to Thielsen's for providing an overview of this region.

On the lower south slopes of Tipsoo Peak just north of a broad saddle, the PCT becomes quite plain as it starts a descent northeast. About halfway to a saddle, the PCT bends north across an open gully, then hugs the forested lower slopes of Tipsoo Peak as it continues northeast to that saddle (7300–0.8). Here one can inspect the severely glaciated north face of red-black Tipsoo Peak.

From our saddle hikers used to zip northeast straight down to Maidu Lake, but the route has been changed so that now we make a long, counterclockwise traverse around a flat, volcanic summit. This traverse provides us with three scenic viewpoints that reveal Red Cone and Miller Lake, then the trail veers northwest across the county-line crest to a switchback. The trail then makes a long, winding, viewless descent to the west end of a broad saddle, on which we cross Maidu Lake Trail 3725A (6190–4.3).

Here the Maidu Lake Trail starts north, and it proceeds to cross the county-line saddle, then descends a gully to the south shore of shallow, semi-clear Maidu Lake. Most hikers will want to make the 0.9-mile trek down to this lake's relatively warm waters, for the next PCT campsite with near-water access is the sometimes over-

D3   **D3, D4, D5, D6**

see MAP D4

see MAP D5

crowded Tolo Camp, 6.2 miles farther. The lake's shore has abundant space for camping, though until early August a tent is necessary to provide refuge from the myriad of mosquitoes.

From the PCT's crossing of the Maidu Lake Trail, you can also start south on this trail, which winds 2.0 miles down to Miller Lake Trail 3725, which you can then follow 0.8 mile south over to the Digit Point Campground. Few hikers will want to make this longer excursion.

The PCT leaves the Maidu Lake Trail, quickly crosses that trail's former tread, and then climbs to a spur-ridge view of Miller Lake. After getting several views of the lake, we cross the spur ridge and follow it north to a crossing of the main, county-line ridge (6490–1.3). Beyond it we climb gently up to an auxiliary saddle, then in an equal climb we top out at a junction from which the abandoned Oregon Skyline Trail once descended southwest to Maidu Lake. The PCT now contours for ¼ mile, then begins a gradually steepening descent to a crest saddle (6470–2.3).

We now climb up to the long Mule Peak crest, cross it, diagonal northwest down the peak's west slopes, and then diagonal northeast to a

D6, D5

D5, D7, D6

see MAP D10

D8

VABM Cowhorn Mtn
7664

BM 5956

7096

Nip and Tuck Lakes

F O R E S T

OLDENBERG

LAKE 45

3643

WAY

WAY

Windigo Lakes

ROAD

60

BM
5710

60

Windigo Pass

5662

LAKES

Windigo Butte

NATIONAL

BOUNDARY

FOREST

60

CASCADE

Creek

BM
4586

Creek

HIGHWAY 138 7 MI.

Bradley

Warrior

Tenas Peak

Lookout
6530

MT. THIEL.

WILD.

see MAP D6

saddle (6300–1.9). Continuing our crest route, we descend to a second saddle, where lies Tolo Camp (6190–0.7), which has camping space for about six hikers. From the camp, Trail 1411 switchbacks eastward ⅓ mile down to a large spring that has no available camping space. From Tolo Camp there will be no reliable water until Summit Lake, 17.0 miles farther. However, near-trail water and campsites are found at several places north of Windigo Pass.

From the Tolo Camp saddle, we traverse over to another saddle (6235–0.6), then traverse across the south and west slopes of Tolo Mountain to Tenas Trail 1445 (6610–1.3), which starts west down a ridge to the old Cascade Lakes Road. Now outside Mt. Thielsen Wilderness, our trail turns east and descends to the ridgecrest, then follows it for over 2½ miles before swinging west across a broad, low saddle to the lower north slopes of a pyroclastic cone called Windigo Butte (6420). We now descend less than ¼ mile along its north spur, then curve northwest over to a junction with a spur trail (5845–3.7), which goes 250 yards

west to a trailhead parking area immediately west of the old Cascade Lakes Road.

Starting north from the junction, our trail quickly drops into a gully, climbs over a low ridge and reaches the new Cascade Lakes Road 60 (5820–0.3) only 140 yards east of Windigo Pass. The old road, which starts by the trail's west side, takes you ¼ mile southwest to the Windigo Pass trailhead parking area, used by north- and south-bound hikers alike.

*   *   *   *

Many hikers still prefer to take the old Oregon Skyline Trail, which closely approaches Odell Lake and which certainly has more lakes at which you can camp. These lakes, of course, have mosquito problems, at least before August, so before then you can choose between mosquitoes on the OST or snow patches on the PCT. If you decide on the Oregon Skyline Trail, then hike northeast down the Cascade Lakes Road to a trailhead (5710–0.7), just 15 yards past a seasonal but obvious creek.

D6, D8

D8

Shallow arm between Nip and Tuck Lakes

DIAMOND

D10

PEAK

13

18

17

16

WHITEFISH

Whitefish

42

TRAIL

WILDERNESS

20

21

24

19

6010

Creek

ett lake

Farrell Lake

60

Whitefish
Horse Camp

Crescent   Lake

SPILLWAY   4853

BM
5503

Creek

5557

25

ek Lake

30

29

Tandy Bay Picnic Area

Contorta Point
Campground

H   U   T   E   S

Crescent Lake
Organization Camp

BM 4856

28

Spring
Campground

36

31

TRAIL

50

Creek

32

33

Cowhorn

Pinewan Lake

LAKES

1

6

5

4

45

LAKE

BM 5388

WINDY

Lakes

12

N   A   T   I   O   N   A   L

7

8

Bingham Lakes

9

TRAIL

KLAMATH CO

DOUGLAS CO

WAY

3643

and Andy

Oldenberg Lake

HWY. 58 and CRESCENT LAKE P.O. 4 MI.

The trail's name has been changed to Oldenberg Lake Trail 45, and on it we start northeast up the OST, contour across gentle slopes of manzanita and sparse forest cover, then descend slightly to the Nip and Tuck Lakes spur trail (5715–1.7). This heads east-southeast for a level 200 yards to the two lakes, which are only one lake in early summer. The peninsula that juts between the two lobes makes an excellent campsite, and the warm, shallow lake water is very inviting. Our trail heads north-northwest and climbs gently at first, but then it makes a short, somewhat sunny, moderate-to-steep climb up to a ridge (5956–1.0), providing us with only one reward—a view south of Mt. Thielsen. The trail ahead is now downhill almost all the way to Crescent Lake.

We start moderately down and head north to the west shore of Oldenberg Lake (5475–1.3), then north past two of the Bingham Lakes to a junction (5450–1.1) with a west-northwest trail to the third. This third Bingham Lake, at the end of the hundred-yard spur trail, is the largest and perhaps the clearest of all the shallow lakes between Maidu Lake and Crescent Lake. Continuing north along our route, we pass through an "Oregon desert" of sparse lodge-poles, then descend gradually and cross a seasonal creek whose luxuriant green vegetation contrasts vividly with the surrounding sparsely needled lodgepoles. We round a low ridge and then reach the northeast end of murky, man-made Pinewan Lake (5180–2.0), which has a habit of drying up in late summer. Here, and for a short distance west, the trail follows the immigrant road built and used by the Elliot Wagon Train in October 1853.

We go about 100 yards before our trail forks right (northwest) from the road and winds ¼ mile down to a gully. Ahead, it wraps around a minor ridge, then descends ¼ mile to a junction with an abandoned trail (5010–0.7). Ahead, the old Oregon Skyline Trail once wove its way northwest down to an organization camp at Crescent Lake's southwest corner. Today, it goes but 80 yards northwest to a gully, then turns northeast, dying out before reaching close-by Road 60. If you'd walk ¼ mile west on that road, you'd reach Road 260, which descends ½ mile to Crescent Lake's Spring Campground.

From the junction we're now heading west on the Metolius-Windigo Horse Trail. It rapidly reaches the gully, curves around a minor ridge, and then weaves northwest down to a junction

D8, D10   D10

Diamond View Lake reflecting Diamond Peak

Asymmetrical Cowhorn Mountain, viewed from the southwest

(5030–0.9). Northeastward, a spur trail heads 150 yards over to Road 60, then continues just beyond it to a trailhead parking area for the Oldenberg Lake and Windy Lakes trails. Just ¼ mile southeast up Road 60 you'd find Spring Campground's Road 260. Westward, we go about 220 yards before meeting southwest-climbing Windy Lakes Trail 50. Anyone who abandons the high and dry PCT and descends about 4 miles down this trail will join us here.

Onward, our Metolius-Windigo Horse Trail almost touches Road 60 as it traverses from northwest to north over to Summit Lake Road 6010. We cross it, parallel it 100 yards north, walk 100 feet up the road, and then relocate trail tread. In ½ mile we wind down to the boggy environs of Whitefish Creek, then 200 yards past it reach Road 220 (4870–1.4) only 60 yards west of its junction with Road 60. We follow this road north through Whitefish Horse Camp and in ⅓ mile reach a campground loop. Immediately before it is a faucet, which for late-season hikers could be their last reliable water until Diamond View Lake, 5½ miles away. Branch left and locate the Whitefish Creek Trail 42 trailhead along the northwest part of the loop. From the loop's north part the Metolius-Windigo Horse Trail heads northeast.

We start northwest on Trail 42, enter Diamond Lake Wilderness in about ½ mile, and then climb rather gently to a fairly reliable tributary of Whitefish Creek (5080–1.6). The trail remains within hearing distance of White-fish Creek—when it's running—as we climb northwest, then north up to a flat and a linear pond at an intersection with Crater Butte Trail 44 (5770–3.1), four miles due east of Diamond Peak (8744).

From the junction our trail heads north past several shallow, somewhat stagnant ponds before arriving at large but shallow Diamond View Lake (5780–0.7). Photographs are best when the peak is snow-clad, which, unfortunately, is when the lake is mosquito-clad. We pass campsites, then leave the lake behind as we make tracks north through swampy lodgepole flatlands to the headwaters of Trapper Creek. This creek remains unseen and unheard for two miles until the trail reaches slopes above the creek where it cascades north down toward a marsh. In the third mile, the trail reaches the creek and more or less follows it to the marsh, then goes east through a shady mountain-hemlock forest. In order to avoid the creekside's wet ground, the trail generally stays on the lower slopes just south of the creek. We follow the creek as it meanders east past tempting campsites, then cascades northeast down past a small breached dam. Almost immediately after sighting this concrete structure, we reach a trail junction (4870–4.9–21.1), where an access trail continues northeast, but our trail turns north.

The access trail descends 240 yards to the Southern Pacific railroad tracks and crosses them 20 yards west-northwest of a huge, steel overhead signal. Head east across the tracks and

D10   **D12, D13**

see MAP D9

under the overhead signal to a dirt road that descends 150 yards to Road 5810 along the west shore of Odell Lake (4788). This lake was named for William Holden Odell who, with B. J. Pengra, surveyed the military wagon road up the Middle Fork of the Willamette in 1865. On July 26th Odell climbed a butte and discovered this lake; both butte and lake now bear his name. If you walk ¼ mile northwest on Road 5810, you'll reach the entrance to Trapper Creek Campground. If you walk 250 yards southeast on it, you'll reach the Shelter Cove Resort, which has a small store and, more important, the Cascade Summit Post Office. The store's selection is

D13

D13

quite limited, so be sure to mail sufficient food and supplies.

After backtracking to the Trail 42 junction (mile 21.1), we curve west 150 yards down to a bridge that crosses Trapper Creek only 35 yards below the breached dam. Leaving this creek behind, we contour the slopes and reach an intersection with Yoran Lake Trail 49 (4900–0.5). This trail goes northeast moderately to steeply 250 yards down to the railroad tracks, from which you follow a dirt road 70 yards to Road 5810. You can follow this road a quarter mile east to the Trapper Creek Campground, then 0.4 mile farther to the Shelter Cove Resort.

see MAP D11
see MAP D12

North of the trail intersection, our trail parallels the railroad tracks below and passes seasonal creeklets before reaching a spur road (4850–0.7), which climbs northwest 0.4 mile to Pengra Pass. We start along this road from a point 70 yards west of the tracks and follow it up 80 yards around a bend to a resumption of the trail, which branches right and ascends 130 yards northwest to a small creek under the shade of a Douglas-fir forest. Here we find shooting stars, bluebells, bunchberries and Oregon grapes, which are typically associated with this type of forest. Our trail now climbs gently northeast and reaches a junction with the Pacific Crest Trail (5040–0.5–22.8). We now follow that trail eastward 1.1 miles to Section D's end near Highway 58's Willamette Pass.

*   *   *   *

From Windigo Pass on the Cascade Lakes Road, the Pacific Crest Trail begins a 7-mile-longer route to Willamette Pass. It climbs ½ mile, to a crest crossing, from which you could head due north ¼ mile, staying east of the crest as you descend to the southwestern Windigo Lake, about 130 feet below you. Avoiding

water, the PCT closely follows the crest for about one mile, then climbs 400 vertical feet on a winding course to a minor crest saddle (6620–2.3). From here you can traverse 200 yards northwest across relatively flat terrain to a lakelet with acceptable water and a possible campsite.

Beyond the unseen lakelet, the PCT climbs the crest over to a saddle (7100–1.6) by the southwest ridge of pointed Cowhorn Mountain. The short, rewarding climb to the top of this miniature Mt. Thielsen is an obvious though steep one. The trail now descends northwest along the crest, eventually switchbacking down to the edge of a forested bowl that contains a small, somewhat stagnant pond (6380–3.1). This, unfortunately, is the only *permanent* trailside water between Summit Lake, 3.8 miles ahead, and Thielsen Creek, 29 miles behind! It's too bad that PCT hikers must go out of their way to get water or to camp. This relatively new section of the PCT could have easily been routed past springs, creeks and lakes. From the stagnant pond you can head cross-country over the low crest and drop ¼ to ½ mile into the Windy Lakes basin for water and a campsite.

D13, D8   **D8, D10, D9**

About ½ mile beyond the pond, we start a diagonal descent across a considerable escarpment and soon reach an amorphous terrain on which we cross an imperceptible crest. A little over 3 miles of viewless meandering bring us close to Summit Lake's south shore (5560–4.1), and a short traverse west brings us to Road 700 (5570–0.2), at the lake's southwest corner. This we cross three times as we follow the PCT north along it to a crossing of Road 6010 (5590–1.4). From here you can head 200 yards over to Summit Lake Campground, above the lake's northwest corner. This lake is a good one for a layover day, for, like *large* Cascade Range lakes, it has clear water and relatively few mosquitoes.

From Road 6010 our trail starts northeast, and we enter Diamond Peak Wilderness as we wind northwest past a series of seven ponds and lakelets shown on the map and even more smaller, unmapped ones. After leaving the west shore of the last mapped one (5670–1.1), our trail winds north up a relatively dry stretch to a slope above the south shore of one of the few accessible lakes we'll see (5860–0.9), near which adequate camps can be established. The trail curves down to the lake's east shore, then, in ⅓ mile, crosses a "spring" from an unseen pond only 30 yards from the trail. Continuing north, we wind up to a forested flat across which the Fawn Lake Trail once traversed. Beyond it, we climb north, then northwest easily up to a switchback (6560–2.8), from which we get one of several forthcoming views of stunning, steep-sided Mt. Thielsen. The trail northeast climbs gently-to-moderately across the imperceptible Lane/Klamath county line and levels off in a severely glaciated bowl just east of Diamond Peak. Hikers wishing to climb this peak can scramble west from here up Class 2 rubble slopes.

Leaving the bowl, we traverse east and catch a view in the south of Crater Lake's rim framed between Mt. Thielsen (9182) on the left and Mt. Bailey (8363) on the right. Closer to us, in the southeast, is large Crescent Lake. We round the curving, northeast ridge of Diamond Peak and soon exchange southern views for northern ones. In open breaks in the mountain-hemlock forest, one may see—if weather permits—South Sister (10,358), Middle Sister (10,047), Mt. Washington (7794) and very distant Mt. Jefferson (10,497). Closer by stand two imposing monoliths, Mt. Yoran (7100) and Peak 7138, the latter of which we'll traverse beneath. Before

that northeast traverse, however, our winding course makes a broad arc northward, passing by some reliable creeklets then by tiny tarns before commencing a steady descent past Peak 7138.

Leaving the ridge slopes behind, we descend to lake-and-pond-dotted slopes and arrive above the north shore (6030–7.2) of a green, unnamed lake, near which you could camp. All the lakes and ponds between it and the Rosary Lakes, north of State Highway 58, are less attractive. Not too far beyond it, we see an even larger lake, east of us, through the trees, and the trail descends to within about 100 feet of its northwest corner (5840–0.6). Lack of adequate level ground makes camping at this corner of the lake undesirable, but more-distant shores offer better potential. (Remember that in wilderness areas your camp must be at least 100 feet from the shore.)

Beyond this lake, we descend for 1¼ miles past shallow, mosquito-infested ponds before angling southeast and descending to a broad flat of silver fir, mountain hemlock and western white pine. A bend northward takes us up to a low saddle from which we descend to within 70 yards (5370–2.5) of fairly well hidden Midnight Lake, which has only a poor camping potential. You may wish to stop for water here or at a nearby pond ¼ mile farther along the route. Beyond both bodies of water we cross a saddle, then steadily descend to a closed road at Pengra Pass (5003–1.5), just 80 yards southeast of its junction with Road 5899.

To get food or mailed packages at Shelter Cove Resort (mentioned in the alternate route), follow this road ½ mile southeast, down to Road 5810, then follow it southeast one mile over to the resort. To return to the PCT, either backtrack or else follow the last part of the alternate route—a maintained section of the defunct Oregon Skyline Trail.

At Pengra Pass we leave the wilderness, and then contour east to a junction with the old Oregon Skyline Trail (5040–0.5), at which the alternate route ends. Here you'll also find an old trail that descends steeply south ¼ mile to Road 5810. The PCT now climbs a short ⅓ mile to a small bluff that provides the hiker with the only good view of Odell Lake he'll get along the route. Our trail climbs a few yards beyond the viewpoint, then contours over to a pond, on our right, past which the trail makes a short, switchbacking descent to Highway 58 (5090–1.1), which you reach ¼ mile southeast of Willamette Pass.

D9, D11   **D11, D13**

This section's PCT
Other trails
Hwys and major rds
Other roads
Campgrounds

0 1 2 3 4 5   10 mi

THREE SISTERS WILDERNESS

Section E: Highway 58 near Willamette Pass to Highway 242 at McKenzie Pass

Introduction: In Section E the Pacific Crest Trail traverses across three types of terrain. The first third of this section's PCT traverses across slopes that are deficient in both views and lakes. On the middle third, which starts at Irish Lake, the trail traverses flatter land that is still generally viewless, but is peppered with very enjoyable lakes (once the mosquito population dwindles). On the northern third, the trail skirts around the Three Sisters, and views abound of glacier-draped peaks and spreading, sinister lava flows. Like Section C's Sky Lakes Wilderness, this section's Three Sisters Wilderness, which dominates most of the section, is flooded with weekend hikers. And for good reason—it is very scenic and readily accessible.

Declination: 18¼°E

Mileages:

	South to North	Distances between Points	North to South
Highway 58 near Willamette Pass.................	0.0		75.8
		2.2	
Lower Rosary Lake	2.2		73.6
		6.8	
Moore Creek Trail to Bobby Lake	9.0		66.8
		7.6	
Charlton Lake Trail	16.6		59.2
		5.6	
Road 600 at Irish Lake	22.2		53.6
		13.4	
Cliff Lake Trail	35.6		40.2
		8.9	
Island Meadow Trail to Elk Lake..................	44.5		31.3
		5.7	
Camelot Lake	50.2		25.6
		4.5	
North fork of Mesa Creek	54.7		21.1
		10.3	
Glacier Way Trail	65.0		10.8
		3.1	
Minnie Scott Spring	68.1		7.7
		3.4	
South Matthieu Lake	71.5		4.3
		2.9	
Trail to Lava Camp Lake........................	74.4		1.4
		1.4	
Highway 242 at McKenzie Pass	75.8		0.0

Supplies: No on-route supplies are available, but you can make a 1¼-mile detour over to Elk Lake Resort, which has a cafe and a small store that caters to fishermen. The resort also holds PCT packages (address: Elk Lake Resort, P.O. Box 789, Bend, OR 97709). Before mailing packages, contact the resort to verify that it still offers this free service.

Problems: Long-distance PCT hikers seem to agree that the trail's worst concentrations of mosquitos are found either in Sky Lakes Wilderness in Section C or in the lake-and-pond dotted south half of Three Sisters Wilderness. Therefore, bring a tent and plenty of mosquito repellent if you are hiking through this section before August.

The Pacific Crest Trail in Section E begins from Highway 58 about ¼ mile southeast of Willamette Pass and just yards away from a road that peels south-southeast down toward Odell Lake. To reach this highway's PCT trailhead parking lot, go down the highway 200 yards from the PCT to a short Highway Commission road that branches north. This road is about 200 yards northwest of a second road that branches down toward Odell Lake (the two Odell Lake roads quickly unite to become Road 5810). After starting north on the Highway Commission road, you immediately take a short road 150 yards east to the trailhead parking lot. From it, a short trail goes 80 yards north to the PCT.

Starting our hike from Highway 58 (5090), we follow the PCT as it curves east behind the Highway Commission's long cinder-storage building, and then we meet the trailhead-parking spur trail (5130–0.2) immediately past it.

Our trail now climbs steadily east through a forest of Douglas-fir, western white pine and mountain hemlock to a saddle, then curves north and passes a hundred-foot-high rock jumble before reaching the ridge above South Rosary Lake (5730–2.0). This clear lake is deep in early summer, and in this it contrasts strongly with the other lakes its size we've seen so far along our entire route. By late summer, however, the lake level can fall more than twenty feet, due to seepage through the porous volcanic rocks, and leave its eastward drainage channel high and dry. We quickly encounter a very good ridgetop campsite, then curve northward, cross the lake's outlet, and reach an equally good campsite. Now we climb northwest to a campsite near the southwest corner of deep, blue-green Middle Rosary Lake (5830–0.6), which is even more impressive than the south lake because it lies at the base of 400-foot-high Rosary rock. On a weekend, you're likely to see climbers scaling this rock. We walk alongside the lake, then pass by the low dividing ridge between the middle and north lakes, on which is an excellent campsite. We reach shallower North Rosary Lake (5830–0.3), then follow the trail as it climbs west above the lake's north shore before switchbacking east-northeast up to a junction with Maiden Lake Trail 41 (6060–0.6), which descends east-southeast before contouring east toward that lake.

We continue east for 130 yards, then switchback west up to a saddle (6170–0.5), but not before getting one last glance back at Rosary rock and the Rosary lakes, and in the distance,

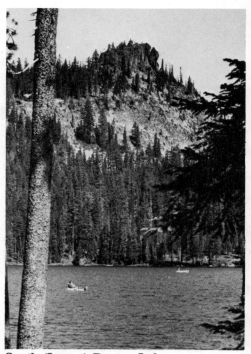

South (Lower) Rosary Lake

Odell Lake, Odell Butte and Crescent Lake—all lakes owing their existence to glacial excavation. Until the late 1980s, the PCT followed the original Oregon Skyline Trail, descending northwest along, appropriately, Skyline Creek. Doing so, it passed three camps: T-M-R, Bark Table and Waithere. The newer stretch, unfortunately, avoids both camps and water and hugs the crest as a crest trail is supposed to do. Still, the lack of camps will be missed by some old-time hikers and equestrians, and will only add to the camping pressure at the Rosary Lakes. Plan accordingly.

After heading north along east-facing slopes of a linear ridge, a stretch that offers Maiden Peak views, the newer stretch crosses the ridge at a minor saddle (6070-1.3) and then soon descends moderately to an intersection of Maiden Peak Trail 3681 (5730-1.2). We continue north on the newer stretch, first dropping moderately to the old OST route (5400-0.6), then traversing northeast a spell before curving north across wet meadows up to a junction with northwest-traversing Bobby Lake Trail 3663 (5440-1.5).

We turn right (northeast) and start up the trail as it curves quickly up to a triangular junction

E1   **E1, E2**

see MAP D12

where two forks of Moore Creek Trail 40 (5470-0.2) branch off from the PCT and merge just east of it. It's best for us now to head east ¼ mile down this trail to a nice campsite at the west end of large, clear Bobby Lake (5408), for our next reliable source of water is Charlton Lake, about 7⅔ miles farther. It seems ironic that as one progresses north into ever thicker, wetter forests, the water sources become spaced farther apart. One expects drought over the miles of pumice-covered lands around Crater Lake and Mt. Thielsen, but it can be frustrating to be in a dense forest during a drizzling rain and yet have to hike miles to obtain running water to drink. In such areas, ground water percolating through the volcanic-rock structures certainly is the major form of water transport.

Back on the PCT, we now head north past two large ponds, climb northwest to a saddle (5980-1.4), curve northeast gently down from it, and then climb to an intersection with Twin Peaks Trail 3595 (6220-1.3). A viewpoint is supposed

Skyline Creek

E2, E3

see MAP E1

to be 50 yards southwest down this trail. It isn't. Don't fret, for about a mile north from this junction you can walk 70 yards west across rock slabs and obtain an unobstructed view westward, from Diamond Peak north to Waldo Lake.

After this side trip, the trail shortly starts a gentle descent and begins to cross gullies one after another. You eventually pass above a small pond, then quickly reach a cluster of three ponds (6320–2.4) grouped around the small knob identified on the map as 6362. The route now descends northeast across gullies, reaches the watershed divide by a small pond, then de-

scends west a short distance before curving north toward gentler slopes above Charlton Lake (5692). We head north through a forested flat area, reach the slopes above the lake, and descend to an intersection with Charlton Lake Trail 3570 (5725–2.5), about a hundred yards north of a small pond. The lakeshore is 100 yards southeast; Road 5897 is 150 yards northwest, just beyond a pond. By heading northeast for 0.1 mile, we reach a closed spur road heading southeast to the lake from Road 5897. Then we diagonal north across the road to a broad trail that we follow north about 45 yards to where it

E3   **E3**

see MAP E2

bends northwest 40 yards to a roadside parking area. From this bend the PCT follows old blazes east-northeast and climbs gently up the divide to a diagonal crossing of Road 5897 (5840–0.6) at a 20° bearing.

Our trail starts north, climbs northwest to the low watershed divide, and then contours north past small ponds and Charlton Butte to a junc-

tion on the right (east) with Lily Lake Trail 19 (5965–1.4), which descends about ¾ mile to that isolated lake. Continuing north, we keep following the divide down a north slope to a small flat, then climb over two low mounds before reaching the southwest arm of shallow Taylor Lake (5550–3.3). Our trail immediately angles away from the lake, heads north past a

E3

E3, E4, E5

see MAP E5

E4

see MAP E3

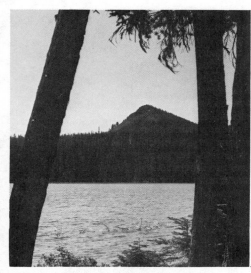

Charlton Lake and Gerdine Butte

pond on the left (west), then reaches Road 600 at Irish Lake (5549–0.3). Popular Irish Lake Campground is ¼ mile east on the road.

We can pick up the trail again by going west 25 yards on the road, then north 50 yards along a spur road that takes us to the trailhead. We enter Three Sisters Wilderness as our route heads north above the west shore of Irish Lake then passes west of shallow but clear Riffle Lake (5575–0.8), which has an adequate campsite on its west shore. We now climb a low ridge and descend slightly to a flat with two large lily-pad ponds before climbing up to a higher ridge

(5730–1.2). The lakes and ponds of this area are shallow, and, like those in the Sky Lakes region, they support a superabundant mosquito population from late spring through mid-July.

We pass a number of stagnant ponds and small lakes in rapid succession as we descend to a nice campsite on the east shore of Brahma Lake (5657–0.6), which is distinguished by a forested island. Our route continues north along its shore, contours west, and then climbs moderately up slopes and through a miniature gorge before reaching the northeast corner of clear Jezebel Lake (5855–1.1). A campsite is perched

E5   E5

Riffle Lake

on the low ridge north of this corner. Climbing northwest above the lake, we reach a shady glen, from which a trail once climbed ¼ mile west-southwest to Rock Rim Lake. Our trail rounds a linear ridge descending east, climbs west along its north slope, then angles north to a good campsite beside the outlet of Stormy Lake

(6045–1.0). The towering cliffs of Irish Mountain over a lakeside evening campfire leaves us with a vivid memory of this choice spot.

Leaving this lake behind, we descend to smaller, slightly cloudy Blaze Lake (5950–0.3), then contour northward past an abundance of ponds before the trail descends a ridge to a low

E5

see MAP E6

E5, E6

see MAP E4

E6

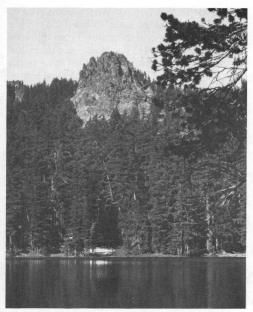

Irish Mountain above Stormy Lake

divide just east of open Cougar Flat (5750–2.1). Our route winds down to Lake 5678, then passes smaller water bodies as it follows the ridge northeast down to Tadpole Lake (5340–2.0), perched on a forested saddle, where you may surprise some feeding ring-necked ducks. We traverse the lake's grassy north shore, then descend north to a grassy pond and a junction with the Elk Creek (#3510) and Winopee Lake (#16) trails (5250–0.4). The Elk Creek Trail climbs northwest over a low saddle and

descends into the Elk Creek drainage; the Winopee Lake Trail curves south around a knoll before descending to Winopee Lake.

We continue northeast across the lower slopes of Packsaddle Mountain (6144), walk north past a polluted lake to the east, and arrive at a junction with Snowshoe Lake Trail 33 (5250–1.2), which descends east. Now we hike north past Desane Lake and enter the Willamette National Forest again as we cross a flat divide and descend into the Mink Lake Basin, where we meet a junction with Mink Lake Loop Trail 3526 (5160–0.4). This 2.7 mile loop climbs northwest up a low, broad ridge before descending north to Mink Lake, stocked with eastern brook and rainbow trout. From there, the loop winds east, dropping to Porky Lake with more eastern brook, then climbs back to the PCT at the Cliff Lake outlet creek.

Our route follows a string of sparkling lakes that make an appropriate necklace for South Sister. In rapid succession we encounter S Lake (5150), Mac Lake (5100) with rainbow, Merrill Lake (5080) and Horseshoe Lake (5039), a very shallow lake with both rainbow and eastern brook. The trail curves around to the north shore of this lake, then reaches a spur trail (5040–1.5) that bears 0.1 mile north to Moody Lake (5020). We cross the usually dry outlet of Horseshoe Lake, then continue north gently up and around a band of cliffs to a reunion with Mink Lake Loop Trail 3526 (5130–0.8) beside the Cliff Lake outlet creek.

Just 130 yards southeast up a spur trail beside this creek is deep, green, rock-and-alder lined Cliff Lake (5138). The web of trails and the abundance of campsites attest to the popularity

E6   E6
A bedrock peninsula cuts deep into Dumbbell Lake

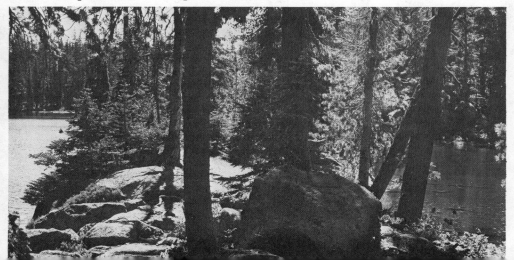

of this lake. The best campsites are atop the cliff along the lake's northwest shore, but should you be caught in foul weather, you can camp in comfort in the Cliff Lake shelter. Good eastern-brook-trout fishing justifies a stop at this lake, as do good diving rocks near large aspens along the northeast shore. Backtracking from these, we pass beargrass blooming between boulders, and, near the shelter, we avoid stepping on delicate bunchberries and shooting stars that grow on the moist, shady forest floor.

Back at the loop-trail junction, we cross Cliff Lake's outlet creek, walk northwest, then round a pile of large boulders and climb gently to a seasonal creek (5225–0.8). We cross it, hike up a switchback, and then work up northeast to a junction with the Goose Rock (#3542) and Senoj Lake (#3534) trails (5330–0.6). The Goose Rock Trail starts northwest down toward a meadow, then heads west and down to Goose Lake; the 5.6-mile Senoj Lake Trail starts southeast to an unnamed lake, heads east to the divide, then continues as Trail 14 east down to Cascade Lakes Highway 46.

We start north, quickly descend to Reserve Meadow, and head northeast along its edge before curving northwest away from its large, east-

end campsite (5320–0.4). We then climb up to relatively deep Island Lake (5438–0.5), which has a patch of grass in its center. From this lake we climb up the trail to a rockpile, contour west past two stagnant ponds, and then hike north until we are just above a 50-yard-long peninsula that juts southwest into Dumbbell Lake (5502–0.7). From this rocky spur you can fish or dive in the lake's warm, clear waters. Our trail now gradually climbs north past many ponds to a low divide (5660–2.2), then descends to a junction with the old Oregon Skyline Trail (5460–0.5), which heads 6.3 miles to Camelot Lake via popular Horse Lake.

From this junction 1½ miles south of Horse Lake, the Pacific Crest Trail branches east. After a few minutes' hiking, we reach an obvious spring seeping from the ground only 10 yards downslope from the trail. This is a good place to obtain water, for the route beyond may be dry until Camelot Lake, 8.8 miles farther. Continuing east, we descend toward Island Meadow, but stay within the forest's edge as we hike southeast along its southern border. We soon reach a bridge across a small, seasoned creek and find a fair trailside campsite above its east bank, 70 yards south of the meadow. Our trail

E6   **E6, E7**

strikes southeast again, but shortly turns and follows a wandering route northeast before descending north to a mile-high meadow across which we traverse north-northeast to a junction with Sunset Lake Trail 3517A (5235–1.9), which passes that lake midway in its descent to the OST. We now go east-southeast on our trail, enter forest and pass a large pond 50 yards south, then snake east over an undetected drainage divide before descending to a junction where the PCT leaves Island Meadow Trail 3/3517 (5250–1.3) and angles north.

The Island Meadow Trail makes a southeast descent 0.9 mile to a trailhead parking area, from which a road descends 270 yards to Cascade Lakes Highway 46. On this you can head south 70 yards to the Elk Lake Resort entrance. Down at the lakeside resort, you can obtain meals plus limited supplies. If you visit the resort by early July, you'll likely see barn swallows nesting in the rafters above its entrance. Large, 57-foot-deep Elk Lake (4884) offers very good trout fishing and is a nice place for a layover day. Although the lake has no outlet and no permanent inlets, its water stays quite clear because fresh groundwater continues to seep into the lake at about the same rate

that groundwater leaves it. Rather than backtrack up the Island Meadows Trail, you can head north on the road 0.2 mile past its trailhead and start up Horse Lake Trail 2 which takes you 1.6 miles northwest up to the PCT.

Back where the PCT leaves the Island Meadow Trail, the PCT climbs north toward a cinder cone (5676), rounds its eastern half, then heads north to a lesser summit before reaching an intersection on a saddle with Horse Lake Trail 2/3516 (5300–1.3). Following the divide, our trail climbs gently north at first, but steepens as it curves over to the western slope of Koosah Mountain (6520). Here we make a long switchback up to the ridge, then contour to its east slope, where, by stepping a few yards east, we can absorb an eastern panorama from Elk and Hosmer lakes north past conical Bachelor Butte (9065) and deeply glaciated Broken Top (9175) to South Sister (10,358). Although we can't see the Cascade Lakes Highway below, we can hear the rumble of the logging trucks on it.

Hiking northwest, we encounter switchbacks down the north slope, then reach a flat and continue north to a junction at the south shore of placid, shallow Camelot Lake (5980-4.4). Here the OST route heads southwest along the Red

E7   **E7, E8, E9**

South Sister, from Koosah Mountain (left) and from Wickiup Plain (right)

Hill Trail. After a brief hike northeast on the PCT, we reach the south edge of Sisters Mirror Lake (5980-0.1), from where you'll see South Sister mirrored in the lake when the water is calm. From here you can head along the west shore to some good camps on a rocky bluff along its northwest shore. Some camps in this general vicinity may be closed, due to previous camper impact, and the Forest Service urges visitors to camp at the lakes lying west of Camelot and Sisters Mirror lakes. On the rocky bluff you'll see a use trail that heads west toward some of these lakes.

The PCT heads north along Sisters Mirror Lake's east shore, and along this short stretch you can climb up to a low bench, which offers small campsites. Next, our trail turns east from

the lake and in about 300 yards it reaches a junction with the use trail heading westward across a meadow toward the lake's rocky bluff. The Forest Service may attempt to obliterate this trail, so don't be too concerned if you don't see it. Near the east end of the meadow, about 130 yards past the junction, you'll come to a junction (5990-0.4) with two official trails. Nash Lake Trail 3527 starts north before turning northwest, while Mirror Lake Trail 20 makes a long, mostly gentle descent south-southeast, eventually reaching Cascade Lakes Highway in about 3.5 miles.

Our route climbs slightly in a traverse east to an important junction (6030-0.3). From here the well-graded Wickiup Plain Trail first rambles about 1¼ miles east across a fairly youth-

see MAP E10

see MAP E11

see MAP E8

Rock Mesa and Elk Lake, viewed from south slopes of South Sister

ful lava flow to a junction with the southwest end of the Moraine Lake Trail. Then it heads ½ mile east along the south edge of the Wickiup Plain to another junction. From it a narrow trail goes 0.5 mile north to an intersection of the Moraine Lake Trail, then continues 1.3 miles northwest over to the PCT. The Wickiup Plain Trail leaves its namesake for a well-graded 2.2-mile descent to the Devils Lake area, with camping, picnicking and fishing (this spring-fed lake is too cold for comfortable swimming). A large trailhead parking area lies just south of Tyee Creek, between the highway and the lake, and is quite heavily used by Bend's residents and visitors. This city, the largest Oregon city east of the Cascades, lies about a half-hour drive away.

From the west end of the Wickiup Plain Trail, the PCT heads north along a minor ridge to the south base of the House Rock and then traverses along its wooded lower slopes up to an arm of the Wickiup Plain. Our trail climbs north gently up this partly forested plain and after ½ mile crosses the broad county-line divide (6210-1.2).

As we approach Le Conte Crater—a low cinder cone to the northeast—we begin to picture a sequence of events that molded this volcanic landscape. The thick stand of mountain hemlock on the northern half of Le Conte Crater indicates that this cone is at least several thousand years old. An educated guess, based upon comparisons with cones of known ages, is that an eruption took place 6000 to 8000 years ago and built up the cinder cone. Immediately following this eruption came outpourings of fluid, basaltic lava that breached the cone's south rim and flowed south down the gently sloping Wickiup Plain. We see this flow today as the forested, undulating surface south of the cone and off to our right (east). The section of Wickiup Plain over which the trail passes is probably no more than 20,000 years old, for it

shows little sign of erosion. We can be quite sure its age is greater than 10,000 years, since it was in existence when the last great Pleistocene glaciers marched down from South Sister and deposited their debris on its eastern side; a conspicuous moraine ends on top of the plain roughly 1½ miles due east of the cone.

Due west from the crater's north base, we meet a previously mentioned trail (6160-0.5) that goes 1.8 miles southeast to the Wickiup Plain Trail. Starting near Devils Lake, that trail provides the fastest way in to the South Sister vicinity. Just north of Le Conte Crater we see a vast, desolate, steep-sided chaotic jumble appropriately called Rock Mesa. The high point near its east side marks the location of the vent from which rhyodacite lava was extruded over 2000 years ago. Because the lava was so viscous, the flow not only solidified before reaching Le Conte Crater, but it also solidified halfway down the relatively steep slopes of the Mesa Creek drainage just north of us. It did succeed, however, in covering up any trace of a conduit that might have given rise to the older flows of the Wickiup Plain.

By now you've probably noticed The Wife (7054)—a conspicuous summit off to the west—and you've probably observed that South Sister (10,358) is a redhead. Should you wish to climb to its summit, strike east from a point just south of Le Conte Crater, then head northeast along the east margin of Rock Mesa. When you reach the peak's lower slope, climb north directly up it and pass between the Clark and Lewis glaciers as you near the summit cone. When you top its rim, you'll find it crowned with a snow-clad lake (10,200) that occupies a crater which may have been active in the last few thousand years. South Sister, with at least three major periods of eruptions, is a geologically complex volcano; its slopes contain over two dozen types of volcanic rocks. This sister is the

see MAP E12

E10

see MAP E11

THREE SISTERS WILDERNESS

see MAP E9

see MAP E12

E11

see MAP E10

see MAP E9

youngest of the three, and it still retains much of its symmetry because it has been exposed only to late-Pleistocene and Recent glaciation. The latest eruption in the Three Sisters area occurred within the last 200 years.

By the time you finish reading the above discussions, you could have been well on your way to the north end of Wickiup Plain. The posts along the route seem unnecessary since the route is so obvious. Newberry knotweed and scattered grass attest to the dryness of the pumice soil, but plentiful gopher mounds indicate that at least one mammal thrives here. At the north edge of the plain, the trail curves northwest over a low saddle, then descends to a creek (6010–1.2) which passes through a large meadow. In early July this meadow is a continuous field of yellow cinquefoil that contrasts sharply with the wintry chill of deep snow patches on the surrounding forested slopes. We regretfully leave this island of sunshine behind and press onward northwest into the forest and down alongside a small gully. Our trail makes a switchback east and leads us down to the south fork of Mesa Creek. Now we step across it, hike north into a large, grassy meadow, and then reach the north fork of Mesa Creek (5700–0.8). You'll find near-creek campsites both east and west of the meadow. Past the north fork you reach a tributary in 100 yards—a scenic lunch spot.

Leaving the meadow and its sparkling creeks behind, we turn our backs on the frozen "tidal wave" of Rock Mesa and climb northwest up to a junction with the James Creek Trail (5920–0.6), which makes a gentle ascent west before curving north along the old OST route. We ascend east, curve north, and then round a murky lakelet just east of us. Continuing to climb north, our route tends to follow the break in slope between the foot of South Sister, to the east, and the Separation Creek headquarters, to the west. Along our course we pass through numerous small meadows and beside a fine, six-foot-diameter mountain hemlock before we descend slightly to a crossing of Hinton Creek (6320–2.1). After hiking to the other side of a low divide, we descend past a cliff of a high-density, parallel-fractured, shalelike flow. Here we cross Separation Creek (6400–0.5), whose flow, like that of Hinton Creek, has usually sunk beneath the pumice by mid-August.

E11, E9, E10

see MAP E13

E12

94

see MAP E10

see MAP E11

We now come face-to-face with Middle Sister (10,047), which can be easily climbed up its south or west slope. Continuing north, we follow posts and rock piles across a pumice flat and reach a shallow, clear lakelet (6460–0.4), beside which good campsites can be found. The fragile timberline ecosystem here is very sensitive to human impact, so treat it gently. Beyond, we tread across level bedrock that has a previous glacier's signature etched upon it in the form of striations. The glacier also left souvenirs of its visit: erratic boulders.

Our route north now crosses half a dozen seasonal, step-across creeks as it descends toward Linton Creek and finally bends west down to a meadow at whose north end we meet Foley Ridge Trail 3511 (6270–1.3), which leads south-southwest down a slope. About 25 yards west, at a forested flat, is a justifiably popular campsite. The Husband (7524), off in the west, is the resistant plug of an ancient volcano that once reigned over this area before the Three Sisters matured. Just after we start north again, we reach a tributary of Linton Creek, then 70 yards farther reach a second tributary.

From these seasonal creeks, our trail climbs gradually north through a hemlock forest to where it meets the Linton Meadows Trail (6440–1.7), descending steeply southwest. The PCT ascends moderately northeast to a spring, then angles north to a gentle slope from which we can look south and identify, from east to west; the Mt. Thielsen pinnacle (9182), the Mt. McLoughlin pyramid (9495) and the Diamond Peak massif (8744). We now follow an open, post-lined, undulating pathway north over loose slopes with trailside rose paintbrushes, yellow cinquefoils, pink heathers and white pasqueflowers. Then we cross a rocky meadow, perhaps while being watched by a marmot, and descend to a junction with Obsidian Trail 3528 (6380–2.1), just above Obsidian Creek. This five-mile trail takes you down to Frog Campground by the McKenzie Highway.

We start hiking east moderately up to a slope, then go northeast up to the trickling, 50-foot-high Obsidian Falls, from which we top a small shelf and cross Obsidian Creek. We now tread north on a trail that sounds and feels like glass. It is. The black obsidian is nature's own glass. Our trail, which passes some outstanding camps past the last junction, soon leaves the shelf, descends a ridge, and then turns east and intersects Glacier Way Trail 3528A (6370–1.6). This path descends moderately 0.7 mile to the Obsidian

Rest stop at Scott Trail junction

Trail, which can be followed 3.4 miles to Frog Campground.

An efficient mountaineering party can follow this route up from the campground, climb North and Middle Sisters via the Collier Glacier col, and return to camp late the same day. From the col, Middle Sister (10,047) can be climbed via its north ridge without any special equipment. Likewise, North Sister (10,085) can be climbed via its southwest ridge to the south aréte, but the climb north along this sharp crest requires a safety rope. The view from Middle Sister is particularly instructional, for from it you can compare the degree of glaciation on all Three Sisters. North Sister, the oldest of the three, has suffered repeated ravages from quite a number of glacial advances. South Sister (10,358), the youngest, retains her symmetry, for she hasn't lived long enough to feel the icy tongues cut deep into her body.

Twenty yards east of the Glacier Way intersection, we bridge Glacier Creek, then reach a

MT. WASHINGTON E13

WILDERNESS

Dee Wright Observatory ×5324 ×5187 BM
McKenzie Pass

Snow Shelter

LANE CO

THREE ×5260 SISTERS WILDERNESS

HIGHWAY 242

Lava Camp Lake
Forest Camp

Black Crater 6582

CRATER TR. 94

6400 5600 5194 BM

pleasant, hemlock-shaded site where Sunshine Shelter once stood. You may find this area closed to camping. We climb briefly north over the western spur of Little Brother (7810), then descend slightly to the steep south slope above White Branch creek (6210-0.9). After climbing along this creek, which can go dry in August, we eventually cross it. Here you can camp above its north bank on a flat called Sawyer Bar.

Our trail bears north 200 yards part way across a basalt flow, then angles east up a ridge of solidified lava to the breached Collier Cone—the obvious source of this flow. Here, mountaineers' paths take off south up to Collier Glacier. We turn north and work our way across several lava ridges before descending north to Minnie Scott Spring (6650–2.2), which is likely to be snowbound through mid-July. You can camp on the level ground west of the spring. Our

trail now makes a curving, counterclockwise descent almost to the Minnie Scott Spring creek, crosses a ridge, descends north to a large, grassy meadow and shortly meets Scott Trail 3551 (6300–0.9).

Descending west to the McKenzie Highway in about five miles, this trail follows the narrow strip of land between the Four in One Cone (6258) basalt flow on its north side and the Collier Cone (7534) basalt flow on its south side. The age of these flows, and of the Yapoah Crater (6737) basalt flow immediately north of us, is about 2600 years. Our route follows the Scott Trail north, which curves northeast and switchbacks up a northwest spur of the Ahalapam Cinder Field. It then curves around the slopes of Yapoah Crater and enters Deschutes National Forest. The crater's lava flow—at least 400 years old—extends north to Highway 242

E12

E12

Views from Dee Wright Observatory: south, the Sisters; north, Mt. Washington and, just barely, Three Fingered Jack

and beyond. Looking north, we can see a row of peaks: Mt. Washington (7794), Three Fingered Jack (7841) and the snowy Mts. Jefferson (10,497) and Hood (11,235).

We now wind along and around ridges of the Yapoah lava flow and are thankful that the rocky trail exists, even when it is covered with snow patches. A cross-country hike across this material would be very exhausting. We reach the edge of the flow and parallel it north on a blocky cinder trail to a junction from where Scott Trail 95 descends east-southeast toward Trout Creek. Just 70 yards north down from this junction is Scott Pass and adjacent, diminutive South Matthieu Lake (6040-2.5). At this pass you get one of your best views eastward of central Oregon, which is drier than the west countryside because of the rainshadow cast by the Cascade Range. Here too, around the 70-yard-wide lake, you'll find several small campsites, which can offer uplifting sunrise views. Just beyond a campsite above this lake's northwest corner, you'll come to a junction with the old OST route (6070-0.1).

*   *   *   *

The OST descended to North Matthieu Lake, and this 2.1-mile stretch is a preferred route over the equally long stretch of waterless PCT. This alternate segment first winds ⅔ mile down to the southeast corner of appealing North Matthieu Lake, then in ¼ mile leaves it at the northwest corner. Along this near-shore traverse you'll spot several campsites. From the lake switchbacks guide you down steep slopes, then you parallel the east edge of the Yapoah Crater lava flow, passing a small pond on the east and then one on the west before rejoining the PCT.

*   *   *   *

From the junction near South Matthieu Lake the PCT first crosses slopes of a fairly young cinder cone, which on a clear day offers you a far-ranging view of northern Oregon's higher Cascade peaks: Mt. Washington, Three Fingered Jack, Mt. Jefferson and Mt. Hood. Then comes a fairly long, viewless, though mostly

E12, E13

well-graded descent to a junction with the old OST route (5450-2.1). Now you have a gentle descent northwest along the east edge of the Yapoah Crater lava flow and soon come to a junction (5310-0.7) with an important lateral trail. This snakes ¼ mile northeast to a fairly large trailhead parking area, which lies along the south side of Road 900, a State Highway 242 spur road that goes over to Lava Camp Lake. Since your next potential source of trailside water is at *sometimes dry* Coldwater Spring, 11.2 miles distant, you should consider camping over at the lake's campground. You'll find the lake just northeast of the parking area, the two separated by a minor ridge. If the weather looks bad, look for a shelter above the southeast corner of the lake. The shallow lake's water is not pristine, so if you'd rather not treat it, you might get safe water from car campers. Should you need supplies, walk out to nearby State Highway 242 and hitchhike 15 miles east to Sisters. When the PCT's "final" route was approved in 1972, Sisters was a sleepy town, but by the late 1980s it had transformed into a prosperous, upscale tourist town.

From the lateral-trail junction the PCT makes a zigzag course west over the blocky lava field and it leaves Three Sisters Wilderness as we cross narrow McKenzie Highway (242) (5280-1.1) 500 yards west of the Dee Wright Observatory—a lookout tower well worth visiting for its views. Just 0.2 mile west down this highway is a parking area with a trailhead for those starting their hike north from McKenzie Pass. This pass was named for the river that was explored in 1811 by Donald McKenzie, a member of John Jacob Astor's Pacific Fur Company. It was opened to travel in 1862 when Felix Scott, with a party of 250 men, chopped their way through the forest, building the road for their 106 ox-hauled wagons as they traveled. They crossed the divide by what is known as the Old Scott Trail, two or three miles south of the present road.

Having crossed the highway, we leave Three Sisters Wilderness and enter Mt. Washington Wilderness. Due to the jumbled nature of the lava flow, our trail must take a twisted route over to the small trailhead parking area (5210–0.3), where our section's hike ends.

E13

The Pacific Crest Trail in Section F

—N—

0 1 2 3 4 5 .... 10 .... 15mi

This section's PCT
Other trails
Hwys and major rds
Other roads
Campgrounds ▲

F14
PCT
Barlow Pass
3530
48
Trillium Lake
F12   F13
Wapinitia Pass
240
2660
2610
4610
58   WHITE
F11   Clear Lake
5890
Timothy Lake   4280   RIVER
528   57   26   216
5270   2651
Clackamas   River   42   F10
Red Wolf Pass

WARM   SPRINGS

46   42   F9   Warm   Springs   Creek   River
4230   INDIAN
4680   Pinhead Buttes   Badger   Mill   Creek   HIGHWAY   26
46   F8   4230
RESERVATION   Creek
706   Boulder   Shitike   Creek
717   F7   720   Olallie Butte
719   4220   Breitenbush Lake
Breitenbush Hot Springs   310   River   Whitewater   River   METOLIUS   RIVER
46   870   4698   Pyramid Butte
2231   3375   3342   Jefferson Park   Jefferson   Creek   1292
DETROIT LAKE   2233   040   F6   68   66   1230   1270
Detroit   2243   3442   F5   Mount Jefferson   67   1260
Idanha   22   2248   3439   Pamelia Lake   68   98   69   1236
2253   3421   F4   3488   70   75   Three Fingered Jack   1230
2257   3443   Marion Lake   73   1210   1216   14
2265   3421   F3   MT. JEFFERSON WILDERNESS   72
3427   3491   Santiam Pass   74
3433   3391   810   2690   F2   500
HIGHWAY 20   2672   685   126   1030   242   1008   20
MT.   F1   Mount Washington   Sisters   HIGHWAY   126
WASH.   Belknap Crater ▲   1008   15
WILD.   2664   850   3579   McKenzie Pass   1018   151
2657   640   PCT   20
2653   EUGENE 74 MI.   BEND 7 MI.

SALEM 43 MI.   ALBANY 46 MI.
BREITENBUSH   NORTH   SANTIAM   RIVER   HIGHWAY 22   McKENZIE RIVER   HIGHWAY 126   830

Section F: Highway 242 at McKenzie Pass to Highway 35 near Barlow Pass

Introduction: The terrain crossed in Section F is an approximate mirror image of that crossed in Section E. Starting from Highway 242, you head north across recent lava flows that also made up the last part of Section E. You then pass three major peaks—Mt. Washington, Three Fingered Jack and Mt. Jefferson—just as you passed the Three Sisters. All six peaks are volcanoes in various stages of erosion. Mt. Jefferson, the northernmost, and South Sister, the southernmost, are the two youngest.

North of Mt. Jefferson you hike through the lake-studded Breitenbush Lake-Olallie Lake area, which is a smaller version of the southern Three Sisters Wilderness. Finally, you hike a lengthy stretch across slopes that are deficient in both views and lakes, just as you did in the first third of Section E. Both sections on the average, are fairly scenic, and it is difficult to say which is better. For many, however, Jefferson Park is the scenic high point of the Oregon PCT. But on this spectacular plain you'll find a backpacking crowd to match or exceed that on any other part of the tri-state Pacific Crest Trail.

Declination: 18½°E

Mileages:	South to North	Distances between Points	North to South
Highway 242 at McKenzie Pass	0.0		112.5
		7.3	
Washington Ponds spur trail	7.3		105.2
		2.4	
Coldwater Spring................................	9.7		102.8
		7.4	
Highway 20 at Santiam Pass	17.1		95.4
		10.2	
Minto Pass......................................	27.3		85.2
		3.7	
Rockpile Lake	31.0		81.5
		6.9	
Start of Pamelia Lake alternate route	37.9		74.6
		1.8	
Shale Lake......................................	39.7		72.8
		4.5	
End of Pamelia Lake alternate route..............	44.2		68.3
		6.1	
Trail north to Scout Lake........................	50.3		62.2
		6.6	
Skyline Road 42 near Breitenbush Lake...........	56.9		55.6
		6.5	
Skyline Road 42 near Olallie Lake Guard Station ...	63.4		49.1
		3.7	
Jude Lake.......................................	67.1		45.4
		6.0	
Lemiti Creek	73.1		39.4
		11.1	
Warm Springs River.............................	84.2		28.3
		8.5	
Miller Trail to Clackamas Lake Campground........	92.7		19.8
		6.8	
Little Crater Lake Trail	99.5		13.0
		8.0	
Highway 26 at Wapinitia Pass	107.5		5.0
		5.0	
Highway 35 near Barlow Pass	112.5		0.0

Supplies: Just 11.1 miles north into this section, at a junction 1.4 miles north of Coldwater Spring, you can descend a broad trail 0.7 mile to the grounds of the Seventh Day Adventists' Big Lake Youth Camp. This camp accepts PCT trekkers' packages. Mail them to: Big Lake Youth Camp, Highway 20, Box 13100, Sisters, OR 97759.

Not far beyond this section's halfway point, you reach the Olallie Lake Guard Station, which in the past has held packages. However, this situation could change in the future, so you might first check with the guard station to be sure they'll hold your parcels. Please send a stamped, self-addressed envelope. Just east of this guard station is Olallie Lake Resort, which has a somewhat limited supply of food.

At the end of this section you could hike several miles out of your way down to the settlement of Government Camp, which has a post office and a moderately well-stocked store.

Our section's PCT begins at a small trailhead parking area just west of ill-defined McKenzie Pass. This trailhead is very easy to find, for it is at a bend in Highway 242 from which the road to the east is very curving but that to the southwest is straight as an arrow.

From the trailhead at the south boundary of the Mt. Washington Wilderness, we make an ascent northwest up the Belknap Crater basalt flows and pass between two forested islands of older, glaciated basalt that stand in a sea of younger basalt. The desolate young basalt flows look as if they had cooled only a few years ago, yet those emanating from Little Belknap (6305) are 2900 years old. The flows seen today on Belknap Crater (6872) and its flanks are mostly 1500–3000 years old. All the flows between

North Sister and Mt. Washington compose a 65-square-mile field that represents the Cascade's greatest post-Pleistocene outpouring of lava. Belknap Crater is an excellent example of a shield volcano, and is quite similar to the shields that the Three Sisters and Mt. Thielsen grew upon.

Our route now takes us up to a junction with a spur trail (6120–2.3) that leads east-northeast up to the summit of Little Belknap. This area we're in looks quite lifeless, yet up here among the rocks you might spot a whistling marmot scurrying for its hole, or even more astounding, you might discover a western toad. Mountain chickadees sing out their name as we enter a strip of forest near Belknap Crater and descend through it to the eastern edge of a fresh-looking

F1   **F1**

Hiking up the Belknap lava field toward Mt. Washington

see MAP F2

F1

Coldwater
Spring

23

24

6323

19

20

6400

Mt Washington

6444

5600

26

25

30

29

MT. WASHINGTON

Washington
Ponds

6000

George
Lake

5200

6175

OREGON

35

5600

36

SKYLINE

31

32

R 7½ E

R 8 E

WILDERNESS

L A V A

5200

5600

5600

Belknap Crater

VABM
6872

TRAIL

Little Belknap
6305

D E S C H U T E S

5600

6000

5864

DESCHUTES CO.

LINN CO.

L A V A

×5560

Dee Wright
Observatory

McKenzie Pass

BM 5324

Snow Shelter

LANE CO.

HIGHWAY 242

BM
5260

Twin Craters

35

see MAP E13

flow (5320–2.5). We first head north, then west up along its edge, which borders the south slope of Mt. Washington. We then switchback northeast and in a couple of minutes switchback west-northwest. From this second you can climb due north rather steeply up fairly open slopes and across minor ridges over to George Lake. If you're on track, you'll reach a steep ridge immediately south of the lake. Some hikers try to avoid unnecessary elevation gain to this ridge by heading north-northeast, hoping to arrive at the east end of the lake. However, if they are just 200 yards east of the lake, they may not see it at all, and could waste lots of time and energy wandering aimlessly. You, however, have been forewarned, and will do better. Follow the ridge down to the lake's east shore, by which you'll find a campsite. Better ones lie above the north shore. Camping at George Lake is superior to that at lower Washington Pond, which in turn is

superior to that at rusty, horse-urine-tainted, seasonally dry Coldwater Spring. When you are ready to return to the PCT (George Lake is good for a layover day), head due south from the east shore, attain a low ridge, and then diagonal south-southwest across undulating slopes to the PCT.

From where the trail switchbacks west-northwest, we climb steadily to the Cascade divide, where our trail levels off. We then traverse northwest for about ¾ mile before curving north for a ⅓-mile stint to a gully in which the easily missed Washington Ponds spur trail starts northeast (5710–2.5). In 200 yards it curves over to shallow, 25-yard-wide lower Washington Pond, beside whose semiclear water desperate hikers have been known to camp.

Beyond this unmarked junction we climb slightly higher through a meadow that affords us an excellent view of the basalt plug that makes

F1   **F1**

see MAP F3

see MAP F1

Mt. Washington, from the southwest

up the steep-walled summit block of Mt. Washington (7794). An ascent of its 500-foot-high south aréte requires a complete set of technical rock-climbing equipment. This extremely glaciated peak probably once stood as high as North Sister at a time when that peak was still undergoing its growing pains.

Our route arcs west and descends moderately alongside the west spur, then descends northward around it to an overused meadow that contains an obvious well (18-inch-diameter pipe) known as Coldwater Spring (5200–2.4). Since this meadow is the only trailside PCT campsite in the Mt. Washington Wilderness that has "fresh" water, it has been overused, so much, in fact, that *it sometimes dries up.* Be prepared. On weekends, as many as two dozen mountaineers will make this their base camp and then climb up the north spur to the 300-foot-high north aréte of the summit block—the easiest summit route, but still requiring ropes and other equipment. The organic evidence lying profusely around the grassy meadow lets us know that horses use this site too. There may be some question about the water quality of the shallow well. It is, however, our last fresh water on route until Rockpile Lake, about 21.5 miles farther. Less desirable ponds and lakes exist near the trail, and snow patches linger through mid-August on the northwest slope of Three Fingered Jack.

Our route continues its northward descent through a hemlock forest occupied by clicking juncos and drilling red-shafted flickers. We pass by an unmarked climbers' trail (5050–0.5) that ascends east-southeast toward the peak's north spur, then we descend north to a fork with a broad trail (4760–0.9), which continues straight ahead. If you sorely need water, descend this old up your mailed parcels, descend 0.7 mile on this old stretch of the former Oregon Skyline Trail to the Big Lake Youth Camp, operated by the Oregon Conference of Seventh Day Adventists. For water, look for a faucet about 60 yards east, by their horse corral. From the grounds you can continue north ¾ mile to Old Santiam Road, then 250 yards east over to the PCT.

Onward, the PCT veers right (northeast) and traverses across slopes that are waterless once the snow patches disappear. We leave the Mt. Washington Wilderness just before we reach the old Santiam Wagon Road (4680–2.0). This waterless spot is very popular with car campers on summer weekends and during hunting season.

From the old Santiam Wagon Road the PCT heads northeast through a ghost forest of burned lodgepole snags and past abandoned logging roads on a route that gradually turns north and reaches a hundred-yard-long lily-pad pond (4790–2.0) just west of the trail. This unsightly

F3

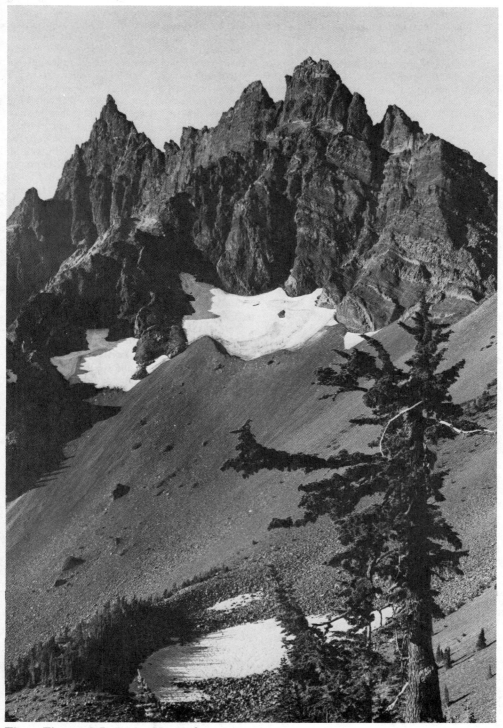

Three Fingered Jack, northeast face

stretch we have just passed through is easy to follow, despite the junctions. Southbound along it, the hiker at least has open, if not scenic, views of Mt. Washington. Just north of the pond, we climb over a low saddle and into a green forest once again. After traversing north over a gentle, open-forested stretch, we hear the drone of automobiles, then our trail turns northeast and heads for a crossing of the Santiam Highway (State 20) (4810–2.0) about 200 yards west of the national forest boundary at Santiam Pass. This pass was first crossed in 1859 by Andrew Wiley. He explored an old Indian trail up the Santiam River and worked his way farther east each year on his hunting expeditions from the Willamette Valley. If you are low on water, head east on Santiam Highway toward Douthit Spring, which can be a bit hard to find. About ¼ mile east of the PCT the highway begins to curve right, and you'll soon see a mile "81" highway sign. Just 30 yards east of it is a minor road, on your right, and just opposite that, on your left, is a small gully. Go up it 50 yards to usually seeping Douthit Spring. Be warned, however, that at times it dries up. You can camp nearby and then return to the PCT's crossing of Santiam Highway.

Just 240 yards west of our crossing is a PCT access road that curves 0.2 mile northeast to a parking area at a popular trailhead. We cross the highway and after 200 yards spy the parking area, immediately west. Our trail bears north, curves northwest and enters the Mt. Jefferson Wilderness, then climbs increasingly steep slopes and passes a few stagnant ponds just before a junction with the Santiam Lake Trail 3491 (5200–1.4), which curves northwest around a prominent boulder pile.

*   *   *   *

Because most of the PCT through Mt. Jefferson Wilderness is rather lakeless, one hiker has suggested we mention an alternative, the old Oregon Skyline Trail. Since Schaffer hadn't had the time to map this route, he is basing the following description on USFS topographic maps and mileages. Take Trail 3491 2.1 miles northwest to Lower Berley Lake, then 1.9 miles farther to more attractive Santiam Lake. Just 0.6 mile north of it you reach a junction, where Trail 3491 turns west. Start northeast on Trail 3494, hike north past South and North Dixie Lakes, and in 1.5 miles reach a junction with Trail 3422. Next, in 1.0 mile you

hike northeast past diminutive Alice Lake and average-sized Red Butte Lake to reach a junction by the south shore of fairly large Jorn Lake. Trail 3422 heads past the lake's west shore, but you head east on Trail 3492 about 0.7 mile to Bowerman Lake, then traverse 2.7 miles beyond it to a junction with Trail 3437, which climbs 2.7 miles southeast up to Minto Pass and the PCT. Next you descend 2.0 easy miles on Trail 3437 to a junction on a descending ridge that juts into Marion Lake. Leaving the wilderness' largest lake, you climb 1.6 miles up Trail 3493 to the John Swallow Grave. From this vicinity Trail 3488 climbs 3.7 miles up to the PCT. Keeping to 3493, you quickly pass aptly named Midget Lake, soon cross Whiskey Creek, find Lake of the Woods just beyond it, turn west at Puzzle Creek, and end your 2.7-mile stretch at a junction with Trail 3421 below the crest of Bingham Ridge (just off Map F5). Northeastward, you soon cross the ridge as your Trail 3493 traverses 2.6 miles, passing pint-sized Papoose Lake before reaching a junction with a trail that climbs 1.8 miles southeast to the PCT, on a saddle near the south end of the Cathedral Rocks. From this junction follow the alternate route description found on page 159. Basically, you drop 1.4 miles to the Hunts Cove spur trail, then 3.1 miles to the north shore of Pamelia Lake, from which you climb 0.7 mile north back to the PCT. The total length of this route is 24.6 miles, more or less, versus 25.5 miles for the comparable stretch of PCT.

*   *   *   *

From the Trail 3491 junction with the PCT just 1.4 trail miles north of Highway 20, we climb northeast up to a forested ridge, then follow it north-northwest toward Three Fingered Jack. The trail eventually leaves the ridge and curves northeast across a prominent cliff above Martin Lake, then heads up a small gully and quickly curves north-northwest (6000–2.5). If you are in desperate need of water, you can now head east cross-country, starting from an obvious flat atop the cliff, then follow markers 0.4 mile north down to sparkling Summit Lake (5800), a favorite among mountaineers.

Back on route, we follow the PCT as it switchbacks up to the ridge again, crosses it, and traverses the lower west slope of Three Fingered Jack (7841), which up close has a totally different appearance than when we saw it from a distance: he seems to have considerably more than three fingers. The easiest route to the

F2, F3, F4   **F4, F5, F3**

F4

see MAP F3

highest summit is a Class 3 ascent that starts on a faint trail up its southwest talus slope, then climbs its south ridge. Most of the routes up to the serrated crest require climbing equipment.

Our trail rounds the peak's northwest spur (6390–2.6), turns east toward a snow patch that lasts through mid-August, then curves northeast up to a saddle (6500–0.5) along the Cascade divide. From this vantage point we can observe the remaining structure of an ancient volcano that stands today as a crest called Three Fingered Jack. This peak is composed of remarkably uniform, thin, alternating beds of cinders and flows that dip west about 20°; their *regularity* over such a great thickness indicates a long period of minor eruptions. The reddish-brown, unsorted cinders consist of ash, lapilli,

F3

F3

see MAP F6

Milk Creek

5600

6800

Waldo Glacier

8000

6800

Pamelia Lake

5884

OREGON

SKYLINE

Hunts Creek TR

4400

799, Grizzly
out Peak

NATIONAL

FOREST

WARM SPRINGS

× 7086

R 8 E   6308

JEFFERSON

MT. JEFFERSON

6000

Goat Peak

7668

INDIAN

RESERVATION

4

WC

9   10

WC BOUNDY

5600

56010

Coyote Lake

Shale Lake

WILDERNESS

× 6221

Hole-in-the-Wall Park

Hunts Lake

Hunts Cove

Hanks Lake

5878

5200

5600

Cathedral Rocks

6444

The Table

6000

Table Lake

68

S   T

am Basin

5600

Papoose Lake

3493

× 5869

6000

JEFFERSON

66

5200

LAKE
Spr

Patsy Lake

SUMMIT   TRAIL

Forked Butte   6483

6000

North
Cinder Rk.   6722

LAVA

SUGAR

PINE

67

6000

3493

4800

Spring

5200

Whiskey Lake

Lake of the Woods

Whiskey

Creek

Creek

SWALLOW

6535

Junction Lake

68

5600

Carl Lake

ridge

John Swallow Grave

Midget Lake   3488

Sad Lake

3493

480

NATIONAL   FOREST   BOUNDARY

Shirley Lake

T   H   E   S

CABOT

Cabo

see MAP F4

blocks and bombs that contrast strongly with the brownish-gray andesite flows.

We now descend several switchbacks, soon recross the divide, and then descend northeast along forested slopes to a smattering of stagnant ponds just southwest of an intersection with the Minto Pass Trail 3437 (5350–3.2) at Minto Pass. This trail descends south one-quarter mile to large, green, ten-foot-deep Wasco Lake, whose shores see a lot campers in August once the mosquitoes have left.

The PCT quickly turns north, climbs to a saddle and reaches the Wasco Lake loop trail (#65) (5430–0.5), which descends southeast half a mile to an unnamed lake before curving west to Wasco Lake. We continue north up the divide, switchback as it steepens, and then traverse across to the southeast spur (6210–2.2) of Peak 6488, from where we can look south and see how Three Fingered Jack got its name. Continuing north, we contour to a saddle, then contour across the east slope of Rockpile Mountain (6559) and pass the Two Springs Trail 70, descending southeast, just before we reach a pond and beautiful Rockpile Lake (6250–1.0). This shallow but clear lake had an excellent campsite above its southeast shore and a very good one at its north end, but now camping is prohibited.

Our trail heads north on the rocky slope along the lake's west shore and then descends the divide to a saddle where a trail (6140–0.5) forks right, dropping generally east, soon as Trail 69, toward roads near Abbot Butte. Our route stays

F3, F4

west of the divide and climbs up to a level, open area just east of a breached cinder cone. Although there are no lakes or ponds near us, we nevertheless find that in midsummer this flat is crawling with one-inch toads. Continuing north, we pass a second cone, South Cinder Peak (6746), which is of post-Pleistocene age, as is the other one. We soon reach a saddle and an intersection with unmaintained Swallow Lake Trail 3488 (6300–1.0), which descends two miles southwest to Swallow Lake and two miles northeast to Carl Lake.

The PCT continues north along the west slope of the divide and reaches a saddle (6400–1.2) on a northwest ridge, from where a spur trail climbs west-northwest to a small knoll with a good view of Mt. Jefferson, six miles north of us. Our trail now crosses a snow patch that lingers through late July, then arcs eastward to the divide and descends it to a level section that contains an adequate campsite beside a small, fresh-water pond 50 yards east of the crest. Hiking a few minutes longer, we encounter an unsigned trail (6240–0.9) that descends southeast about a mile to large, emerald Carl Lake (5500), where camping is prohibited.

From the junction we hike once again up the ridge route, then contour across the forested west slopes of North Cinder Peak (6722) to a small, grassy meadow (6240–1.7) that has obviously been camped at, and for a good reason. A hidden, rock-lined pond lies on the other side of a low pile of rocks that borders the meadow. This is a good water hole to stop at if you are passing through late in the summer.

F4, F5

Mt. Jefferson, from escarpment north of North Cinder Peak

| see MAP F5

After a brief ascent north, we arrive at an escarpment (6340–0.4) where Mt. Jefferson (10,497) towers above us in all its presidential glory. On March 30, 1806, Lewis and Clark saw this snowy peak from the lower Willamette River, and they named it after their president. At the base of its south slope below us lies a bizarre glacio-volcanic landscape. During the last ma-

jor glacial advance, glaciers cut a deep canyon on each side of the resistant Sugar Pine Ridge, seen in the east. After these disappeared, volcanic eruptions burst forth and constructed Forked Butte (6483), east of North Cinder Peak. This butte was subsequently breached by outpourings of fluid basaltic andesite that flowed east down the glaciated Jefferson Creek and

F5

F5

Cabot Creek canyons. A smaller cone with a crater lake, north of us, also erupted about this time, but it was aborted by nature before any flows poured forth. To its north stands the flat Table, and between it and the ridge of Cathedral Rocks is a large, deep, enigmatic depression that may represent a collapsed flow.

Time, which allowed nature to sculpt this surrealistic art work, now forces us to press onward. We descend northwest, still marveling at the configurations below, then leave the ridge and switchback down to a junction where a faint, unsigned trail (6130–0.7) climbs 100 yards back to the divide before descending into the marvelous basin. After more switchbacking down, we reach a saddle (5910–0.5), from where three variations of the Pacific Crest Trail continue northward.

*   *   *   *

The *oldest route* starts north steeply down the glaciated valley and curves west to shimmering, pure Hanks Lake (5144–1.2). Along its north shore, the Hunts Cove spur trail climbs north up to another gem, Hunts Lake (5236–0.4). It also descends west to a junction with a newer PCT route (5020–0.5–1.7).

*   *   *   *

The *newer route,* which was the standard one through 1972, starts on a contour northwest from the saddle, crosses over a low ridge, then makes a descent to the Trail 3493 junction (5640–1.8), near a saddle, before it switchbacks down to the Hunts Cove spur trail (5020–1.4). The older route joins the newer one here, continues a descent into the glaciated valley and finally arrives at the southeast shore of shallow Pamelia Lake (3884). Paralleling the shore, the route curves west to a junction with the Pamelia Lake Trail 3439 (3970–3.1), which takes us down to many campsites near the lake's deeper end. Early in the season, the lake is high and attractive, but by August, Pamelia is reduced to a putrid puddle dotted with hikers who climb the easy 2.4-mile trail to this lake. Leaving this potential eyesore behind, you can ascend north, then northeast up toward Milk Creek and reach a junction (4320–0.7–7.0) with the newest PCT route.

*   *   *   *

The *newest* PCT *route,* completed in the early '70s, starts on a gentle descent north-northeast from the saddle and heads along the lower slopes of the inspiring Cathedral Rocks, which, judging

Russell Creek

by their color, must have been constructed in the Dark Ages. Our route curves northwest to the crest of a lateral moraine well above sparkling Hunts Lake, then leaves this escarpment and winds north to the west shore of placid Shale Lake (5910–1.8), which is a logical spot to stop for the night. However, camping is now forbidden at this lake and at other nearby lakes, so you might try camping on relatively flat ground east and northeast of Shale Lake. The shale implied by the lake's name is actually basaltic andesite that has become highly fractured along many parallel planes.

Just north of this popular lake, we reach a shallow, seasonally larger lake that in late summer dwindles to a mudhole. Beyond it, our trail drops west to the glaciated escarpment, then oh-so-gently descends it before entering a Douglas-fir forest and reaching a junction with the Oregon Skyline Trail (Old PCT) (4320– 4.5), just south of Milk Creek. Those taking one of the alternate routes join us here. We start up the gravelly, bouldery outwash deposits of Milk Creek canyon and pass a lavish display of

F7

wildflowers and shrubs before hiking north past a two-person campsite to a crossing of aptly named Milk Creek (4320–0.2). Its silty color is caused by fine volcanic sediments that may in part be glacially ground to create "rock flour." We shall see many more creeks like it as we encounter glacier-clad volcanoes along our journey north.

Beyond this minor torrent we now make tracks northwest across many small, deceptive ridges before we reach the real Woodpecker Ridge and a junction with lightly used Woodpecker Trail 3442 (5040–1.6), which descends west. We head east gently down from the ridge and soon pass a stagnant pond with a fair, but illegal, campsite at its west end. The open forest here is quite choked with an understory of spiraea, corn lily, gooseberry, rhododendron and the ubiquitous huckleberry. You'll easily identify Whitewater Lake, way below you, by its milky color, due to a high influx of fine sediments.

Not much farther along, we pass a small spring, enter a shady forest, and then cross a creeklet whose gully is a channel for periodic avalanches. Two minutes past it we cross Jeff Creek, cross a nearby two-person campsite, and see more evidence of avalanches. After ½ mile of gentle ascending north, our trail ascends east, sometimes moderately, then quickly drops to a ford of milky Russell Creek (5520–2.8). Plan to cross this creek *before 11 a.m.* The afternoon's warmer temperatures greatly increase the snowmelt from the Russell and Jefferson Park glaciers, and that increased flow has swept some hikers on a one-way trip down the gorge immediately below the ford. This diurnal fluctuation is a second characteristic of glacier-fed creeks that we will encounter on our future traverses around major Cascade peaks.

Our trail now curves around a minor, westward-descending ridge with a poor campsite, soon makes a loop around a small, boggy area, then briefly descends to cross the headwaters of a Whitewater Creek tributary. From its north bank we make a minute's walk west to a junction with heavily traveled Jefferson Park Trail 3429 (5640–0.6). Starting from the end of Whitewater Road 1044, this trail—the shortest one into popular Jefferson Park—climbs 3.9 miles to the main branch of Whitewater Creek, then climbs an additional 0.4 mile to our junction.

From this point our PCT/Jefferson Park Trail makes an easy climb east-northeast to ford that branch (5680–0.4). This crossing can be a wet one, but unlike the ford at Russell Creek, it is always a safe one. We continue our easy ascent in the same general direction, then curve north for a momentary climb to the south rim of beautiful but over-populated Jefferson Park.

Our trail quickly curves northeast (5860–0.5), and at that point a short spur trail descends to the nearby shore of cool, deep, green Scout Lake (5830). Camps rim the lake's shoreline, but like other lakeside camps in Jefferson Park and in *every* wilderness, these are illegal. However, there is no other acceptable camping alternative. You would think that after years of this area's overuse, the Forest Service would build ecologically sound campsites. Funds and/or motivation for such a program have yet to appear.

If you enjoy crowds, camp at Scout Lake. Otherwise, try nearby Bays Lake, more-distant Park Lake, or some dry, nonmeadow spot in between. Beneath hemlocks on the north shore of Scout Lake, you get beautifully framed views across the reflective lake of stately Mt. Jefferson (10,497) with its ermine robe of glaciers. At this lake and the adjacent lakes of Jefferson Park, you might make a strange catch while fishing for trout: Pacific giant salamanders that inhabit these lakes' shady waters.

The PCT turns right (northeast) at the first spur-trail junction, follows blazes past radiating, narrow spur trails, then curves north past a seasonal pond and reaches a spur trail (5930–0.3) that heads west to Scout and Bays lakes. We now hike north-northeast across the open flat of Jefferson Park and obtain impressive views back at the peak all the way to a junction with South Breitenbush Trail 3375 (5870–0.5), which starts west-southwest before descending northwest. Just 30 yards farther, a prominent spur trail branches northeast 250 yards to shallow Russell Lake (5856). Camping is prohibited at this lake, but you might consider camping in this vicinity at a fair distance from the lake. By late season, this lake may be fairly depleted and others in the basin may be completely dry. The PCT turns abruptly northwest at this junction, then quickly descends northeast to a step-across ford of South Fork Breitenbush River (5840–0.1). As you begin your ascent northeast, you can spot an excellent campsite 40 yards southeast just above the other side of the "river." The trail now climbs steeply up a slope and into a glacial cirque, where we again step across the river. Here, a steep shortcut northeast

see MAP F9

West
Pinhead Butte
VABM △ 5577

South
Pinhead Butte

F8

Chinquapin Viewpoint

4354

4220

4276

4800

4230

4387

4480

4230

120

4800

4800

M
O
U
N
T

Car
Pra

SAYLINE

BM
4295

Gravel
Pit

4391

Creek

BM
4220
4264

Lemiti
Campground

BM
4207

Lemiti Butte
4530

140

BM
4230

Slow

4522 ×

Lemiti
Mdw

Lemiti Trooper Springs

4883

South

4400

Creek

Creek

4800

4690

4134

CLACKAMAS CO.
MARION CO.

5073

× 4528

BM
4278 ×

4800

MARION CO.
WASCO CO.

S   T

4220

4800

4800

4920

BM
4439

BLUE

4800

Olallie

River

4400

Creek

ROAD

BM
4989

BM
4508

Olallie
Meadow

5200

LAKE

5200

Olallie Meadow Campground

△

Brook
Lake

716

Jade Lake

5200

× 4172

Russ
Lake

706

4220

Triangle
Lake

MARION CO.
WASCO CO.

× 5395

BM

5200

4400

Campground

see MAP F7

may look more like the trail than the trail itself does. It developed, as so many shortcuts do, when early-season hikers chose to descend straight down the slope rather than follow the buried trail across snow patches. The real trail parallels the trickling river a short way north, then curves and climbs moderately southeast to a spur on the Cascade divide. This is climbed in an arc up to Park Ridge, which is then traversed 70 yards west to a viewpoint (6920–2.0), where you obtain your last look down at justifiably popular Jefferson Park. A short trail climbs 200 yards west up to Peak 7018 for an even better view. In the distance, just east of north, towers magnificent Mt. Hood (11,235), and just to the west of north stands southern Washington's decapitated Mt. St. Helens (8364).

We now descend the trail—or rather, the semipermanent snowfield—toward small, shallow lakes and ponds. As the gradient eases, the trail becomes very obvious as it selects a pond-dotted route north out of the alpine realm and into the hemlock forest. Our path momentarily takes us over a low saddle (6150–2.1), then meanders northeast, giving us some views of locally dominating Pyramid Butte (6095) as we cross many minor gullies and ridges. Views disappear and soon we start through a small flat with a low hill on our left. Here we leave the Mt. Jefferson Wilderness and immediately meet a conspicuous trail—the old Oregon Skyline route—branching right. In 1985 this misleading

trail was conspicuously signed THIS IS NOT THE PACIFIC CREST TRAIL. We hope the sign stands for years.

Our trail rambles onward for ⅓ mile, passing a small, volcanic butte of shalelike rocks before it meets Breitenbush Lake's outlet creek. Beside it is a spur road, which goes east to a large, nearby trailhead parking area, constructed in 1989. Immediately east of it is the Warm Springs Indian Reservation boundary, and squeezed between that boundary and the southwest shore of Breitenbush Lake is the Breitenbush Lake Campground, which is administered by the Forest Service. On the PCT we walk a few paces past the spur road to decrepit Road 4220 (5500-1.6), crossing it just 30 yards northeast of the start of the spur road. Unless Road 4220 is improved, very few people will want to drive up it to the trailhead parking area. East of the PCT, Road 4220 becomes even worse, suited only for 4WDs and motorcycles.

Keeping within Mt. Hood National Forest, we climb a winding trail up to the east shore (5750–0.5) of a shallow lake, curve around to its north shore, and then pass near a smaller, triangular lake. Our trail then traverses the bouldery southwest slope of summit 5975 before winding down to a junction with the old OST route (5510–1.0), now Gibson Trail 708. Starting northwest, we momentarily reach Horseshoe Saddle Trail 712 (5520–0.1), logically, atop a saddle above Horseshoe Lake. You can follow

F6, F7   F7

Mt. Jefferson, from Olallie Lake Resort

Olallie Butte, from Russ Lake

this trail ¾ mile down to its trailhead by Road 4220's Horseshoe Lake Campground.

A short distance northwest along our ridge route, we encounter the Ruddy Hill Trail 714 (5600–0.3), which climbs west. We now contour northward through a thick forest, then climb up to a low knoll before descending slightly to Many Lakes Viewpoint (5660–1.2), which lives up to its description. Mile-long Olallie Lake is the focal point of the basin, and andesitic Olallie Butte (7215) rules above it. ("Olallie" is what the native Indians called the huckleberries.) This volcano has been active in both glacial and postglacial times.

After hiking counterclockwise down the knoll's northern slopes, we reach a dry flat, from which the southbound traveler sees the lofty

F7

see MAP F10

see MAP F8

F10

see MAP F9

crown of Mt. Jefferson beckoning him onward. Here our trail crosses a seasonal creek, then descends north steeply alongside it, and veers northwest to a very good campsite at reposeful Upper Lake (5380–0.9). Continuing north, we pass several seasonal ponds and shallow, linear Cigar Lake (5350–0.4), from where a 0.6-mile

trail first winds northeast down to Top Lake (5170), with a good west-shore campsite, then climbs back to a mile-high crest junction with the PCT. Leaving Cigar Lake, the PCT takes an easier, more direct route to that crest junction (5280–0.4), from which Red Lake Trail 719 goes 1¼ miles northwest to Fork Lake.

F7   **F7**

Cooper

Creek

3600

4000

2

1

4400

11

12

14

13

3600

5890

528

Meditation Point
Campground

23

24

Timothy Lake

Mile
15.8

57

SPILLWAY 3217

528

Gone Creek
Campground

Hood View
Campground

26

25

26

35

36

3600

R 8 E

R 8½ E

BM 3421

BM 3468

Crater Cr.

5890

2

58

2660

ABBOT

58

+

ABBOT

58

Little   Crater
Meadow

11

500

Little Crater Lake

Forest Camp

Little Crater
Meadow   12

ROAD

58

3600

14

14

13

18

1887

3600

23

23

23

24

19

4280

BM

BM
3522

Clackamas
Grove

Oak Grove

26 R.

26

25

42

S42

3600

57

Clackamas Lake
Forest Camp

Guard Station

42

BM
3345

534

4270

*Clackamas
Lake*

35

BM
3444

S549

36

Big   31

BOUNDARY

Oak Grove   Fork

BM
3523

4270

BM 3444

Clear L
Bu

VABM 4458

Look

4000

3600

6

7

LINE

(MC QUINN)

30

BM

35

S549

Stone

The PCT contours north along the divide, curves northeast and crosses it, then follows it east down past a small triangular, semiclear lake (5180–0.9) and arrives at the shore of deep, clear Head Lake (4950–0.7). Here a short spur trail curves eastward 60 yards to the Olallie Lake Forest Service Guard Station beside Skyline Road. For northbound hikers this spur trail is the quickest way to Olallie Lake Resort. A pleasant picnic area separates the resort from the guard station.

From the spur trail, the PCT climbs above the southeast shore of Head Lake, and on it we pass a very good trailside campsite only 50 yards before we reach Skyline Road 4220 (4990–0.1) at a point 20 yards north of its signed 4991-foot divide. *Southbound* hikers can follow the road 100 yards south to a "Y" junction, from where they can follow a spur road 200 yards east to Olallie Lake Resort. It has a limited food selection, as did the store at Odell Lake's Shelter Cove Resort, about 143 miles back. Northward, you can look forward to good, but expensive, meals at Timberline Lodge, 54 miles distant.

From the Skyline Road crossing, the PCT starts northeast, then makes a long, gentle descent north along the lower slopes of Olallie Butte (7215) to an intersection with Olallie Butte Trail 720 (4680–2.2), which descends 220 yards west alongside the southern powerline to Skyline Road. We cross under the three sets of powerlines and parallel the unseen road, going north-northeast until we observe a flat, bushy, open depression on the right (east). Then our trail veers northeast, but a blocked trail continues north. This trail (4570–1.0) is a 230-yard link between the PCT and the old OST (now Lodgepole Trail 706). Our trail now enters Warm Springs Indian Reservation land, and will remain on it almost to Clackamas Lake. (There is ongoing logging on the reservation, and the PCT crosses logging roads in various states of use. Not all are shown on the maps or are mentioned in the text.) We continue northeast on a low ridge, angle north and intersect Russ Lake Trail 716 (4550-0.3), ascending southeast from Olallie Meadow Campground. This trail continues 0.3 mile southeast past an adequate campsite at Jude Lake to a better one at deeper Russ Lake (4600).

We start north, then ramble northeast to shallow Jude Lake (4600–0.2), which has a good campsite on its northwest shore. Get a good drink of water, for the spring 0.4 mile ahead sometimes dries up by mid-August. You then have a long, dry (though shady) walk

around the lower ends of two ridges before you descend to trickling Lemiti Creek (4360–6.0) at the lower end of Lemiti Meadow.

The trail arcs clockwise through the forest around the meadow's northeast fringe to a signed spur trail (4400–0.5) that gently descends 70 yards southwest past a spacious campsite to a five-yard-wide fresh-water hole known as Trooper Springs. On a weekend, you may have to compete with the Scouts as well as with the frogs—your next water will be at a spring 8.3 miles farther.

Our trail continues southeast for 0.1 mile, then turns north and climbs over the low Cascade divide. It more or less follows the divide north through a viewless forest, until South Pinhead Butte (5337), where we reach the trailside Chinquapin Viewpoint (5000–2.8), rather disappointing, but at least it permits us to see over the forest. Better views are just ahead. We contour the butte's slopes northward, cross a saddle (4980–0.8) with an abandoned spur road going west, then reach the southeast slope of North Pinhead Butte (5447), which is the youngest of the three andesite buttes. Looking south, we see Mt. Jefferson once again and are reminded of the beauties of Jefferson Park.

We now descend north to a lava flow, where a signed spur trail (4640–1.4) heads north-northeast 60 yards across it to an open view north of Mt. Hood (11,235) and east of the Warm Springs River basin. We then make a switchback, descend back into the depths of the forest and generally follow a gentle ridge route down to a junction with a spur trail (3860–3.3) that descends moderately west-southwest 70 yards to a seeping spring. You may have to treat the water before drinking it. The slopes steepen, and so does our route, which switchbacks down to a dry creek, contours northward, then turns west and makes a crossing of Warm Springs River (3330–2.3), with a campsite nearby. You've also just crossed the 45°N Latitude line and are midway between the Equator and the North Pole. If you hike the entire Pacific Crest Trail, about 2600 miles long when it is completed, you'll cover only 16½° of latitude, going from about 32½° at the Mexican border to about 49° in Manning Park.

We now climb north above a tributary gully and reach a flat, where we meet another signed spur trail (3450–0.4), which heads 70 yards east-southeast to a spring. Camp can be made almost anywhere in this open-forest area. Beyond it we cross a northwest-trending linear meadow that is being invaded by lodgepoles,

F7, F8   **F8, F9, F10**

Little Crater Lake

then we climb gradually increasing slopes up to a junction with Road 4245 (3720–1.0). Traveling southwest along this road, you would reach Skyline Road in 3.4 miles. We walk 17 yards northeast up Road 4245 to a resumption of the trail and follow it north up to the east slope (4230-1.7) of andesitic Summit Butte (4790). During the mid '80s the PCT was slightly relocated to skirt below an obvious logging operation on the east slopes. Past it we make a gentle descent north, pass under a six-cable powerline, cross northwest past unseen Red Wolf Pass (4120-1.4), and then reach a jeep road (3990-0.8) that diagonals northeast across our route.

Our trail continues its northward descent and parallels a seasonal creek on our right (east), shortly before intersecting closed Road S549 (3580–1.3), which, like our trail, heads toward the Clackamas Lake area. We cross this road and roughly parallel it northwest, leaving the Warm Springs Indian Reservation before we reach a junction with Miller Trail 534 (3400–1.9). The Miller Trail makes a moderate descent northwest before contouring west to fairly large, well-maintained Clackamas Lake Campground, 0.3 mile distant. Why it is so popular is a mystery, for nearby Clackamas Lake appears to be little more than a polluted cattle pond, and campground vistas are virtually nonexistent. Could it be the campground's two old-fashioned, muscle-powered water pumps? Judge for yourself. Actually, the lake's water is better than one would first guess, for it is spring-fed. The PCT turns north and proceeds through the forest bordering the meadow's edge to a usually dry crossing of Oak Grove Fork Clackamas River (3350–0.7) shortly before a junction with now

paved Skyline Road 42 (3370–0.2). The PCT crosses this road just 90 yards northeast of the entrance to Joe Graham Horse Camp, which in turn is 200 yards northeast of a junction with Road 57. We start west on the trail and soon see Oak Grove Fork Clackamas River below us on our left (southwest). We momentarily descend to this creek, then climb a little and pass a spring

F10, F11

F11

F13

MADRAS 51 MI.

⅓ mile before reaching Timothy Trail 528 (3320–1.4), which makes an eight-mile traverse around Timothy Lake (3217), passing campgrounds, picnic areas and creeks before rejoining the PCT near the lake's northeast end.

You can see the lake from this junction, from which the PCT winds gradually down to its unappealing east shore. The shoreline improves as you head north, where you are perhaps tempted to swim across the lake's narrow arm or make an adequate campsite beside it. Farther north, the arm enlarges to a shallow bay that in late summer becomes a swamp, and the trail contours northeast around it, passing several trailside springs, some of them seasonal, a few minutes before you reach a bridge over wide,

F11

F11

see MAP F13

clear Crater Creek (3220–4.3). Just north of this crossing, Timothy Trail 528 rejoins our route from the west.

About 250 yards beyond this junction, we reach another, where Little Crater Lake Trail 500 (3230–0.2) strikes east 220 yards to 45-foot deep, extremely clear Little Crater Lake, which is an oversized artesian spring. Its purity is maintained by a fence that keeps out the cattle. You can camp either back near the trail junction or at pleasant Little Crater Camp-ground, which is just 200 yards east of the lake. Little Crater looks like the ideal swimming hole, but stick your arm down into it—brrrr!—as with most springs, its water stays an almost constant year-round 40°F. We re-enter forest and get back on the PCT.

Our path north to Mt. Hood is now deficient in views, lakes, creeks and hikers, but it is great if

F11

you like the solitude of a shady forest, such as this one, that has Douglas-fir, western and mountain hemlocks, western red and Alaska cedars, silver, noble, grand and subalpine firs, and western white and lodgepole pines. Our trail starts northwest, then gradually curves north up to Road 5890 (3360–1.6), which gently de-scends northeast to a crossing of Crater Creek. We bear north for 30 yards on a diagonal across the road, then continue north up to Abbot Road 58 (3860–1.4), which would lead you back to Little Crater Campground and Skyline Road. Traversing through a forest of mountain hem-lock and lodgepole, we next reach Linney Creek Road 240 (3880–0.8). Not far beyond it, we pass through a small campsite (3910–0.2), which has a seeping spring. This could be your last on-trail water until the upper Salmon River, 13.7 miles farther. However, water can be ob-

F11, F12

tained ½ mile off the PCT at the Frog Lake Campground, about 4¾ miles away.

The PCT now climbs north to a saddle (4010–0.5), then makes a long northeast traverse through a beautiful forest with rhododenrons to a junction with Blue Box Trail 483, which strikes south to Clear Lake (3500). In 50 yards you reach U.S. Highway 26 (3910–3.5) at Wapinitia Pass. We used to recommend that hikers should follow this highway 7.7 miles to the post office and village store at Government Camp. While you can still take Highway 26 over to that settlement, you'll find the route noisy—in 1978 it was widened to four lanes to meet the demands of ever-increasing traffic. We now recommend another route that starts from Barlow Pass and is described at the end of this chapter.

Walking 70 yards closer to that pass, we reach a spur trail that goes 40 yards to the Wapinitia Pass PCT trailhead parking lot, beside the busy highway. From the parking lot, Road 2610 curves southeast and after ⅓ mile gives rise to Frog Lake Road 230, branching southwest. Starting on it, you'll come to the entrance to the new Frog Lake Campground, built in 1978. You might plan to camp here, or at least get water at it.

Only 120 yards past the parking-lot trail, the PCT meets southbound Frog Lake Trail 530, which quickly crosses Road 2610, then soon crosses Road 230 and parallels it to the northwest lobe of Frog Lake. Leaving Trail 530, the PCT continues northeast through a solemn forest of western hemlock, curves southeast upward, then makes a switchback north to a near-crest junction (4360–1.2). From here the Twin Lakes trail immediately crosses a crest saddle, visits the two glistening orbs, and then, after a total length of 2¾ miles, rejoins the PCT. This lake loop used to be a part of the PCT, but the easily accessible Twin Lakes became overused and the PCT was rerouted in the mid-70s. Still, many PCT hikers prefer this longer route, if not for its aesthetics, then at least for its water. No reliable water is found until off-route sources near Barlow Pass.

Beyond the near-crest junction, the PCT makes a shady, viewless traverse north to a broad saddle (4450–1.1), then continues northwest to a reunion with the loop trail (4500–0.5). From this junction our route heads north, passes by southeast descending Palmateer View Trail 482 (4550–0.5), then soon hugs the crest for a 1.2-mile descent to an *old* section of Highway 35 at Barlow Pass (4157–1.5). You'll find a

PCT trailhead parking area immediately west of here. Then, as you start to parallel the old highway northeast, you immediately cross Road 3530, descending south. Past it, the PCT soon becomes an abandoned road, which takes the hiker on a minute's walk to this section's end, a crossing of a new section of Highway 35 (4155–0.2). You should be able to find water in a gully about 130 yards east of this crossing. If not, and you're desperate, then start down the following alternate route, which begins 0.2 mile back.

*   *   *   *

Most hikers will continue along Section G's PCT to Timberline Lodge, which serves good, but expensive food, and which also holds parcels mailed to it—for a fee (see Section G: **Supplies**). Long-distance PCT hikers on a shoestring budget may want to have their parcels mailed to Government Camp Post Office, rather than to Timberline Lodge.

You can reach Government Camp by descending west along the old section of Highway 35, now Road 3531. Starting at Barlow Pass, this takes you down past an obvious roadside spring (4074–0.6) to a scenic hairpin turn, then down to a pioneer woman's grave, on your left, about 100 yards before crossing the East Fork Salmon River. Just ⅓ mile west of the crossing, Road 3531 ends at the new section of Highway 35 (3665–1.9).

Continuing west, you soon pass through the large, high-speed interchange of Highways 26 and 35, then follow traffic over to the start of the Timberline Lodge road (3980–2.7), opposite the Summit Ranger Station. Just ¼ mile past it, you fork right and take the Government Camp road through town, reaching Government Camp Post Office (3840–0.8–6.0) just 250 yards past the moderately well-stocked village store.

Now backtrack to the Timberline Lodge road (3980–0.8) and follow it up past the entrance to Alpine Campground (5450–4.5), then up to road's end at giant Timberline Lodge (5940–2.2–13.5). At the north end of the large hikers' parking lot, below the lodge, register at a small hut. You'll find the Pacific Crest Trail making an obvious slice across the slopes just above the lodge. Although you've bypassed part of the PCT by taking this alternate route, you can see from a distance the best part of what you've missed by following the PCT a long half mile eastward to the White River Buried Forest Overlook, described in Section G.

F12, F13, F14   F14, G1

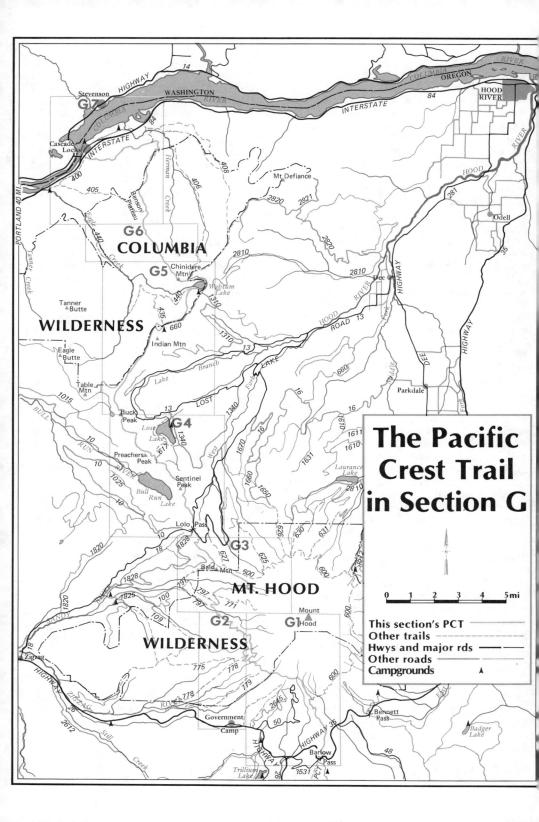

The Pacific
Crest Trail
in Section G

0 1 2 3 4   5mi

This section's PCT ——————
Other trails ----------
Hwys and major rds ■■■■■■
Other roads
Campgrounds   ▲

Section G: Highway 35 near Barlow Pass to Interstate 84 at Bridge of the Gods

Introduction: In this short section, the hiker traverses around Oregon's highest and most popular peak, glacier-robed Mt. Hood. If you start your hike at Timberline Lodge, you can traverse around the peak in one long, though relatively easy, 18.7-mile day. However, hiking in the opposite direction requires considerable effort, for in that direction you have a *net* (not total) gain of 2520 feet instead of a net loss.

From Bald Mountain north past Lolo Pass to Wahtum Lake, the scenery is subdued—a typical, forested Oregon Cascade crest. North of Wahtum Lake, the Pacific Crest Trail has the potential to be highly scenic if the route were only slightly relocated. As it now exists, it has a noticeable lack of views, particularly as you're descending into the spectacular Columbia River gorge. We therefore recommend the unusually beautiful, dramatic Eagle Creek Trail as an alternate route, for it abounds in waterfalls within a steep-walled canyon.

Declination: 18¾°E

Mileages:

	South to North	Distance between Points	North to South
Highway 35 near Barlow Pass	0.0		54.4
Join the Timberline Trail	3.6	3.6	50.8
Timberline Lodge	5.0	1.4	49.4
Paradise Park Shelter...........................	9.6	4.6	44.8
Ramona Falls	15.6	6.0	38.8
Leave the Timberline Trail	20.9	5.3	33.5
Lolo Pass......................................	23.7	2.8	30.7
Huckleberry Mountain Trail	28.0	4.3	26.4
Indian Springs Campground	36.2	8.2	18.2
Wahtum Lake at Eagle Creek Trail junction.........	38.8	2.6	15.6
Camp Smokey saddle...........................	43.6	4.8	10.8
Teakettle Spring...............................	47.3	3.7	7.1
Lateral trail to Herman Creek....................	50.3	3.0	4.1
Bridge of the Gods, east end....................	54.4	4.1	0.0

Supplies: This section is short enough so that most hikers don't worry about supplies. However, the long-distance hiker will certainly want to pick up packages he mailed to Timberline Lodge, which lies only 5 miles into this section's route. Packages are held at the lodge's Wy'East Store, and the rate charged for this service is $1.50 per week and $4 per month *per package*. Therefore, try to send only one package and not too early (address: Timberline Lodge, Wy'East Store, Timberline, OR 97028). You could avoid this charge by picking up your package at Government Camp, a few miles off the route. An alternate route at the end of Section F tells you how to reach this small settlement. Timberline Lodge, like other premier mountain lodges, is expensive. Those who can afford it can get rooms, meals and showers, plus use of a hot pool and a sauna.

Half way through your trek you can take the Huckleberry Mountain Trail down to a small store at the north end of Lost Lake. However, few hikers do so.

Finally, at trail's end in Cascade Locks, you can find almost anything you need. If you can't, take the bus west into Portland or east to much closer Hood River.

Section G begins where the PCT diagonals across the east end of a relatively new stretch of Highway 35. This crossing is 40 yards northeast of the new Barlow Pass elevation sign (4161), which in turn is 40 yards northeast of the old stretch of Highway—*now* Road 3531. (The *real* Barlow Pass is ¼ mile southwest of the PCT crossing.) Road 3531 goes ¼ mile southwest to a PCT trailhead parking area—the start of Section F's alternate route that goes to Government Camp. If you must stock up on water, get it at an obvious roadside spring ½ mile southwest past the parking area or in a gully about 130 yards east of where the PCT crosses Highway 35.

From Highway 35 (4155), the PCT starts northeast, but immediately angles west for a climb to the Cascade divide. Ascending north, it stays close to the crest of the divide, then quickly curves northwest over to a gully (4870–2.7) with a campsite and with *usually* flowing water. From this cool forest retreat, our trail methodically climbs over to the slopes of the Salmon River canyon, where we can look west toward Alpine Campground and see a cliff below it of loose hornblende andesite debris. Our trail then climbs northeast up to a junction with Timberline Trail 600 (5340–0.9), which starts a descent east to the White River. This trail, which stays near timberline as it circles Mt. Hood (11,235), offers an alternative 22.7-mile route if you take it counterclockwise to a reunion with the PCT near Bald Mountain. Clockwise, it coincides with the PCT, which starts northwest up a ridge of loose, gravelly debris, and soon ramifies into a number of sandy paths that parallel one another up the ridge.

If you look east at the cliff composed of unsorted volcanic debris that is above the White River, you'll get an idea of the type of sediments you're walking on. These deposits, which are on the south and southwest slopes of Hood, are remnants of a huge debris fan of hornblende

andesite that was formed 1700–2000 years ago when a crater was blasted out near the mountain's summit and a plug dome of viscous lava welled up, melting the surrounding ice field. The sudden release of frozen water created devastating mudflows that carried the volcanic debris down to these slopes that the PCT crosses today. Due north of us, we can identify Crater Rock (10,560), which is a remnant of that plug dome. Just north of it, numerous fissures still emit steam and hydrogen-sulfide gas. On clear, windless days the gas emissions from these fumaroles are visible from as far away as Portland. Mt. Hood had minor eruptions during the last century, and we can be sure that it is still alive today.

Our paths eventually merge, and we reach the White River Buried Forest Overlook (5790–0.8), which in 1978 was signed with an incorrect elevation, as many such signs are. If you scrutinize the *lower* mudflow sediments in the canyon's wall opposite you, you should be able to recognize a few buried snags. It was these snags that provided radiocarbon dates for eruptions mentioned in the previous paragraph.

Leaving the overlook, we soon curve northwest away from the canyon views, cross a dry creek bed, then cross the upper Salmon River (5900–0.3), which derives its flow from an arm of the Palmer Glacier. This flow is your first reliable on-route water since a seeping spring just past Linney Creek Road, 13.7 trail miles south. The trail now contours southwest past an ascending dirt road, then quickly reaches a spur trail (5960–0.2)—one of many—that descends to the east side of gigantic Timberline Lodge (5940–0.1). No hiker should pass up the opportunity to inspect this grand structure built by the Works Progress Administration in the late 1930s.

Just east of and below the lodge's parking lot is an even larger lot for backpackers and mountaineers; and at its north end is a small hut

G1   G1

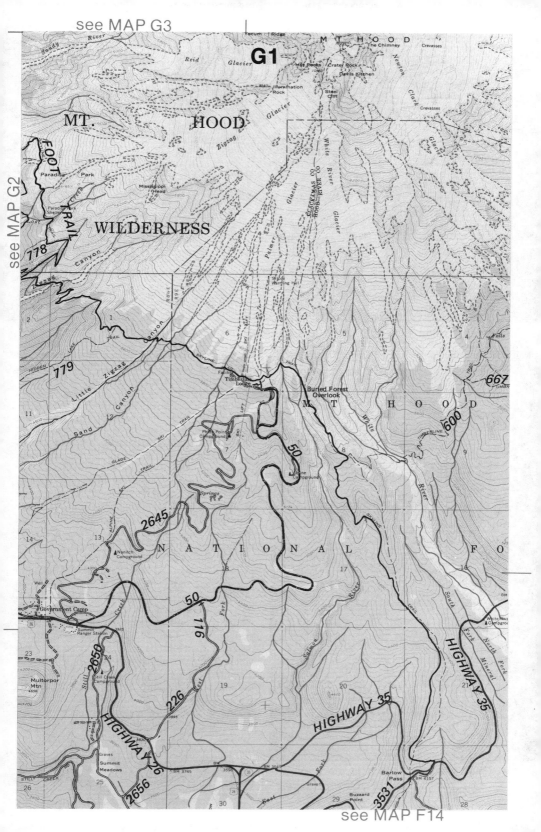

see MAP G3

G1

see MAP G2

see MAP F14

Southbound hiker near the White River Buried Forest Overlook

Mt. Hood's White River Glacier

in which you should register if you plan to hike any farther or if you plan to climb Mt. Hood. Mountaineers who climb Mt. Hood often try to reach its summit by sunrise in order to avoid avalanche hazards generated by warming snow and ice. By early July rockfalls can become a real danger along south-slope routes. Don't attempt to climb the peak unless you are an experienced mountaineer and are familiar with Hood's routes and hazards.

After ascending one of the spur trails or roads from the lodge back to the PCT, we hike west under the ski lift and past a microwave tower (5980–0.2) below us, then gradually descend westward with views south across a rolling topography to lofty Mt. Jefferson (10,497). Several seasonal creeks are crossed before we make a three-yard boulder-hop across silty Little Zigzag creek (5760–0.9), enter Mt. Hood Wilderness, then continue our descent to a junction with Hidden Lake Trail 779 (5680–0.4), which goes southwest down a morainal ridge to Hidden Lake. Our trail continues its rambling descent, then climbs to a narrow ridge from where we get a great view of Mt. Hood and glaciated Zigzag Canyon. We switchback down the steep slope, jump across the silty Zigzag River (4890–1.3), and climb moderately into a tributary canyon, then out of it up to a slope where the PCT (5140–0.5) splits into two routes.

*   *   *   *

G1

The newer horse trail starts west-southwest and switchbacks up to a broad ridge where we intersect Paradise Park Trail 778 (5390–0.4), a footpath that climbs northeast. The horse trail ascends north across the ridge and passes a camping area below us just before it turns northeast and descends to splashing Lost Creek (5390–0.6), which cascades down a cliff just east of us. We cross it and its more reserved tributary, then pass another camping area below us as we make a climb west up to a ridge, top the ridge, and descend once again—this time to a crossing of Rushing Water Creek (5440–0.6) just below its narrow waterfall. After climbing steeply north out of this cliff-bound canyon, we follow a rather direct trail down to a reunion with the foot trail (5400–0.5–2.1).

*   *   *   *

The older foot trail, which is by far the more scenic route, starts northeast and zigzags up the tributary canyon of Zigzag Canyon. If you're wondering about the composition of the loose cliffs—yes, they are part of the debris-fan deposits that originated from the Crater Rock area. Our ascent finally eases off just after gaining access to a ridge and meeting Paradise Park Trail 778 (5740–1.0), a footpath descending west-southwest through an alpine meadow. We now hike over to Lost Creek (5720–0.2), whose banks are ablaze with common and Lewis monkey flowers, lupine, bistort, corn lily, Mariposa lily, yarrow, paintbrush, pasque-flower, aster and eriogonum.

Remembering that campsites must be at least 100 feet from any creek or body of water, we push onward and quickly reach the Paradise Park Shelter (5730–0.1) in an open forest of dwarf hemlock. This ten-foot-square shelter, constructed with andesite blocks from the surrounding lava flow, once had an operable fireplace. Beyond it, our trail makes a slight climb, then contours across more alpine meadows, and perhaps gives us a chance to spot a pair of sparrow hawks before it switchbacks down to a reunion with the PCT horse trail (5400–2.2).

We now make a switchbacking descent and obtain two fantastic views: up toward the glacier-mantled summit above and down upon the mountain's anatomy below, exposed by the incising Sandy River. We get one more view—from a vertical-sided ridge at the end of a 50-yard spur trail—and it is the most revealing of all: the cliffs of the Sandy River canyon and its tributary canyon are composed of andesite flows and interbedded pyroclastic deposits. As if this flood of magnificent scenery were not enough to satisfy, our trail takes us down to the west side of the ridge where, from a viewpoint, we are saturated with the impressive, naked

G2

see MAP G3

G2

see MAP G4

G3

see MAP G2   see MAP G1

cliffs of Slide Mountain (4872) and of the Rushing Water Creek canyon all around us.

After such a day as this, one is bound to reminisce about his alpine adventure, and a good place to stop and talk it over is at large, flat Scout Camp (3400–3.0) which is beside Rushing Water Creek at the bottom of the switchbacks from the viewpoint. Leaving this forested site, which is closed to camping, we descend the trail northwest 100 yards and arrive at the bouldery, bushy bottom of the Sandy River canyon. We immediately make a log crossing of the three-yard-wide river, which in high runoff expands to fill its 30-yard-wide channel. Continuing northwest downstream on a sandy trail, we wind 270 yards between bushes and over bars to a low cliff of unsorted, poorly bedded sediments of a glacial moraine. Our trail makes a short climb up it and reaches a flat bench (3270–0.3), which is suitable for camping. From it, a steep path climbs about 50 yards east to Upper Sandy Guard Station, which is often locked and unmanned. From the bench, the PCT climbs north to a quick junction with Ramona Falls Loop Trail 797 (3320–0.1), which de-

scends northwest from the rim of a high stream terrace. If you need help or if the weather is terrible, you can abort your trip by descending 1½ miles along this trail to Muddy Fork Road 1825–100, which you take 1½ miles west to Road 1825, then 1½ miles down to Riley Horse Camp, or ¼-mile farther to McNeil Campground. One-fourth mile past this campground, Road 1825 ends at Road 1828, which goes ½ mile southwest to Lolo Pass Road 18. This continues southwest 4¼ miles to the settlement of Zigzag, beside Highway 26.

The Ramona Falls Loop Trail, the Muddy Fork Road and other trails and roads between these and Interstate 84 were ordered closed on November 24, 1976, when James Burns, a Federal judge, issued a final decree. This decision stemmed from a 1973 lawsuit brought against the Mt. Hood National Forest by a coalition of environmentalists who wanted to halt logging operations in Portland's watershed, the Bull Run Reserve. Judge Burns agreed with the environmentalists, but added that a strict interpretation of the legislation that banned logging in the first place—the 1904 Bull Run

G2, G3   G3

Trespass Act—also prevented any kind of trespass. Hence the trails were closed and environmentalists (not to mention the general public) were banned from enjoying the land they sought to preserve. Fortunately, Congress in 1977 drew up and passed the Bull Run Watershed Management Act, which changed the watershed boundaries, and popular trails such as the Ramona Falls Loop Trail and the Eagle Creek Trail were again opened to the public.

Bearing this legal lesson in mind, we start southeast along the loop trail, then follow it east across the broad terrace, which sprouts a dry, open forest, to beautiful Ramona Falls (3460–0.4), splashing down moss-draped rocks. Due to overuse in the past, no camping is allowed within 500 feet of the falls. Just a few yards after we cross the falls' creek, we leave the loop trail, which descends along the creek while we climb high above it to a ridge junction with Yocum Ridge Trail 771 (4000–0.6). During the mid-70s, this trail was extended southeast up to alpine slopes near the south edge of Sandy Glacier.

The PCT climbs as it leaves this ridge trail, then it levels and traverses in and out of gullies, and drops to a cluster of small campsites (4100–2.0) about 70 yards before the first glacier-fed tributary of Muddy Fork. You may have to wade across the first three tributaries, particularly if you are crossing them on a hot afternoon. Between the second and third fords, you get particularly impressive views up-canyon of a serrated, pinacle-studded ridge that separates cascading creeks which descend from spreading Sandy Glacier.

Beyond the third ford we make a minute's stroll over to the jump-across fourth ford, which, unlike the others, flows beneath forest cover. Another minute down it, we come to a spur trail (4060–0.4) that immediately crosses the creek to an official, south-bank, four-person campsite. Just past it the PCT leaves the canyon floor, then in ½ mile makes a gentle ascent westward. We

G3
Exposed sediments of Slide Mountain

G3

G4

see MAP G3

HIGHWAY 26 9 MI.

pass several creeklets before we traverse Bald Mountain's south slopes. On these we get unrestricted views of towering Mt. Hood, forested Muddy Fork canyon, and the canyon's east-end, glacier-fed cascades.

Views disappear as we curve north out of Mt. Hood Wilderness, enter forest cover and make a ¼-mile easy descent to a shady-crest junction with the old Oregon Skyline Trail (4270–2.3), climbing from the west. Here, Timberline Trail 600, which has been with us since mile 3.6 of this section's hike, strikes east for a 22.7-mile traverse around Mt. Hood back to that mileage point.

G3

G3

Ramona Falls

From this junction, our route is mostly downhill to the Columbia River. Descending northwest 50 yards, we reach a junction with Top Spur Trail 785, which starts a westward descent toward Road 1828–118. We continue our forested route northwest to the crest's end (4200–1.4), then start north down a series of switchbacks. The thorny gooseberries, thimbleberries and giant Devil's clubs attest to the cool, moist slope of this forest, which we leave behind as we descend a drier north ridge to a flat clearing immediately south of Lolo Pass Road 18 (3420–1.4) at Lolo Pass. A quarter mile west of here, you can find water running down to the road. The north trailhead is about 20 yards southwest along paved Road 18 and 30 yards before this road's junction with paved Road 1828. Immediately east of the PCT, Road 1810 branches southeast from Road 18, taking one 0.4 mile to spring-fed water.

We start northwest from Lolo Pass, quickly cross north under four sets of buzzing power lines, and then glance back northeast at Mt. Hood's deeply glaciated north face. Before the glaciers performed their cosmetic surgery, the peak's summit towered to about 12,000 feet. You soon reach a gully with a trickling creek (3520–0.4), then climb gradually north to the divide, and circle around the east slope of Sentinel Peak (4565). Rejoining the divide, we contour northwest past two low summits before arriving at a junction with Huckleberry Mountain Trail 617 (4020–3.9), which descends slightly for 0.3 mile to a trickling creek in the gully below the Preachers/Devils saddle. If you descend this trail farther, you reach Lost Lake (3143–1.7), follow its east shore north to Lost Lake Campground (3160–0.8), then finally reach a small store (3160–0.3–2.8) by the lake's north end. The Oregon Skyline Trail once followed this shoreline route, but the trail segment has since been abandoned.

From the junction we contour 270 yards to a sharp bend in the trail, where a spur trail descends 50 yards to a trickling creek and a small flat called Salvation Spring Camp. Back on route, we continue north to an obvious gully and then switchback up to the Preachers/Devils saddle (4340–0.9). Avoiding sermons from its two summits, we follow a huckleberry-lined path in a forest of hemlock and fir, descend to a saddle, climb north up the ridge above Lost Lake, and then descend west to a notch (4250–1.9). Now, a short, stiff climb north takes us to a saddle and a junction with Buck Peak Trail 615 (4500–0.5), which continues along the ridge up to Buck Peak (4751). We descend north across the west slope of this peak and discover a small spring (4340–0.4) a couple feet below the west edge of the trail. A little farther down the trail, we reach the ridge (4230–0.3) again, then switchback down to a long saddle, from which we can get a glimpse below of Blue Lake (3780) to the southwest. As we arc northeast, we leave Portland's Bull Run Watershed behind for good, and with it the posted *no camping* signs that have bothered us while within that section of the county since Lolo Pass. They don't want fires.

Ahead, we'll flirt with the southeast boundary of Columbia Wilderness for more than 7 miles, as both the PCT and the wilderness boundary parallel an old crestline road northeast. Columbia Wilderness, about 61 square miles in size and containing about 125 miles of trail, was officially created in 1984. Before that date the area had long been a *de facto* wilderness, spared the logger's ax. It's good to know we don't see any clearcutting once we reach Wahtum Lake. We'll

G3, G4   **G4, G5**

G5

Hicks
Lake

Wahtum Lake
Guard Sta

406

670

Chinidere
Mtn
1873

Wahtum
Lake

Blue Ridge Camp

Tunnel Falls

Falls

434

440

600

1600

Falls

East

Fork

670

Forest

3½ Mile Camp

440

F   O   R   E   S   T

Scout
Lake

660

4400

4400

COLUMBIA

WILDERNESS

660

Falls

1600

Creek

435

3200

3600

Indian
Springs

Forest
Camp

419

2800

2030

4000

Indian

Indian Mtn
Lookout (site)

4400

No

Name

4400

Creek

2800

13

Creek

2400

3200

WAUCOMA

2800

BRANCH

13

ROAD

Branch

2400

TRAIL

BASE   LINE

3600

3600

Sawtooth

Mountain

SKYLINE

5

LAKE

Creek

Lake

4

3

Raker Pt

2

Lost

223

TRAIL

13

Washout

2800

3600

13

LOST

Blue
Lake

8

Buck Pk

2800

9

10

Lost Lake Butte

11

Mt. Hood, from one mile north of Buck Peak

certainly see enough of it to the east of us as we make a crestline traverse.

This stretch follows a fairly level crest northeast, contours across the southeast slope of a low, triangular summit, then, just below a saddle, reaches the abandoned Oregon Skyline Trail (4190–2.2), which climbs from the southwest to merge with the PCT. Climbing gently northeast, we quickly reach Larch Mountain Road 2030 (4240-0.1), which is momentarily atop the ridge. We locate the trail on the northwest side of the road, parallel it northnortheast and then round the narrow north spur (4400–1.6) of Indian Mountain (4890), from which we see Mts. St. Helens (8364), Rainier (14,410) and Adams (12,276). Then we descend eastward to Indian Springs Campground (4300–0.3), which has few car campers because of the rough, rocky nature of Road 660, which is used to reach it. Unfortunately, this area had to be logged over to remove snags left by a devastating 1920 fire. The camp's spring is just beyond the west end of the camp's road loop, and just beyond it, the brushy, unmaintained Indian Springs Trail 435 starts northwest toward the north spur, follows it, then steeply descends it two miles to Eagle Creek Trail 440.

The PCT recommences at the east end of the loop and parallels the road, first below it, then above it to a saddle, where it leaves the roadside and winds gently down a forested slope, then northeast down to a junction with Eagle Creek Trail 440 (3750–2.6) just above the southwest shore of Wahtum Lake (3732).

*   *   *   *

The hike from Wahtum Lake down to the Columbia River is far more scenic along the Eagle Creek Trail than along the PCT, and is therefore described here as a highly recommended alternate route. From the Wahtum Lake outlet (3740–0.1), which is the East Fork of Eagle Creek, Trail 440 begins as a typical trail, for it descends through a Douglas-fir forest with an understory that includes inconspicuous annuals such as coolwort, false Solomon's seal, queen's cup, bunchberry and vanilla-leaf. In a north-draining canyon, we reach an adequate campsite beside a trickling creek (3300–1.2), then arc westward gently down to a ford of the Indian Springs fork (3040–0.8) of Eagle Creek, which could be tricky to cross in early summer. Along its banks is a very good campsite.

We now begin a descent northwest that takes us past rhododendron, gooseberry, red elderberry, thimbleberry, huckleberry, Devil's club and Oregon grape. Along this cool descent, you may see Indian Springs Trail 435, which climbs two steep miles up to Indian Springs Campground. After reaching a viewpoint (2350–1.6) at the tip of a north spur, our trail turns south and descends past a campsite (1920–1.0) by a shallow gully, crosses seasonal creeklets, and then makes a switchback (1600–0.7) north.

The slope is now much gentler, and in the near distance we can hear Eagle Creek splashing merrily down its course. In a short distance we reach a rockbound creek (1440–0.5) and pause for a drink. Don't be too surprised if a red-spotted garter snake is climbing up a rock behind you; he needs water too. It is not uncommon to encounter half a dozen of these beneficial snakes in a day's hike along this verdant route. Just beyond this refreshing creek we meet several trails that descend about 50 yards west to 7½ Mile Camp (1380–0.1), complete with a primitive shelter. If you intend to camp before reaching the trailhead, this certainly is a good place to stop at. Before us lies the string of impressive waterfalls that make this last half of the trail so popular.

Our trail gradually descends to the bank of Eagle Creek, and we see a 50-foot cascade (1180–0.7)—not too impressive—but a sample of what's to come. The creek enters a safe, very deep, crystal-clear pool (1120–0.3) that is extremely tempting for an afternoon swim, but the cool water will ensure that you won't stay in for long. Immediately beyond it is a two-stage, 100 foot-high waterfall, sliced into a narrow gorge, which we don't see until we round a vertical cliff, where our precariously exposed trail, blasted from the cliff, heads toward 150-foot-high Tunnel Falls (1120–0.2). This trail is definitely not for the faint-hearted, nor is its ceiling sufficient for those on horseback. The fall, in its grotto of vertical-walled basalt, is spectacular enough to make it the climax of this route, but our sensations of it are heightened even more as we head through a wet tunnel blasted behind the fall about midway up it. Exuberant from the wall of water around us, we leave this grotto of the East Fork in expectation of more high adventure. Below us, Eagle Creek cascades 30 feet down to another layer of this Miocene Columbia River basalt.

Our trail's exposure decreases considerably as we leave the falls' narrow gorge. We soon reach pleasant Blue Grouse Camp (1120–0.3), then continue on to a junction with Eagle Benson Trail 434 (1000–0.5), which climbs steeply up to the PCT. This narrow footpath is not recommended by the authors, who believe it is too narrow to be safely climbed or descended with a heavy pack. In places it is quite easy for you to slip on loose gravel and then fall over a hundred-foot cliff. Just around the corner from this junction, our trail enters another side canyon and bridges a murmuring tributary a hundred yards downstream from its slender, 80-foot-high fall. Unseen above it is the Eagle Benson Trail, which descends near the mossy brink of this graceful fall.

Continuing northwest, we soon enter another side canyon, and this one provides us with Wy East Camp (960–0.5), which is just above the trail. Progressing farther downstream on this trail, we reach a bridge (710–0.7) across Eagle Creek, 20 feet below. A daredevil instinct may urge some to jump from the bridge into the tempting 8-foot-deep pool below, but better judgment takes hold and we pass up the opportunity for another time.

Now above the creek's west bank, we follow the singing creek down to the popular, excellent 4 Mile Camp (680–0.6), also known as the "Tenas Camp." How many campsites do you know of that have a beautiful waterfall near them? We've seen just a few. This one has a two-step, 40-foot fall, and near it, you'll find the dipper, or water ouzel, which is a gray, chunky, water-loving bird that tenaciously clings to the bottoms of swift streams in search of aquatic animal life. The name "dipper" refers to the bird's bobbing motions while standing on land, and, taking that word as a suggestion, we decide to take a dip in the 57°F creek ourselves. After a quick, invigorating frolic in the pools below the lower fall, we stretch out in the afternoon sunlight to thaw out before hiking once again.

Back on the trail, we walk spiritedly north to a bridge (690–0.3) across a 90-foot-deep gorge that is only 30 feet wide. A hundred yards downstream from this crossing, the swirling creek has cut, with the aid of churning boulders, deep potholes that would make superb swimming holes were it not for the cool temperature. The six-inch trout don't seem to mind it though. Above the potholes, wispy Loowit Falls emerges from the vegetation to flow silently down the polished rock and into one of the pools.

Continuing downstream, we soon enter another side canyon, bridge a creek 50 feet above it, then pass by massive, vertical-walled flows of this Columbia River basalt. The contact between two flows tends to be a weak point, and both the creek and its tributaries tend to flow along such contacts. The height of a waterfall often represents the thickness of a single flow. The minutes pass by quickly, and before we know it, we cross Tish Creek and arrive at an overlook (500–1.4) above Punch Bowl Falls, which drops 40 feet into a churning cauldron

Along a part of the Eagle Creek Trail below Tunnel Falls

below us. It's hard to judge just how deep this huge pool is, but right beneath the falls a depth of 20 feet wouldn't be much of an exaggeration.

Here our trail starts to climb high above the now-impassable gorge, and we soon see more reasons why horses aren't allowed on the trail. At times, the overhanging walls seem to press us terribly close to the brink of the dead-vertical cliff below us, and we're thankful that the trail crew installed cables along these stretches. We now reach another overlook (520–0.7), where we can look 200 yards upstream to Metlako Falls, whose silvery course plummets another step down into the inaccessible gorge.

Our route gradually begins to descend toward the trailhead, and we leave the threatening, moss-covered cliffs behind as we descend into the realm of a cedar-and-Douglas-fir forest. Alder, maple, dogwood, ocean spray, blackberries, thimbleberries, moss, three species of ferns and dozens of wildflowers harmonize with the conifers on these canyon slopes to create a symphony of nature at her best. All too soon, our verdant route reaches the trailhead (150–1.5), which is by a bridge that spans Eagle Creek. On the creek's west side, you'll find a short, looping nature trail that splits off from climbing, 1.8-mile Wauna View Point Trail 402.

To reach Bridge of the Gods, we take Gorge Trail 400, which starts from the parking area. This trail climbs through a picnic area, crosses the short road up to Eagle Creek Campground (200–0.1), passes between the campground and Interstate 84, then quickly reaches a part of the abandoned, narrow Columbia River 'highway.' On this we curve over to Ruckel Creek (230–0.6), where, on its east bank, Ruckel Creek Trail 405 makes a 5.3-mile climb to the Pacific Crest Trail.

Our shady gorge trail continues northeast, and at times it almost touches Interstate 84. After traversing a few hundred yards across grassy slopes—absolutely miserable in the rain—the trail ends at Moody Avenue opposite the PCT (280–1.9–16.3). From here the PCT route follows a road under nearby Interstate 84, then as a trail again it curves 200 yards over toward the toll booth at the south end of Bridge of the Gods. See the end of this section's PCT description for a list of the available services in Cascade Locks.

*   *   *   *

The Pacific Crest Trail, which is 0.8 mile shorter than the Eagle Creek route, starts a

Eagle Creek gorge just above Loowit Falls

G7, G5

see MAP G7

see MAP G5

see MAP G6

traverse east along Wahtum Lake's southwest shore. It then meets a lateral trail (3750–0.2) that climbs ⅓ mile up to the Wahtum Lake Campground, atop a saddle. From that saddle Road 1310 descends southeast toward other roads that lead out to the city of Hood River, and crest-hugging Road 660, from Indian Springs Campground, crosses the saddle and traverses northeast high above Wahtum Lake.

From the lateral-trail junction, the PCT, like Road 670, circles Wahtum Lake, leaving its popular south-shore campsites behind. The trail's gentle, long, counterclockwise climb ends high above the lake at a junction with a ¼-mile-

G5

G5

long spur trail that heads northeast to Road 670. In 200 yards our now-level trail reaches a junction with the Chinidere Mountain Trail (4270–1.8). If you're having good weather, don't pass up this ⅓-mile long, 400-foot ascent to its superb, panoramic summit. From the summit you can see decapitated Mt. Helens rising skyward above the north-northwest horizon, massive Mt. Adams lording over the north-northeast horizon, and graceful Mt. Hood dominating the south-southeast horizon. You also see the Columbia River and Wind River canyons, due north, while closer by, you're surrounded by deep, slightly glaciated canyons.

Leaving the Chinidere Mountain Trail junction, the PCT curves northwest around this miniature mountain to a saddle (4140–0.6), then contours across the southwest slopes of summit 4380 to a crest viewpoint. It then drops to a second saddle (3830–1.4) and traverses to a third saddle (3810–0.8), this one signed *Camp Smokey*. Perhaps someone once smoked too much, for these two saddles and the southwest-facing slopes between them were part of an area burned by a large forest fire. A small campsite is found at the Camp Smokey saddle, but a better one is found 180 yards down the Eagle Benson Trail. You'll find a refreshing spring just 50 yards past the campsite. Beyond the spring, the Eagle Benson Trail, descending to Eagle Creek, is usually unmaintained.

Pushing toward the deep Columbia Gorge, we leave the Camp Smokey saddle and climb up to the southeast edge of spreading Benson Plateau, which is a preglacial land surface that is being slowly devoured by back-cutting tributaries of Herman and Eagle creeks. In a gully on the plateau's southeast edge, we meet lightly used Benson Way Trail 405B (4100–0.5), which starts west but eventually curves north over to the Ruckel Creek Trail.

Staying near the plateau's east edge, the PCT winds north to the Ruckel Creek Trail 405 (4110–0.9), which you can follow west ½ mile to a large campsite. This campsite is the only one between Wahtum Lake and Dry Creek that is suitable for equestrians, so don't be surprised if you find horses at it. Forty yards south of this campsite you'll find a spring in a small meadow. From this campsite you could continue about 4.8 miles down the trail to Gorge Trail 400, which is mentioned at the end of the alternate Eagle Creek Trail route, described earlier.

Beyond the Ruckel Creek Trail junction, the PCT descends gently northwest along the pla-

teau's east edge and it soon meets the abandoned-but-visible Benson Ruckel Trail (3980–0.7), which once traversed west-southwest one mile to the Ruckel Creek Trail. Past this junction the PCT curves northeast and leaves Benson Plateau by the time it arrives at a junction with the *second* Benson Way Trail 405B (3760–0.7). Here you'll find a waterless campsite that will accommodate four persons.

We now hike north along a forested crest and pass another waterless campsite (3680–0.6) just before the trail curves east to begin a descent into the deep Columbia Gorge. Our moderately-to-steeply dropping trail briefly descends crest, then heads west to a switchback. Immediately past this turn we encounter Teakettle Spring (3360–0.3), which can easily be missed when its sign is gone.

Past the spring our trail switchbacks once again down to the crest, on which it reaches a barren area that gives us revealing views of the giant Columbia Gorge. We can identify the towns of Cascade Locks, Stevenson and Carson, and with the use of this book's maps can mentally sketch the winding route of the PCT up the gorge's north wall. You can also identify large landslides (see the beginning description of Section H). To the west we see an impressive set of cliffs that are composed of the same kind of volcanic rocks that compose our barren area—pyroclastic rocks. These indicate that in pre-glacial times a volcano may have existed at this site or close by.

From the barren area atop the crest, our trail starts west, turns north, soon crosses the crest, then makes a fairly steep, viewless descent into the deep Columbia Gorge, recrossing the crest—now a ridge—near its lower end. From it, the PCT traverses ⅓ mile west to a junction (1120–3.0) with a 1.8-mile trail that provides a fast way out to the highway, ending at the Columbia Gorge Work Center.

The hiker who intends to cross into Washington should continue along the westbound Pacific Crest Trail. Departing from the lateral trail down to Herman Creek, the PCT continues its traverse across open talus slopes, then enters a cool, mossy forest of Douglas-fir and maple. A creek is soon crossed (960–0.5), just beyond which we pass through a shallow saddle and then round a steep bowl. As our trail reaches a ridge and turns west to leave the bowl, a spur trail heads northwest steeply down the east side of a small gully. The PCT traverses southwest for about a mile, dropping slowly, then turns south and

G5, G6, G7   **G7**

Bridge of the Gods

southeast. Our trail contours over toward a saddle and joins a power-line road (680–0.7) that climbs up and over it. We head northwest down this road only 70 yards, then branch left on the trail. This segment rollercoasters west ½ mile around the north slopes of a low summit, turns north and descends to Moody Avenue. The Eagle Creek Trail alternate route ends here, opposite the PCT.

Down this dirt road we go 70 yards to its junction with SE Undine Street (240–1.0), where it becomes paved. Moody Avenue immediately crosses under the freeway, and 5 yards west of the freeway's largest pillar, the PCT resumes, curving 200 yards northwest over to the paved loop road that leads up to the Bridge of the Gods (200–0.1). Section G ends here and Section H begins on the other side of the Columbia River, at the bridge-road junction with Washington's Highway 14, 0.5 mile distant. In 1989 it cost 25 cents to walk across Bridge of the Gods.

If you're a long-distance hiker, you'll want to resupply in Cascade Locks. Walk down to the town's nearby thoroughfare, old U.S. Highway 30, which here is known as Wa Na Pa Street. On it you walk 0.4 mile northeast to the Cascade Locks Post Office, which is conveniently located opposite the Columbia Gorge Center, with a general store, a restaurant and other stores. In another 0.4 mile you'll reach a road that heads north to the Cascade Locks Marine Park. It has a campground and nearby, in the visitors center, it has showers. One great feature of the park's campground is its roofed cooking area, with tables, under which you can keep dry on those all too often rainy days. In this park you can visit the shipping locks, built in 1896, which allowed ships to travel up-river beyond the Columbia River's Cascade Rapids. The town of Cascade Locks was spawned by the resulting commerical activity. The park's museum used to have an exhibit that said a Bridge of the Gods was a natural bridge that spanned the river. Not so. However, the river was likely dammed for a while by a huge landslide from the north, whence the Indian legend.

If you are waiting for the weather to improve, then you might spend time at the city hall, on Wa Na Pa Street ⅓ mile east of the park entrance. Most of this building is, surprisingly, occupied by an indoor basketball court, but there is also a neat little library tucked away in an upstairs room. Here you can catch up on all the gruesome news you've been missing while out on the trail.

quickly descends to a bridge across perennial, misnamed Dry Creek (720–1.8). Camping is possible here and at other spots along this creek. Immediately beyond it, we encounter a dirt road, which can be followed 0.2 mile up to its end, where you'll see an ideal shower—a 50-foot-high waterfall.

From the dirt road, the PCT starts west and after a few yards passes a spur trail branching

G7   **G7**

Section H: Highway 14 at Bridge of the Gods to Highway 12 near White Pass

Introduction: Because this is the longest section and because it has the greatest elevation change, it is the most diverse. It starts near the west end of Bridge of the Gods, which at 180 feet elevation is one of the lowest points on the official Pacific Crest Trail (the lowest point—140 feet—is met just one mile southwest from the start of Section H). Near this section's end, the PCT climbs to 7080 feet elevation—its highest elevation in Washington—before it makes a traverse across the upper part of Packwood Glacier.

Between these two extremes we pass through several environments. After starting in a lush, damp Columbia River forest, we climb usually viewless slopes, wind past an extensive, recent lava flow, traverse through a lake-speckled, glaciated lava plateau, and climb to a subalpine forest. We then circle around a major, periodically active volcano, Mt. Adams, traverse high on the walls of deep, glaciated canyons, and finally climb up to an alpine landscape at Packwood Glacier. Along Section H, then, we pass through all of the landforms and vegetation belts that one sees along the PCT from central Oregon to trail's end in southern British Columbia.

Declination: 19°E

Mileages:

	South to North	Distances between Points	North to South
Bridge of the Gods, west end	0.0		147.5
		3.8	
Gillette Lake	3.8		143.7
		5.9	
Spring near Table Mountain	9.7		137.8
		5.6	
Spur trail to Three Corner Rock water trough	15.3		132.2
		5.0	
Rock Creek	20.3		127.2
		5.8	
Sunset-Hemlock Road 41	26.1		121.4
		4.0	
Road 43 alongside Trout Creek	30.1		117.4
		5.4	
Road 65 near Panther Creek Campground	35.5		112.0
		8.7	
Big Huckleberry Mountain summit trail	44.2		103.3
		6.8	
Road 60 at Crest Campground	51.0		96.5
		7.4	
Blue Lake	58.4		89.1
		3.0	
Bear Lake	61.4		86.1
		6.3	
Road 24	67.7		79.8
		8.8	
Road 88	76.5		71.0
		5.8	
Road 23	82.3		65.2
		6.6	
Round the Mountain Trail	88.9		58.6
		8.8	
Killen Creek cascade	97.7		49.8
		5.0	
Lava Spring	102.7		44.8
		3.6	

Mileages:	South to North	Distances between Points	North to South
East-west road near Midway site	106.3		41.2
		11.7	
Walupt Lake Trail	118.0		29.5
		4.5	
Sheep Lake near Nannie Ridge Trail	122.5		25.0
		4.5	
Trail 86 to Bypass Camp	127.0		20.5
		2.1	
Dana May Yelverton Shelter	129.1		18.4
		6.9	
Tieton Pass	136.0		11.5
		7.9	
White Pass Chair Lift spur trail	143.9		3.6
		3.6	
Highway 12 near White Pass	147.5		0.0

Supplies: When Schaffer first mapped Section H in 1973, it was 136½ miles long. You could pick up mailed parcels at Stevenson, early in the hike, and at Midway Guard Station, about two thirds of the way through. Unfortunately for the long-distance hiker, the guard station burned down in 1976 and, with the completion of the last segment of trail in 1984, Stevenson no longer lies along the route. No supplies—mailed parcels or otherwise—can be found along Section H, which today is 10½ miles longer. Only the southern and central High Sierra has a bleaker logistical problem. If you aren't up to such a rigorous hike, you can bypass the first 35½ miles of the PCT, taking an alternate route on roads through the towns of Stevenson and Carson. Doing so will cut 21 miles off Section H's length and will save you about a vertical mile of unnecessary climbing. In Stevenson you should be able to purchase almost anything you'll need, but in Carson you'll find very little. Both towns have post offices, but the Carson Post Office is preferable because, being 4½ miles closer to White Pass, it shortens your walk with a full pack just a little. PCT adherents avoiding these towns will have to resupply at Cascade Locks (end of Section G) and at White Pass (end of Section H). At the pass you can pick up mailed parcels and usually can get a hot meal. Don't expect much else.

Special Restrictions: The Forest Service would like to see you camp at least 200 feet from the Pacific Crest Trail when you are in an official wilderness area. Unfortunately, topographic and/or vegetative constraints often make this impossible. Nevertheless, try to choose a site that will have a minimal impact on the environment and on other trail users. Packers mustn't let their animals graze within 200 feet of lakes, and if they pack in feed, it must be processed so as to prevent seed germination. All these rules apply to *all* of Washington's wilderness areas.

View toward crest, from climb north up the west slopes of Table Mountain

The Cascade crest lies to the east, but the Pacific Crest Trail begins westward, which makes for a very roundabout—and hilly—route. In general terms this 35½-mile route climbs 3300 feet to a ridge, drops 2000 feet to Rock Creek, climbs 1700 feet to Sedum Ridge, drops 2200 feet to Trout Creek, then climbs and drops hundreds of feet as it rolls east to Road 65 near Panther Creek Campground. Your net elevation gain from Bridge of the Gods is a mere 750 feet, yet with a fully laden backpack, you could take three days to do this arduous stretch. However, if you take the most direct route to Road 65, you can reach the PCT near Panther Creek Campground in a mere 14.7 mlles. Furthermore, if you start with a light pack and wait until you reach the Carson post office to pick up your mailed parcels, then you have to hike with a full pack only 7.6 miles to reach the PCT. Following this plan, Panther Creek Campground is reached by a relatively easy one-day hike. This short, alternate route will be described first.

* * * *

The alternate route starts north from the west end of Bridge of the Gods toll road (180–0.5, if you're counting the mileage from the end of section G). Our Highway 14 curves past Ashes Lake, then heads northeast to the town of Stevenson (110–2.7), which has stores and cafes, plus the Stevenson Post Office, located at the corner of First and Russell, one block south of the highway. In Stevenson you should be able to buy food, boots, packs and other equipment.

East of Stevenson, our highway climbs rocky bluffs and provides us with scenic views up and down the river. Douglas-fir and maple provide plenty of shade even if you're doing this stretch on a rare sunny afternoon. Our road eventually descends slightly to a junction with the Wind River Road (280–3.4), an "all weather" route we take northeast. It curves over to the sleepy settlement of Carson (450–1.0), which has a post office on the road's east side. This is the last one you'll find until you reach White Pass Village, a very long 119 miles away. If you're doing the whole PCT or at least the Oregon-Washington part, you'll want to mail your heavy packages here rather than carrying them from the Cascade Locks or the Stevenson post office.

The Wind River Road leaves Carson, bends northwest, crosses a bridge spanning the 200-foot-deep Wind River gorge (570–2.5), and reaches a junction (802–2.3), where we turn right and follow the Old State Road briefly east to Panther Creek Road 65 (802–0.1). On this we walk one mile north, then soon begin a winding stretch of road up along Panther Creek to the Pacific Crest Trail (930–2.7–14.7). This trail crosses our road only 230 yards south of Warren Gap Road 6517 and its adjacent Panther Creek Campground. This is a good place to spend the night, for the next near-trail campsite with *good* water is at Blue Lake, about 23 miles farther.

* * * *

From the west end of Bridge of the Gods toll road (180) you head south on Highway 14 past Ice House Lake—an oversized pond—and just 90 yards beyond it reach the PCT trailhead (150–0.2). You'll find limited parking space nearby, but an official trailhead parking area is lacking. Your "trail" at first is along an old powerline road which parallels Highway 14, just below you. Because the roadbed is rather overgrown, the trail sticks to the road's outer edge, which in one short stretch is very exposed—one slip and you'll fall off a vertical cliff to almost certain death. Here, the trail needs a guard rail or needs to be moved to the road's inner edge. The short clifftop stretch soon gives way to safer slopes, and presently you reach a road that climbs briefly up to a nearby cistern, which is your first source of reliable water. You follow the road for 280 yards, angle right from it, then in 110 yards cross a paved road (140–0.8), which climbs from Highway 14 to Wauna Lake.

Leaving civilization, we first climb to a ridge (250-0.4) from where Tamehnous Trail 25 starts southwest, meandering ¾ mile over to a large parking area opposite the Bonneville Lock and Dam North Shore Visitors Entrance. Ahead, the forested, often-fern-bordered PCT takes a convoluted, rolling route across a giant landslide.

Large and small landslides have descended from both walls of the Columbia Gorge. In part this is due to the steepness of the gorge's walls. However, it is also due to another factor. The volcanic flows and associated volcanic sediments composing the walls belong to two distinct time periods. The lower layers are about 25 million years old, while the upper ones are about 15 million years old. The surface of the lower layers thus had about 10 million years to deeply weather to clay in its warm, humid, preglacial climate before it was buried under a sea of younger deposits. This clay layer is the

H1   **H6, H5, H1**

see MAP H1

VANCOUVER 33 MI.

H1

Rock Creek
Butte

CG 2000
2030

Rock

1200

2000

Spring Creek

22

23

24

Nelson

800

225

1200

2000

Hot Springs

28

27

26

25

33

34

CG 2000

35

800

400

36

Kanaka

STEVENSON

Cem

BM 103

830

4

WIND RIVER ROAD 2.7 MI.

449

Mosley
Lakes

44

Fan
Marker

HIGHWAY 14

PORTLAND

CLARK

COLUMBIA

WASHINGTON
OREGON

BM 105

Airport

84

THE DALLES 38 MI.

Quarry

11

Bowles
Lakes

Gravel
Pit

10

Blue
Lakes

Ashes Land

Piling

Lights

Old
Locks

Park

BM
105

BM
133

Cascade Locks

Res

see MAP G7

Evergreen
Lake

Smith
Lake

L Ashes
Lake

37

BM
104

12

13

Gillette Lk

Black
L

Wauna L

Ice House
Lake

BM

Bridge of the Gods

PINE

Kidney
Lake

Spring
Lake

Airway
Beacon

Fern L

Rand
Lake

SPOKANE

RIVER

400

Rudolph Creek

1600

16

15

Hazel L

Sheridan
Point

PACIFIC

296

105

14

Boat

COLUMBIA

BM 185

Bass Lake

HWY 14

BM
98

SHERIDAN WAYSIDE
STATE PARK

BONNEVILLE

PORTLAND 42 MI.

see MAP H2

structurally weak element that causes overlying layers to give way, as in the landslides from Table Mountain and the Red Bluffs.

The gorge's north wall is more prone to landslides than is the south wall because the volcanic rocks that compose both walls dip to the south. Naturally, then, rocks tend to slide south along this incline, and resulting landslides push the Columbia River against the south wall. Such landslides can temporarily dam the Columbia River, and such temporary dammings perhaps provided a basis for the Indian legend about the Bridge of the Gods. It is known that certain Oregonian Indians witnessed the eruption of Mt. Mazama 6900 years ago, leaving Crater Lake basin in its aftermath, and it is therefore quite likely that the Multnomah Indians witnessed one or more devastating landslides in the last few millennia.

After about an hour of seemingly aimless wandering—more of it up than down—you temporarily break out of forest cover at a utility road (410–2.1), which serves three sets of Bonneville Dam powerlines. Across this major road the PCT follows an abandoned road down toward Gillette Lake (280–0.3). You'll find a 75-yard spur trail heading east to the lake's northwest shore, which may be your first possible Section H campsite. On private land in a setting that is anything but pristine, the lake is, nevertheless utilitarian, and swimmers will find the water relatively warm.

We re-enter forest and in a couple minutes pass the lake's seasonal inlet creek, then climb for ¼ mile to a "firebreak." From it you follow an old road 70 yards west before leaving it. Eastbound trekkers could be led astray if they miss the PCT tread starting from the east side of the firebreak. On trail tread westbound trekkers make an easy climb to a lily-pad pond before momentarily dropping to a horse bridge across Greenleaf Creek (510–0.9). This is your last totally reliable *on-trail* water source until Rock Creek, 15.5 miles farther. Fortunately, some near-trail water sources are available.

We switchback upward from the creek and get our only views of sprawling Bonneville Dam as we make a short traverse southwest. We then angle northwest to a gully with a seasonal creeklet, ramble west to a second creeklet, then climb north along a third before switchbacking up to a low ridgecrest (1100–1.9). Here, we turn north and parallel a little-used road up Cedar Creek canyon. Along this stretch you can drop to the nearby road, camp along it, and wade through dense vegetation to get water from Cedar Creek.

H1, H2

After a crest walk northward, we cross the road (1300–0.6), and then in ⅓ mile recross it. Ahead, the trail unfortunately climbs above the creek's headwaters, leaving you high and dry, so plan accordingly.

In about ⅓ mile our climb north takes us to a creeklet, just beyond which we meet an old trail that climbs very steeply up a minor ridge. On a moderate grade we climb northwest, then southwest up to a larger ridge (1970–1.2), it too having an old trail along it. Now we exchange the Cedar Creek drainage for the larger Hamilton Creek drainage. We drop a bit, quickly emerge from forest cover, then drop some more to avoid steep slopes on the west side of towering Table Mountain. Enjoy the panoramic views while you can, for you still have 1500 feet of climbing ahead. On a hot, muggy summer's day you may be too tired to enjoy anything, particularly with that heavy pack on your back. The earlier in the morning you make this protracted climb out of the Columbia Gorge, the better.

On a shady bench due west of Table Mountain the PCT latches onto an abandoned roadbed which, fortunately, is alder shaded along its first half mile. You'll need the shade, for the gradient averages a stiff 17%. Just before the gradient abates you'll get a view (2480–1.3). Stop and listen for music to your ears—a never-failing creek. Reaching it is another problem. It could use a spur trail down to it, but unfortunately the creek is on private land. Drop your pack and cautiously head downslope, trying to keep slipping and sliding to a minimum. (Equestrians have a real dilemma: horses can't reach this spring-fed creek, and they may not be able to reach Cedar Creek, mentioned earlier. Horses could get heat prostration on a hot summer

afternoon—you may have to walk your horse up this perspiring stretch.)

Onward, in about 140 yards you re-enter forest cover and bend west. Soon you leave the old roadbed, pass under a buzzing powerline, traverse a short stretch of beargrass turf, and then ramble over to a nearby road (2790–0.8). You climb briefly north, then east on a rather steep, very rocky tread across a rubbly open slope that offers fine views south down Hamilton Creek canyon. Mt. Hood also comes into view, poking over the shoulder of multilayered Table Mountain. With a final burst of effort you reach a ridge (3120–0.5) above a powerline saddle. Welcome back to a crest route; you've struggled 11 miles to reach it.

Having put most of the elevation gain behind us, we can enjoy the next stretch, which has views east past Greenleaf Basin and Peak to the Columbia Gorge and south past Table Mountain to Mt. Hood. Typical of a crest route, the PCT climbs to a saddle and crosses it (3400–0.7), giving us our first view of Three Corner Rock—a conspicuous knob to the northwest. The trail climbs briefly, topping out at just over 3400 feet, then makes a minimal descent over to flowery, bushy slopes, immediately beyond which we come to a seep (3370–0.3). It may be dry, so don't count on it.

Next we wind around a ridge, absorbing panoramic views to the south, west and northwest, then submerge in a forest canopy for a descent to a saddle with a crestline road (3020–1.3). This jeep road heads over to Three Corner Rock, and the PCT parallels it in the same direction. Traversing along the PCT we get sporadic views to the north and east, with Mt. Adams and

H2   H2

PCT bridge across Trout Creek

see MAP H5

see MAP H3

see MAP H2

H5

Creek
BM 1001
15
16
1021
Whisky Cr.
14
2400
60
1200
1200
417
REA
21
22
Bunker Hill
2383 Lookout
1600
1200
54
23
993
BM 1015
Warren Gap
6517
Panther Creek
Campground
938
F O
2000
65
Panth.
8C
Gaging
Sta.
Stabler
BM 947
Wind River
Ranger Station
Trout Creek Picnic Ground
ROAD
43
28
Creek
26
WIND
Pilot Knob
25
BM 985
1200
BM1109
27
Creek
41
WIND RIVER ROAD
BM 918
34
Martha
1600
35
1200
36
1200
NATIONAL
FOREST
BOUNDARY
1903
1825
2400
TRAIL
4
2798
3
2600
2974
2
2400
1
2000
Creek
9
10
2400
11
12
Bunger
Spring
Creek
2000
16
15
14
13
GIFFORD PINCHOT
NATIONAL FOREST
13

clearcuts catching our attention. Views disappear about ¼ mile before our trail touches the jeep road, and ahead we climb, first viewlessly southwest, then viewfully west up to a spur trail (3320–2.0). Your next on-trail water is way down at Rock Creek, a hefty 5.0 miles away. If you really need water, you can gamble and take the narrow, bouldery spur trail ⅓ mile over to a water trough. You'll find it about 30 yards west of the trail at a point just 40 yards before the trail ends at a jeep road. The trough is bathtub size, and when Schaffer visited it, it looked like folks had bathed in it. You'll certainly want to treat the water! The trough, unfortunately, could have sprung a leak, leaving you thirsty and frustrated. If you've hiked as far as the water trough, you might as well scramble up the jeep road to close-by Three Corner Rock for unrestricted views, which include Mts. Hood, Adams, St. Helens and, weather permitting, Rainier.

From the junction we get a few views of unesthetic clearcut slopes as we wind and switchback northward down to a viewless saddle (2360–1.9), which is crossed by Road 2090. Next we skirt east just below a ridgecrest, soon enter a clearcut, then gratefully leave it just before ducking through a crest gap (1980–0.5). After immediately switchbacking west below the gap, we quickly plunge into a deep forest and wander in and out of numerous usually dry gullies before crossing Road 2000 (1720–1.8). If you need to abort your trip, take this well-maintained road 11 miles down to Stevenson. Otherwise, follow the PCT down and across gullies to an ultimate bridging of Rock Creek (1420–0.8). This 5.0-mile stretch from the spur trail has been a well-graded, very steady descent across a generally viewless, intricately complex terrain. Our hats are off to whoever surveyed this route; it must have been a formidable task, particularly with such dense vegetation.

Your water problems are now over, at least until you leave Panther Creek Campground, some 15+ miles ahead. You quickly climb above Rock Creek, traverse east to a junction with the Snag Creek Trail, then in 120 yards reach its namesake, Snag Creek (1470–0.4). Ahead we soon emerge from forest cover, cross a clearcut with crowding, waist-high vegetation (very miserable on a rainy day), then reach Road 2070 (1450–0.3). If you're in need of a campsite, you can head about 250 yards down this rocky road and set up camp along the North Fork of Rock Creek. Otherwise, prepare for a challenging ascent.

At first we have a pleasant stroll through a forest of Douglas-firs, alders and vine maples. The North Fork stays close by for the first ¾ mile, then we enter and leave a prominent gully and climb to a north-trending North Fork tributary. It is usually flowing, but is a problem to reach because the PCT typically stays 100 feet above it on steep, densely vegetated slopes. Finally we cross a seasonal creeklet (2080–1.8), one's last hope for any water until a Trout Creek tributary 7.0 miles away. Switchbacks carry us up to gentler slopes, across which we climb to a lushly vegetated, though dry, gully. Ahead, we climb east to a ridge and then north to the base of steep slopes below crest-hugging Sunset-Hemlock Road 41. Southeast, we climb a short half mile, obtaining poor views before we reach a south-trending ridge (3080–1.8). Next we skirt over to an adjacent crest saddle, then just beyond it have our first good views as the trail skirts the base of a lava cliff. At a second saddle (2985–0.7) we almost touch Road 41, and here you might note the abandoned Sedum Ridge Trail, descending 4 miles to Road 2000, along Rock Creek. We climb once more, topping out at 3130 feet near a viewful, south-trending ridge,

H4

1978 PCT bridge construction at Wind River

H2, H3, H4

and then we descend to Sedum Ridge, where we finally cross Road 41 (2950–0.8).

Leaving the road, the PCT hiker meets what's left of Greenknob Trail 144 in ¼ mile, and on his PCT descent he is likely to see traces of this former trail. The PCT reaches a gully, descends briefly north, turns east around a knifeblade ridge, then drops north through a lush forest to the main ridge (2550–1.0). Here we get our first good view north and see Bunker Hill, to the east, standing alone in a flat-floored valley.

The view disappears and once again we disappear into a lush forest. If you are hiking the

trail on one of those damp misty days so common to this area, you may see a dozen or more rough-skinned newts. The trail quickly reaches gentler slopes and angles northeast down to a viewless saddle (2150–0.7), then continues northeast down into several gullies which often though not always provide water. The trail leaves these gullies and in ⅓ mile crosses a wide, splashing tributary (1210–2.0) of Trout Creek. Now on nearly level ground, we curve east to Trout Creek and cross it on a concrete span built to last as long as the PCT does. This is a good spot to camp. Immediately past the bridge, our

H4   # H4, H5

trail crosses Road 43 (1180–0.3), which gently descends 1.3 miles to the Trout Creek Picnic Ground, with a good swimming hole.

From the road we hike 280 yards over to a bend in the trail, and here a faint path heads 75 yards west over to a nearby campsite at the end of a short spur road. Past the campsite, the PCT soon parallels unseen Road 43 southeast to Road 417 (1120–0.8). Walking east 30 yards on this road, we locate the PCT's tread, which follows the road's north edge 120 yards to a road junction (1120–0.1). From here a road goes ½

mile southeast to the Wind River Ranger Station, which is near the picnic ground. Road 417 heads northwest along one edge of a tree farm while our trail heads east along its fenced-in south edge.

We briefly parallel the farm's east edge hiking northward, then in 100 yards angle northeast for a steepening walk up to the Bunker Hill Trail (1210–0.5), which switchbacks up to the summit. The PCT now winds, dips and climbs eastward along the hill's viewless, lower slopes, crosses a crest (1250–0.7), then descends north

H5

H5

see MAP H8

see MAP H6

Lake Nahe
4716
Rock Lake
Little Rock Lake
East Crater

H8

Lake Toke Tie

INDIAN

Lake
Umtux

Indian Heaven

Lake
Sahalee Tyee

HEAVEN

Blue
Lake

Gifford Peak
5368
Lake
Sebago

Tombstone Lake

EAST CRATER

48

6035

WILDERNESS

Dry

Cre

4987

Berry Mtn

Forlorn
Lks C G

Forlorn
Lakes

Creek

65

Trail
171

Spring Camp

040

6040

171A

Racetrack

CREST

4570

240

3600

Goose
Lake

Forest
Cam

60

N   C   H   O   T

4297

Red Mtn
Lookout
VABM 4968

Spring   Creek

BM 3452

300

Sheep
Lakes

ROAD

260

BM 3496

6048

TRAIL

The Wart

BM
3438

Crest C G
BM 3527

B
E
D

60

GULER

65

BM 3134

H9

gradually down to a crossing of Little Soda Springs Road 54 (940–0.8).

East of the road a row of trees bisects a large meadow, and our trail stays along the row's north side as it traverses east. It leaves this meadow just before crossing Wind River (940–0.3) on a major bridge, built in 1978, which is one of the largest bridges to be found along the entire PCT. You could camp in this vicinity, but Panther Creek Campground, less than an hour's walk ahead, is better for logistical reasons.

From this river we climb to busy Wind River Road (1020–0.2) and cross it just 0.2 mile northwest of this road's junction with Warren Gap Road 6517. The PCT starts a climb southeast, almost touches Road 6517, eventually crosses it (1180–0.8) just past Warren Gap, then winds east down to Panther Creek Road 65 (930–1.2). The entrance to Panther Creek Campground is just 230 yards up the road, opposite the end of Road 65. You should plan to camp there, for once you leave Panther Creek, you won't have any campsite with *good* water until Blue Lake, 23 miles farther.

From the Panther Creek Road, the PCT winds east 300 yards to Panther Creek and from it we switchback upward, passing two trickling springs long before we reach the westernmost end of a ridge (2100–2.3). Now we largely follow the old Big Huckleberry Trail up to Big

H5, H6

Fern-decked path north of Crest C.G.

Huckleberry Mountain. We start by paralleling a slightly climbing ridge crest northeast to a saddle (2300–1.1), from which a good dirt road starts a northeast descent and a vegetated one starts a southeast traverse. We take the vegetated road and follow it for 300 yards, curving around a brushy wash and then meeting a trail once again just before the road curves south around a ridge. We hike east, up this trail, recross the head of the wash, and wind around two minor ridges before coming to a saddle. This we cross; then, after a ½-mile climb across south slopes, our trail becomes an old road that quickly arrives at a junction with Road 68 (2810–1.3), on a saddle.

The trail continues east from the road, staying just south of the crest as it traverses a logged-out area, then, just before a saddle, curves around the forested south slopes of the ridge, soon returning to the crest. We now stay fairly close to the crest, which narrows to 5 feet in one spot, then descend to a broad, open saddle (3214–1.7). Now we climb, aided by occasional switchbacks, moderately up along the crest to a junction with the old Cascade Crest Trail (4000–2.2) near the summit of Big Huckleberry Mountain. From here we climb steeply for 130 yards up to a junction with the Big Huckleberry Mountain summit trail (4070–0.1), which climbs steeply east 200 yards to the summit.

Our path now eases off, curves northward and descends a "fog drip" ridge route, crosses a saddle ⅓ mile past our last junction, then skirts across slopes that give us views of Mt. Adams before we make a second saddle crossing (3730–1.2). Past it we descend to a gully (3550–0.5), which has a fairly reliable spring. This spring, 10.3 miles beyond Panther Creek, will probably be your last water until the Sheep Lakes, 7.0 miles farther. From this spring we contour northward through a shady forest of Douglas-fir, western hemlock and western white pine, reach a viewless, broad saddle (3580–0.8), and then wind down toward Road 6801, coming within 150 yards of it (3220–0.8) near an open saddle.

Contouring counterclockwise around Summit 4170, we follow the edge of geologically recent Big Lava Bed, cross one of its western overflow channels—which reveals the detailed intricacies of the flow—and then contour around another summit and cross another channel to the back of the Crest Campground (3490–3.5), which is on the south side of Carson-Guler Road 60.

H6, H7, H8

The campground has a horse corral but no water, so we pick our packs off the tables, put them on our backs and trudge north up the signed Pacific Crest Trail. This moderate ascent up a fern-decked path is really quite nice if you aren't running short of water. We climb to a flat and reach a duck pond (4020–1.9), which is no more than an oversized mud puddle after your arrival frightens the ducks away. Nevertheless, it boasts the name *Sheep Lake*. You can camp near it, if necessary. After climbing northwest through a more open forest, we enter Indian Heaven Wilderness and reach another pond, a 35-yard-wide puddle, Green Lake (4250–1.1), which gets as deep as a foot in early summer and serves as a vital water supply.

When one of the authors (Schaffer) visited this "lake" in late August 1973, it had just been converted into an oversized latrine by an unscrupulous packer and his family who let their eight horses defecate and stomp around in it. Having followed in his tracks for several days, I observed that he always let his horses do this, presumably after the family first got its share of water. I wish I could say that he was the only packer I encountered who had such disgusting trail manners, but in fact, *every* packer I saw camped near water disregarded the 200-foot Forest Service shoreline limit and allowed his animals to graze and defecate right up to the water.

Since you may find Green Lake too polluted to suit your standards, prepare for a dry march and start northwest past a meadow, then reach a junction with Shortcut Trail 171A (4240–0.4), which strikes west-northwest half a mile to a large, stagnant pond and to the Racetrack, which supposedly was used by Indian horsemen. We hike north-northwest through a forest, then climb several long switchbacks up the sunny south slope of Berry Mountain before reaching its crest. The abandoned Cascade Crest Trail, on the shady slopes way below us, led thirsty hikers past a spring. Our trail provides us with excellent views of Mt. St. Helens (8364) to the northwest, Mt. Adams (12,276) to the northeast and Mt. Hood (11,235) to the south. Upon reaching the north end of linear Berry Mountain, we descend short switchbacks to a saddle (4730–2.9), follow a rambling path down past the seasonal outlet creek of Lake Sebago (4640–0.9), and come to an overlook of a 100-yard-wide stagnant pond beyond which we finally reach the welcome, clear waters of Blue Lake (4630–0.2), nestled at the foot of Gifford Peak

(5368). Here you'll find the first good campsites since Panther Creek Campground, 23 miles back. Starting along the lake's east shore, Thomas Lake Trail 111 heads ¼ mile northwest over to an additional good campsite at shallow, circular Lake Sahalee Tyee. Camp at it if the Blue Lake campsites are full.

The Pacific Crest Trail, which barely touches Blue Lake, starts northeast from the lake's southeast corner, then winds north up to a west arm of East Crater. The trail curves northeast around this youthful feature, then angles north for a short drop to a junction with East Crater Trail 48 (4730–1.9), which starts along a skinny west finger of pleasant Junction Lake. You'll find a good campsite near its southwest shore and a poorer one near its northwest shore.

At the tip of the finger we cross the lake's outlet and meet Lemei Lake Trail 33A (4730–0.1), which climbs east before swinging north past Lemei Lake to Indian Heaven Trail. Whereas the old Cascade Crest Trail skirted along Indian Heaven's mosquito-populated ponds and lakes, the newer Pacific Crest Trail stays on lower slopes just east of and above them. We'll see parts of the old trail as we hike north toward Road 24.

By adhering to the lower slopes, the PCT avoids the bogs that were found along the old CCT, but in early season, snow patches may be quite a problem. One-quarter mile past our crossing of the usually dry Lemei Lake creek, we discover Elk Lake Trail 176 (4790-1.0). From above the southeast corner of Bear Lake, this trail first skirts along the southwest shore, offering you access to a campsite or two. Both Acker and Elk lakes, which are nearby, are less desirable. Onward, we traverse above Bear Lake and then over to a slope (4830-0.4) above the east end of Deer Lake, whose shoreline camps are fewer and poorer than those at Bear Lake. Rounding slopes above the lake, we meet Indian Heaven Trail 33 (4880-0.1). This 3.8-mile-long trail takes the long way out to fairly large, and often popular, Cultus Creek Campground, which usually has a summertime host present, should you need help. By going just ⅓ mile on this trail, you can reach an adequate campsite by the northeast corner of Clear Lake. A couple of more remote lake campsites can be reached with some cross-country effort.

With no more trailside lakes before Road 24, we continue north, pass two seasonal ponds and

H8   **H8, H9**

then soon reach Placid Lake Trail 29 (4980-1.1), offering neither nearby camps nor water. Still northbound, we cross a saddle, then traverse northeast to another one, almost touching the old Cascade Crest Trail at each. At the second (5110-0.5) you can hop on the old CCT and follow it 150 yards down to a campsite by a pleasant, unnamed lakelet. From that lakelet, Wood Lake Trail 185 heads ½ mile northwest over to its namesake, which is not worth a visit.

Staying high, the PCT contours around the lakelet and soon meets an old, supposedly abandoned trail climbing ¼ mile northeast from it. At this junction we also meet the west end of Cultus Creek Trail 108 (5150-0.4). This climbs briefly northeast to a wooded saddle, then drops 1.5 miles at a hefty 15% gradient to the aforementioned Cultus Creek Campground, along Road 24.

Our trail now stays close to a well-defined crest, which it eventually crosses and thereby gives us views of massive Mt. Adams and the terrain being logged around it. Just past our crest crossing, the trail heads briefly south, only to switchback north and descend to a crest saddle. At the switchback you'll see a prominent huckleberry field just below you, with berries in season from about mid-August until mid-September. You might sample these if you haven't already made a side trip to huckleberry fields back near Indian Heaven.

From the crest saddle (4850–1.2) a 1.7-mile-long footpath switchbacks almost up to the knife-edge crest of Sawtooth Mountain before switchbacking down to the PCT. From the serrated crest, which can be reached by a short scramble, you get an exhilarating view down its east cliff as well as an unobstructed view of Mt. Adams. On a clear day you also see three other snowy peaks: distant Mt. Hood in the south, bleak Mt. St. Helens in the west-northwest, and distant Mt. Rainier in the north.

The PCT stays low as it traverses north gently down the west slopes of Sawtooth Mountain to a reunion with that summit's footpath (4570–

H9

H9

see MAP H11

see MAP H9

1.4). It then leaves Indian Heaven Wilderness as it descends into the Sawtooth Huckleberry Field, reaches a spur road, and parallels it 60 yards northeast to a signed PCT crossing of Road 24 (4260–1.2). The large berry field at this flat was being harvested by Indians when George B. McClellan's exploration party came through in 1854. Needless to say, it had probably been harvested for countless generations. Roads were built up to it around the turn of the century, and today the Indians have exclusive rghts only to the berries *east* of the road. Frankly, we were hard-pressed to find many bushes on that side, and wondered whether some midnight raiding party of pioneers had transplanted some of the bushes to the west side.

Our trail now descends gently east-northeast, enters forest, and passes above the little developed Surprise Lakes Campground, which is for *Indians* only. Continuing northeast on the 1972 Surprise-Steamboat lakes section of the PCT, we descend to a saddle (4070–1.4), then climb northwest up this well-graded trail and round the west slopes of East Twin Butte (4690). We reach a platform between the two Twin Buttes, which are obvious cinder cones, descend northwest below unseen, dumpy Saddle Campground, switchback northeast, and descend to a crossing of a trickling creek immediately before reaching Road 8851 (3915–2.5) at a junction 35 yards southeast of the west-trending Little Mosquito Lake road. Our trail bears northeast from Road 8851 and quickly reaches the wide, refreshing outlet creek from Big Mosquito Lake (3892).

The PCT leaves the creek and climbs gently east along the upper margin of a sheep-inhabited clearing, then rounds a spur and shortly crosses a dirt road (4090–2.5) that snakes northwest 130 yards up to Road 8854. We continue northeast and descend to a small gully with a seasonal creek, and here the Steamboat Lake spur trail (3980–0.4) climbs north moderately 0.2 mile up to that lake (4022), from which you can then follow an east shoreline road northward. By the time you've reached the lake's northeast corner, this road deteriorates to a log-strewn trail. Then you can take a steep trail northeast up to Road 8854 and small, waterless Steamboat Lake Campground, ¾ mile from the PCT. At the northeast edge of the camp, a ½-mile-long trail descends to a shallow, unnamed lake and then rejoins the PCT at a bend.

From the Steamboat Lake spur-trail junction, the PCT curves counterclockwise from the gully and makes a gentle descent to an outlet creek 70 yards downstream from an unseen, unnamed lake, then climbs briefly northward to a saddle, where it meets the end of the alternate trail (3970–0.8), which climbs west to Steamboat Lake Campground. Here our trail descends first northeast, then east, weaving through a quiet forest down to a junction with Road 88 (3470–1.2). The swath this road cuts through this forest is so oriented that we have an open view directly at Mt. Adams.

H10, H11

see MAP H10

see MAP H12

H9, H10

TROUT LAKE 11 MI.

Our trail recommences at a large sign 50 yards northeast up this road, and on it we top a minor ridge before descending to three-yard-wide Trout Lake Creek (3310–0.4). North of the trail at a point 25 yards east of this creek, we see a very good campsite, and 100 yards later we cross the smaller Grand Meadows Creek. Our trail now ascends eastward, steeply at times, but momentarily descends to a tributary before making a final, stiff climb up to Road 8810 (4140–2.1). Continuing east up the slope, we reach the crest (4570–0.6), then begin a gen-

erally descending route north-northeast along the ridge down to a trailhead at Road 8810 (3854–2.7). We walk east 50 yards to this road's junction with north-trending Road 23 and a trailhead for the Mt. Adams Wilderness.

Our trail drops to a two-yard-wide creek just east of Road 23, then climbs north around the slopes of a low summit to a crossing of east-trending Road 521 (4020–0.9). After hiking ¼ mile north, we reach a small, good campsite near a bridge over a permanent creek. In the next ¾ mile we cross two usually flowing creeks.

H11, H12

H12

see MAP H12

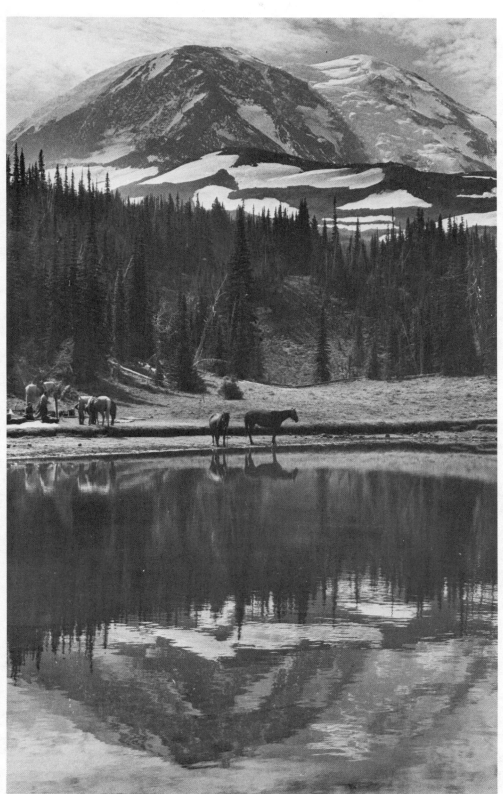

Mt. Adams and Adams Glacier

see MAP H15

H14

see MAP H13

Now we continue up an increasingly steep trail to the Mt. Adams Wilderness boundary, switchback northeast, traverse east, and finally drop gently to a barely recognizable, often dry creek known as the White Salmon River. About 100 yards past it (4900–2.7) you'll see a spring gushing from thick vegetation 50 yards below the trail. This is your last reliable water until Sheep Lake, 6.5 miles later.

Our trail then switchbacks, crosses the "river" in a shady bowl, switchbacks again, and then makes a long, snaking ascent to a junction with Stagman Ridge Trail 12 (5790–2.5), which starts a descent south. Pressing onward, we climb east up to a junction with Round the Mountain Trail 9 (5900–0.5). This traverses ¼ mile east to dry Dry Lake Camp, then continues 6¼ miles to Timberline Camp, above the end of Road 8040. The easiest and most popular route to the summit of Mt. Adams (12,276) starts there and climbs up the south ridge. You should have no trouble attaining the summit in good weather, for this is the route that mule trains used in the 1930s. Back then, a sulfur claim had been staked out on the summit, but it didn't pay off. This massive andesitic stratovolcano, like the others we've seen, should still be considered active. Its last eruption may have been 1000 to 2000 years ago, and in May 1921 its near-surface magma generated enough heat to initiate a large snow slide that eradicated the forest on the slope below it.

On the high slopes east of our junction with Trail 9, we can see the White Salmon Glacier. Some PCT mountaineers prefer to climb Mt. Adams via that icy route, which starts from our junction and crosses Horseshoe Meadow.

The Pacific Crest Trail climbs northwest around a ridge that separates this glacier from the Pinnacle Glacier, immediately north of it. Our northward, round-the-mountain route is quite a contrast with that of Mt. Hood; it stays at a relatively constant elevation, and where it climbs or descends, it usually does so on a gentle gradient. To the north and northwest, we can often see Goat Rocks and Mt. Rainier. After traversing to a saddle (5950–3.2) just east of Burnt Rock, our trail descends toward 70-yard-wide, 5-foot-deep Sheep Lake (5768–0.3), which is 40 yards northwest of the trail, then reaches milky jump-across Riley Creek (5770–0.2).

Next on our menu, Mutton Creek (5900–1.3) is approached, and we follow it up beside a geologically recent, rather barren lava flow over

which we eventually diagonal quite a distance up. Our route then bounds from one wash to the next, crosses milky Lewis River (6060–1.3), and in 200 yards reaches a spur trail that goes 110 yards north to a viewpoint. From it you'll see distant, snowy Mt. Rainier standing above a nearer, clearcut-patched landscape. Our PCT quickly crosses some silty tributaries of West Fork Adams Creek before it curves north-northwest to a junction with Divide Camp Trail 112 (6020–0.3), which descends northwest toward Road 2329. Directly upslope from us is the overpowering, steeply descending Adams Glacier, which appears to be a gigantic frozen waterfall rather than an advancing snowfield. Along our journey north, our glances back toward this massive peak will always single out this prominent feature.

We head northeast across a 330-yard swath of bouldery glacier outwash sediments, then jump across silty Middle Fork Adams Creek. After climbing its bank, our route contours northeast past a 70-yard-wide pond (6110), and in a few minutes we arrive at a junction with Killen Creek Trail 113 (6084–1.4), which starts beside a seasonal creek as it descends northwest toward Road 2329. We contour onward, descend to a large flat through which flows clear Killen Creek, then cross this creek as it reaches a brink (5920–0.8) and cascades merrily down 30 feet to a small meadow and a beautiful campsite nestled under a cluster of subalpine firs.

As we are about to head north away from the mountain, we reflect upon another charac-teristic of this crescentic trail which distin-guishes it from its counterpart on Mt. Hood: this trail stays on the mountain's lower slopes, and we never feel like we've set foot on the mountain itself—the upper slopes don't begin until a "distant" 2000 feet above us. In this respect, the trail resembles those around Mt. Jefferson and the Three Sisters. A short distance from the campsite, our trial meets Highline Trail 114 (5900–0.2), upon which you may find *foot-prints* leading east toward the Yakima Indian Reservation. About 100 yards along this trail you'll find a shallow lakelet, near which you can camp.

Just north beyond this junction we spy a 70-yard pond a hundred yards northwest of us. It is better to descend 80 feet down the slope to this pond than to continue onward to a second, readily accessible one (5772–0.4) that receives too much impact from packers. The PCT now becomes a rambling, evenly graded pathway

H12, H13　　　　　　　　**H13, H14**

see MAP H14

that descends north-northeast into a subalpine-fir/lodgepole-pine forest whose monotony is broken by an intersection with a trail (5231–2.0), which starts east-northeast toward a junction two miles later with the Highline Trail.

Meeting no traffic other than perhaps chickadees or juncos, we continue northward and eventually reach a sturdy bridge across the 5-yard-wide Muddy Fork (4740–1.6), by which we find a small campsite. Curving northwest, our path soon reaches and then parallels an alder-and-willow-lined silty creek westward to a very good campsite (4590–0.5), nestled between two of this creek's branches. A short distance farther we round the nose of a recent lava flow and head north to the vibrant, crystal-clear waters gushing from trailside Lava Spring (4520–0.3) at the foot of the flow. Since its water is among the best you'll find along the *entire* PCT, you might as

well rest and enjoy it. An American dipper—a drab, chunky bird—may be camped here.

Leaving it, we follow the 40-foot-high edge of the flow a short way, leave Mt. Adams Wilderness, then climb gently through a predominantly lodgepole forest to a small trailhead parking lot a few yards north of paved Road 5603 (4750–1.6). From the lot we walk northeast 50 yards along an old jeep road, then veer north-northeast along a trail that ascends gently toward Potato Hill (5387). Although motorized vehicles are specifically barred from the PCT, they or their tracks are likely to be encountered along this rather unscenic stretch through second-growth forest. We quickly reach the jeep road again and follow its northwest-curving path around Potato Hill, then take this dusty road north-northwest past huckleberries and mountain ash to a junction with Road 115

H14

H14, H15

H16

GOAT ROCKS WILDERNESS

YAKIMA INDIAN RESERVATION

(4490–2.0). By walking 0.3 mile west on it, you'll reach the site of Midway Guard Station (which burned down in 1976) beside Road 2329 and Midway Creek. Although you can't pick up mailed packages as you could in the "good old days," you can find ample room to camp. We walk 50 yards up a road, then branch left for a grassy diagonal up a trail to closed Road 655 (4520–0.1), which descends west-southwest 0.1 mile to Road 115. We'll walk across no more roads until at Highway 12 near White Pass, 40½ miles distant.

Our trail starts west-northwest up toward Midway Creek, crosses it (4690–0.4), then climbs up through alternating forested and

cleared land toward the crest. As the gradient eases off, we enter forest for good and follow a winding path that takes us past eight stagnant ponds. You could have an adequate campsite at any of them if you're willing to purify the water. After leaving the last pond (5070–2.8), on our left (west), we hike around the west slope of a knoll, descend gently to the west side of a broad saddle, then climb moderately to a switchback (5220–1.6), from which Trail 121 descends to Walupt Lake Horse Camp. Now within Goat Rocks Wilderness, we climb east to a saddle (5450–0.7), and pass two small ponds, on the left. We then climb north to a prominent ridgecrest (5600–0.8), that stands directly south

H15
Mt. Adams, from Sheep Lake campsite

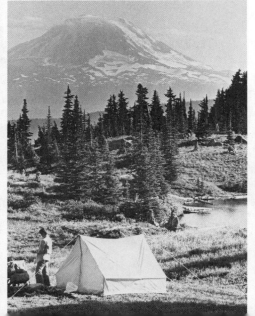

H15, H16
Ives Peak and Cispus River headwaters

H17

YAKIMA INDIAN RESERVATION

GIFFORD   PINCHOT   NATIONAL   FOREST

GOAT   ROCKS   WILDERNESS

Nannie Peak

WALUPT LAKE

of Walupt Lake (3926). North of us we see the glistening summit of Old Snowy Mountain (7930), in the heart of the Goat Rocks country, over whose slopes we must soon climb.

Our route now winds southeastward down auxiliary ridges and enters a forest of mountain hemlock, western white and lodgepole pines, and Alaska yellow cedar. We pass near two undesirable ponds before we cross a trickling creek (5140–1.4) that you shouldn't overlook, for it contains the best water you'll taste for miles. After descending gently eastward, we curve counterclockwise around boggy Coleman Weedpatch to a 50-yard pond (5050–0.5). An old trail east from it goes to a nearby, shallow lake (5058) on a forested, flat saddle immediately within the Yakima Indian Reservation. On the PCT we arc eastward, north of the unseen lake, then follow our easy path northwest through a dense mountain-hemlock forest across the lower slopes of Lakeview Mountain (6660). As we veer east, our forest transforms into an open stand of lodgepoles, and we finally curve southeast to a junction with Walupt Lake Trail 101 (4960–3.4), which goes 4.4 miles to its trailhead at Walupt Lake Campground. You will find several fair-to-good campsites ⅓ to ½ mile down this trail.

Beyond the junction the countryside is quite open, and the topography stretches out below us as we hike the trail up the west slope of a long, north-trending ridge. Fireweed, yarrow, lupine and pearly everlasting proliferate along the trailside before we reach the shady confines of a coniferous forest. We now contour for several miles before reaching the diminutive headwaters

Glacier-striated rocks

of Walupt Creek (5480–3.9). If there were enough level ground here, a primitive campsite by the stream would be nice. Instead, it is better to continue west up toward a saddle where you'll see shallow, clear 130-yard-long Sheep Lake (5710), which has good but open campsites. Just north of it, we meet a junction, with Nannie Ridge Trail 98 (5760–0.6), which descends 4.5 miles to its trailhead at mile-long Walupt Lake.

Our route north through the Goat Rocks country will take us on ridges high above glaciated canyons. Walupt Creek canyon was the first major one we've seen in this wilderness, and the ones north of it are even more

H16, H17   H17

Forty-foot-high "Split Rock" along PCT

see MAP H19

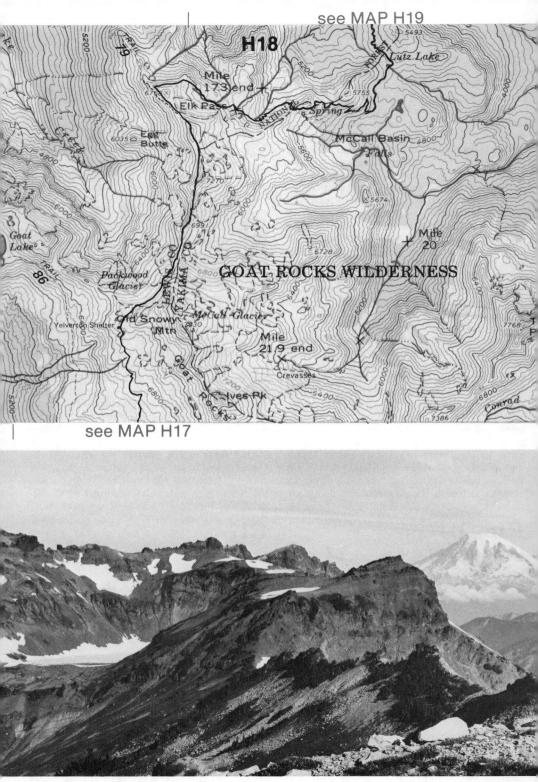

H18

GOAT ROCKS WILDERNESS

see MAP H17

Goat Lake and Mt. Rainier

spectacular. From our junction we descend ⅓ mile before diagonaling up a mid-70s stretch of PCT to a crest saddle (6100–1.4). Now in Yakima Indian territory, we traverse north across barren slopes that have snow patches through most of the summer. Our trail steepens as it approaches often snowbound Cispus Pass (6460–0.9), where we leave the Indian reservation.

Our timberline trail drops north and passes by dwarfed specimens of mountain hemlock and subalpine fir as it descends toward the headwaters of the Cispus River. The basin is much smaller than it first appears, and we quickly reach an open campsite beside the easternmost tributary (6130–0.6). The scale of the canyon is put in true perspective when backpackers hike past miniature conifers that are now seen as only 30 feet high instead of as 80, as we originally presupposed. After descending west, we jump across the base of a splashing, 20-foot-high waterfall, then make a winding contour to a junction with Trail 86 (5930-1.6). This trail goes 0.6 mile west down to wind-shielded Bypass Camp, on the east side of Snowgrass Creek. West, the trail continues 0.2 mile to Trail 96, which offers the shortest route into the Goat Rocks area. Trail 96 goes about 3 miles southwest to a fork, from which the south branch goes over to a nearby hikers' trailhead on spur road 405, and the north branch goes about ⅓ mile farther to an equestrian's trailhead near the end of Road 2150.

Leaving the Trail 86 junction, the PCT switchbacks up to a saddle, traverses slopes above Snowgrass Flat, and arrives at the Trail 96 junction (6420-1.0). After a fairly steep climb north for 0.2 mile, you pass the old junction with the abandoned route of the old Trail 96, which is about 40 yards from a 40-foot-high "Split Rock." This broke apart eons ago, for full-sized conifers now grow in the gap between the two halves.

Our route next climbs north-northeast up past the rock, then switchbacks west, over to a nearby ridge. From about this point north to Elk Pass and then east to the saddle above McCall Basin, you can expect to find quite a number of snowfields through most of the summer. About ¾ mile past the newer Trail 96 junction, we tread across rocks with deep striations, convincing "fingerprints" of past glaciers. Climbing up to the low west ridge of Old Snowy Mountain, we find the Dana May Yelverton Shelter (7040-1.1), 12 feet square, which provides plenty of protection from the frequent summer storms (no

fires allowed). The 6-inch-high junipers here attest to the severity of this environment. Above us lies the realm of rock and ice—the habitat of the alpine mountaineer.

As you climb briefly north from the shelter, you may see one or two low windbreaks, neither giving you much protection if you are caught in a storm. Crossing a snowfield takes us to the brink of the severely glaciated, 3000-foot-deep Upper Lake Creek canyon, which will become even more impressive as our northbound trail provides us with even better views down and across it. To the northwest we see usually frozen Goat Lake (6450) nestled in a classic glacial cirque at the southeast end of the Johnson Peak ridge. At the brink, ¼ mile beyond the shelter, former hikers used to start a traverse northeast across the gentle upper slopes of the Packwood Glacier, rather than climb 550 feet higher to the north shoulder of Old Snowy Mountain (7930)—the route that is sometimes passable for stock. In 1978 the Forest Service blasted a route that more or less follows the one taken by former hikers. Typically, it is mostly snowbound and potentially dangerous, and therefore is not much different from the pre-trail traverse. When you start across it, you leave the highest PCT point in Washington—7080 feet.

In a way it is unfortunate that the old trail up Old Snowy is not taken by everyone, for from it you have an almost full-circle panorama of the Goat Rocks country. Looking above the canyons to the northwest, you see the monarch of the Cascade Range—mighty Mt. Rainier (14,410)—ruling above all the other stratovolcanoes. To the south is Mt. Adams (12,276), the crown prince and third highest peak in the range (California's Mt. Shasta, at 14,162, rivals Mt. Rainier in size). Off to Adams' west lies the youthful princess, Mt. St. Helens (8364). The Multnomah Indians had a legend about these two peaks and about Mt. Hood (11,235), the Cascades' fourth highest peak. They said a feud developed between Klickitat (Adams) and Wyeast (Hood) over the beautiful Squaw Mountain (St. Helens), who had just moved into the neighborhood. (In geological terms, it is the youngest of these stratovolcanoes.) She loved Wyeast, but Klickitat triumphed in a fight, so she had to reside in Klickitat's domain. She refused to bed down with him, however, and after a while, as would be expected, his flames of love for her died, and both volcanoes became dormant. A modern-day account would say she couldn't stand Klickitat any longer, so finally on

H17, H18   **H18**

May 18, 1980, she blew her top. Literally. You'll find traces of Mt. St. Helens' ash along the PCT in much of Section H.

The newer PCT cuts rather precariously across the upper part of Packwood Glacier before curving north down to a crest saddle (6850-1.0). This Egg Butte section of the PCT, constructed with heroic efforts in 1953-54, now continues along the jagged ridge, contours around its "teeth" and provides us with alpine views across McCall Glacier toward Tieton Peak (7768), due east of Old Snowy. We reach a small saddle, from which the trail makes a precarious descent across a steep slope as it bypasses summit 7210. You can expect this narrow footpath to be snowbound and hazardous through most of July. Crampons may be required, particularly in early summer, and stock animals may be forced back. Reaching the ridge again, we follow it down to Elk Pass, where we meet the upper end of Coyote Trail 79 (6680-1.3). Here the windswept whitebark pines stand chest-high at most, and the junipers creep but inches above the frost-wedged rocks.

Pushing toward supplies at White Pass, we first drop northwest, paralleling Coyote Trail 79, below us, then in ⅓ mile angle east across the sometimes snowy north slopes of Peak 6768. We trade breathtaking views down Upper Lake Creek canyon, to the northwest, for views north down larger Clear Fork Cowlitz River canyon. Just below the peak's northeast ridge, we reach bleak, alpine campsites (6320-0.3), which you would not want to use unless you absolutely had no choice. If you're hiking south, these are the last campsites you'll see until the west flank of Old Snowy.

Our trail descends east-southeast to the foot of the Elk Pass snowfield, down which hikers sometimes ski. We cross its runoff creek and several others, pass by glacially striated bedrock, and then slip and slide down short, steep switchbacks etched on a narrow ridge. The grade abates and ends near a small pond at the foot of another snowfield. By late afternoon the snowfields in this basin are melting at a good rate, as evidenced by the roar of the cascade to the west. From the pond we now switchback steeply but briefly up to a saddle (5820-1.3). From it the Cascade Crest Trail formerly dropped east-southeast to wet, meadowy, overused McCall Basin, but the PCT switchbacks east. It almost touches a crest saddle (5580-0.6), on which one could set up an emergency camp, then it switch-

H18

H18

Old Snowy Mountain and McCall Glacier

H19

Campground
Leech
Lake

White Pass

South

HIGHWAY 12

HOGBACK

1144

Creek

Picnic Area

Knuppenburg
Lake

Millridge

Ginnette
Lake

Hell Lake

JEEP

5967

TRAIL

5401

5200

5600

Hogback Ridge

6000

Miriam

6375

4800

Hogback
Mtn

Miriam
Lake

5663

6783

6000

6406

6717

Shoe Lake

6650

6000

Scatter

Creek

6427

5600

5723

1207

Fork

Hidden
Spring

North

Fork

1117

TRAIL

1118

Mile
15

Mile
15

3320

TRAIL 61

5535

BOUNDARY

Tieton Pass

NORTH

TIETON

Tieton
Meadows

Clear

Fork

River

Mile
15

GOAT ROCKS WILDERNESS

GOAT ROCKS WILDERNESS

Mt. Rainier above the Chimney Rock-Elk Pass crest

backs down into forest cover to a junction with the old CCT (5200-0.5). Following it about ¼ mile southwest would take you down to McCall Basin.

On the PCT we traverse over to a saddle that holds knee-deep Lutz Lake and several small campsites (5100-0.6). Beyond this viewless spot we descend north around the west slope of Peak 5493 to Tieton Pass (4570-1.0). Here by a dry campsite, North Fork Tieton Trail 1118, which at 4.6 miles is the shortest trail approach to this pass, descends east before curving northeast down to North Fork Tieton Road 1207. You can usually find creek water by descending about ¼ mile along this trail. Clear Fork Trail 61, starting a moderate descent west-northwest from Tieton Pass, takes a long way out toward U.S. Highway 12.

H18, H19   H19

Mt. Rainier poking above Shoe Lake-Hogback Mountain crest

Our trail starts a gentle descent northwest, gradually makes a winding route north past two stagnant ponds, then crosses east over the divide (4930-1.5) and rounds Peak 5472. We now continue on our viewless path east until we climb the southeast spur of Peak 6427 and then reach a junction with Trail 1117 (5520-1.8). This first goes about 280 yards east to the abandoned northern segment of the Shoe Lake Trail. On this trail you can head southeast about a similar distance to an area with several small campsites. One or more short spur trails in this vicinity head east to Hidden Spring, which lies just above a beautiful meadow. Note that this is your last real opportunity for camping and for good water this side of U.S. Highway 12, about 8.5 trail miles from the spring.

On the PCT we climb north, then northwest, and where an old segment of the PCT bends northeast, we branch west (6040-0.9) on a mid '80s segment. This first curves southwest as it climbs toward Peak 6427, then it curves north, leaving forest cover as it approaches a ridge. This we cross and then traverse steep slopes on the west side of Peak 6652. These at first are bouldery and open, and we have views west into deep Clear Fork Cowlitz River canyon, whose floor lies a half mile below our trail. Boulders give way to firs and hemlocks, and through midsummer, some snow problems. We soon recross the ridge and have views southeast of Shoe Lake as we contour over to the old Shoe Lake segment of the PCT. Overuse at the lake led to the creation of the newer, less desirable route. We meet the old segment, which still switchbacks down to the lake (no camping allowed!), and then in 90 yards top a narrow ridge (6620-1.2). From it we see Mt. Rainier poke its head above Hogback Ridge while Mt. Adams just manages to lift its crown above Goat Rocks.

The volcanic flows around us here superficially resemble sedimentary rocks, for they have broken along close, evenly spaced horizontal joints to give the illusion of alternating, stepped beds of sandstone and shale. We make one switchback, descend a well-graded trail past a thumb above us and Miriam Lake below, then reach the stepped slope of Hogback Mountain (6789). As we descend its northeast ridge, we obtain more views of Mt. Rainier, then we enter forest once again, cross a vaguely defined sad-dle, and climb gently to a nearby junction with Chairlift Trail 1112 (5830-2.5).

*   *   *   *

This shortcut route to White Pass is used mainly by day hikers, who start below at the White Pass ski lodge (4480). Trail 1112 goes about 500 yards north to a tight bend in the chairlift's road, which you then follow north 330 steep yards up to the lift (5961). In 1989 it cost $3 for a one-way ride down to the ski lodge, and the lift ran from 9 A.M. to about 4:30 P.M. from late June until mid September. The lodge houses the Continental Cafe, open year-round. From it you can walk east 100 yards to White Pass Village, with its Nor'wester Restaurant, then 70 yards more to the Kracker Barrel Grocery and post office at a gas station. Minimal supplies are available here but you can wash your clothes and make a phone call home. A half-mile walk northeast on U.S. Highway 12 takes you to the Leech Lake spur road, just beyond which the PCT crosses the highway.

*   *   *   *

From the Trail 1112 junction the PCT makes a viewless, winding descent northeastward to a junction with little-used Hogback Trail 1144 (5400-1.2), which starts on a gentle descent east before curving north. Our trail curves northwest, passes a small, stagnant pond, and reaches green, 100-yard-long Ginnette Lake (5400-0.2). We now leave Goat Rocks Wilderness, get a glimpse of the chair-lift jeep road northwest of us, and then switchback down to a trailhead parking lot 50 yards south of U.S. Highway 12 (old state Highway 14) (4405-2.2). The short road to the trailhead begins just 30 yards east of the Leech Lake spur road to White Pass Campground. About 200 yards up that spur road, where it bends from west to north, an old, closed road starts south and then quickly bends southwest for a rambling traverse over to White Pass Village, reaching a north-south road that starts from the west side of the village. This usually soggy, mosquito-ridden route is supposedly for campers, hikers and equestrians, but Schaffer much prefers walking southwest along the broad highway shoulder to reach the Kracker Barrel Grocery and White Pass Village.

H19   **H19**

Section I: Highway 12 near White Pass to Interstate 90 at Snoqualmie Pass

Introduction: Graphic contrasts in land use separate Section I into two very different segments. The southern half is largely a subalpine parkland glistening with lakes cupped in forests and meadows. Long-appreciated, most of this backcountry lies protected within the boundaries of two recently designated (1984) wilderness areas and Mt. Rainier National Park. The northern half, on the other hand, being lower, is totally within the montane forest belt so favored by the lumber industry, and it blisters with a lot of barren earth, some of the most extensively clear-cut land in the West.

Moderate topography characterizes both halves of Section I, and fit border-bound hikers can make good time. From White Pass the trail sloshes through soggy muskeg country, crossing a plateau pocked with pools and lakes. As the Cascade divide rises into a knobby backbone, the trail follows it faithfully, swinging from saddle to subalpine saddle, passing within 12 miles of massive Mt. Rainier. Not quite one third of the way through Section I at Chinook Pass, the broadest of these flower-rich saddles, State Highway 410 crosses the crest.

Halfway through Section I the craggy divide slopes below the subalpine zone, and though fir and hemlock forests dominate here, meadows and crest-top vistas keep the hiking varied and interesting. Still 40 miles from Snoqualmie Pass, the trail enters land shared in a checkerboard pattern by the Forest Service and Burlington Northern railroad. The railroad received title to every other square mile during the railroad subsidies of the 1880s in return for laying tracks across Stampede Pass. Neither owner being fully responsible for the territory, the forests have been mined, and nearly one half of this last stretch goes through clearcuts laced with logging roads and bulldozer tracks. By 1984 most of the Burlington Northern sections that the PCT passes through had been logged and the trail permanently rerouted through them, whereas most of the Forest Service sections were roaded but still holding their forests.

Declination: 19½°E

Mileages:	South to North	Distances between Points	North to South
Highway 12 near White Pass	0.0		98.6
Buesch Lake	5.9	5.9	92.7
Bumping River ford by Bumping Lake Trail........	14.6	8.7	84.0
Dewey Lake...........................	26.3	11.7	72.3
Highway 410 at Chinook Pass	29.5	3.2	69.1
Sheep Lake	31.7	2.2	66.9
Big Crow Basin Spring near Norse Peak Trail	40.2	8.5	58.4
Arch Rock shelter spur trail	47.3	7.1	51.3
Camp Urich at Government Meadow	52.3	5.0	46.3
Unnamed spring 2.1 mi. n.e. of Windy Gap........	57.1	4.8	41.5
Granite Creek Trail on Blowout Mountain	63.1	6.0	35.5
Sheets Pass	71.1	8.0	27.5
Stampede Pass	80.4	9.3	18.2
Stirrup Creek..................................	85.5	5.1	13.1
Mirror Lake...................................	89.9	4.4	8.7
Lodge Lake	96.8	6.9	1.8
Interstate 90 at Snoqualmie Pass.................	98.6	1.8	0.0

Supplies: Restaurant food, post offices, and the typically minimal foodstuffs can be found at White Pass and Snoqualmie Pass (see page 225). Similar amenities can be found about one third of the way north from White Pass, at Crystal Mountain, a couple miles away from and 1400 feet below the PCT. Snoqualmie Pass also features a bed and breakfast inn popular with PCT hikers (see page 253).

Wilderness Permits: No wilderness permits are required along this section, unless you venture some distance west of the PCT into Mt. Rainier National Park (see page 20).

Problems: Mosquitoes can be especially bad in the marshy terrain north of White Pass. On the crest-top route between Government Meadow and Stampede Pass, though, water is scarce, partly because logging has obliterated some springs. By mid-July only one reliable water source can be found for the last 23 miles of this stretch, and even it is somewhat inconvenient. In early season, snow clinging to north and east slopes between Bumping River and Blowout Mountain can make carrying an ice axe worthwhile.

In some of the logged areas, blowdowns and generally battered soil make following the trail less than easy, although few hikers get off route. The trail crosses many logging roads and follows a few for very short distances. *Most* of these crossings and followings are clearly posted with PCT emblems or diamonds, but a few require a brief search. Finally, active logging operations can temporarily reroute the PCT, in which case hikers follow impromptu signs, blazes and surveyor's tapes.

Hikers driving to White Pass will want to turn north off Highway 12 just 0.5 mile northeast of White Pass and park, after 0.2 mile, at the trailhead parking lot near Leech Lake. The PCT crosses Highway 12 only 30 yards east of the Leech Lake PCT trailhead turnoff and passes an old shelter on its way to this parking lot.

Pulverized duff and "trail apples" evince this trail section's popularity with horsemen as we start from the lot (4415–0.2) in a gentle switchbacking climb, crossing a bulldozer track before entering William O. Douglas Wilderness. A staunch conservationist, the late Supreme Court Justice Douglas grew up near

I1   **I1**

I1

see MAP H19

Sand Lake

Yakima, and he hiked throughout his life in the lands now named after him, loving the area enough, despite his world travels, to establish his home in Goose Prairie, on the Bumping River. After leveling out in the fir-and-spruce forest, we pass a junction with Dark Meadows Trail 1107 (4780–1.1), which descends east to Dog Lake. Resuming a gradual climb, we skirt a meadow, rise beside and then cross Deer Lake's outlet creek, and switchback up to a much larger meadow just before reaching Deer Lake (5206-1.0). Here there is an extensive and beaten-down camping area.

Ahead, a barely ascending walk north through forest and lupine-rich glades brings us to Sand Lake (5295–0.5) where, from the base of the lake's peninsula, a spur leads south to a renovated shelter that's barely large enough to sleep three. Just beyond this spur a sign points west to Highway 12, along obscure Sand Lake Trail 60. We, however, continue north on an essentially level track, noting the curious spikes of beargrass, and meet Cortright Creek Trail 57 (5520-2.0) coming from the southwest. Under subalpine firs we contour around a rocky knob to a gap, where we start winding down a few steep switchbacks.

The brief descent ends at Buesch Lake (5081–1.1), entry point onto the heart of the plateau that caps this part of the gentle divide

between the Cowlitz and Yakima rivers. Andesite lavas erupted in the Pliocene and Pleistocene epochs to form this plateau, and during the cooler Pleistocene, a small ice cap formed over it and helped smooth it out. For half a dozen miles now the trail runs across hummocky flatlands riddled with ponds, puddles, mudholes and muskeg. Patchily forested with droopy hemlocks and pointy subalpine firs, and carpeted with heather, huckleberry and azalea, this area supports only acid-tolerant plants.

We turn east along the north shore of Buesch Lake and soon come to Dumbbell Lake Trail 56, which forks south between two pools. From here we curve north to pass within close view of Pipe Lake and then pass a long, slender lake with a good picnic spot (5180-1.1). A few minutes north from here we arc northeast around a couple of grassy ponds and arrive at ill-defined Cowlitz Pass (5160-0.5). In this open area, snags from an old fire stand over spiraea and azalea, and allow a view of Mt. Rainier. Trail 44 heads east from here for Shellrock Lake.

The PCT soon turns northwest, leaves the westbound stretch of Cowlitz Trail 44 (5140-0.2), and starts a twisting, winding course, first northeast, then trending northwest. Although the topo map shows almost no contours through here, dozens of hillocks and gullies dimple this land, and the trail takes great pains to avoid every hint of meadow or soggy ground. On our way we pass just north of one unnamed lake, and wind into dark forest, then down to Snow Lake (4935-2.1).

We cross a bridge over Snow Lake's outlet and weave a north-trending course, barely descending. Peeking in and out of fir groves, we come to Twin Sisters Trail 980 tracking east, then intersect Pothole Trail 45 (4900-0.8), which to the south meets Trail 44 and to the north parallels us east of the PCT. Still avoiding meadows while trending north-northwest, we hike just west of a creek that is gradually gathering water and momentum. Our track channels into a steady, gentle descent as we pass the forested slopes of Fryingpan Mountain, and a junction with southbound Jug Lake Trail 43. With more easy walking we come to a bridge over the creek, at a packer campsite (4620-2.9).

From this bridge the PCT skirts east of a large meadow and decidedly drops off the Cowlitz-Yakima plateau. The steady descent ends at the outlet of Fish Lake (4100-1.1), headwaters of the Bumping River. Across this creek is a large campsite and a junction with Bumping Lake

I1   **I1, I2, I3**

Trail 971, where our path cuts west to touch the north shore of long, shallow Fish Lake. It promptly leaves the lakeside path and starts working up long switchbacks that take us above Buck Lake, across Crag Lake's outlet, and then back to a spur that drops to Crag Lake itself, where there are some comfortable campsites. As the PCT contours just beyond this spur, it passes a reliable drinkable rill (5170-2.7).

A couple more long, lazy switchbacks have us rising across meadowy slopes verdant with aster, spiraea, blueberry, and corn lily. Marveling at Mts. Rainier, Adams and St. Helens, we then turn north around the Cascade divide and pass Laughingwater Trail 22 (5690–1.6), which drops southwest. Here at the start of a long tour high along the Cascade backbone, you can in good weather look forward to miles of glorious, expansive views; in bad weather you'll find yourself shrouded in clouds, exposed to the brunt of wet westerly storms.

Contouring now, we soon recross the divide to traverse above One Lake, and eventually to Trail 380 (5660–1.6), which descends 0.3 mile to Two Lakes. Next, a quick climb takes us back to the west side, where Mt. Rainier's overwhelming presence hardly lets us notice the many wildflowers at our feet, of which partridge foot is the most common. Along here we meet Cougar Lakes Trail 958A, which heads back over the crest, and we start another long traverse, contouring through forest and meadow across a couple of spur ridges before dropping via abrupt switchbacks to a saddle and Ameri-

can Ridge Trail 958 (5320–2.6), which departs eastward. Just past this junction we come to a campsite, although finding water here would require a bit of a walk downhill. Here we look down the long, forested (and previously glaciated) valley of the American River.

Now the PCT makes a brief climb north to cross a crest saddle, then contours through subalpine-fir groves before winding down to visit Anderson Lake (5340–1.4), just within Mt. Rainier National Park. It has a nice campsite, and you won't need a permit to camp at it. Continuing north, the trail barely climbs as it crosses a seasonal trickle, traverses scree, and rounds a spur ridge. It then arcs down toward Dewey Lake, first meeting Dewey Way Trail 968A, which splits northeast to connect with Trail 968. Just beyond the junction, Dewey Lake's expansive waters and numerous campsites along the shore-hugging PCT invite a pause (5112–1.8).

After rounding Dewey Lake's shore and bridging its inlet, our route passes Dewey Lake Trail 968 (5130–0.5), which branches east to the American River valley, and then our route climbs out of the soggy lake basin, working west through dark forest before emerging onto meadowland. After this it switchbacks and immediately meets the Tipsoo Lake Trail, a day hiker's path that reaches Highway 410 only ⅓ mile south of Chinook Pass. Here is an introduction to some amazingly colorful flora. Paintbrushes, pasque flowers, lupines, avalanche lilies and a galaxy of other blossoms spill over

I3, I4   **I4**

see MAP I3

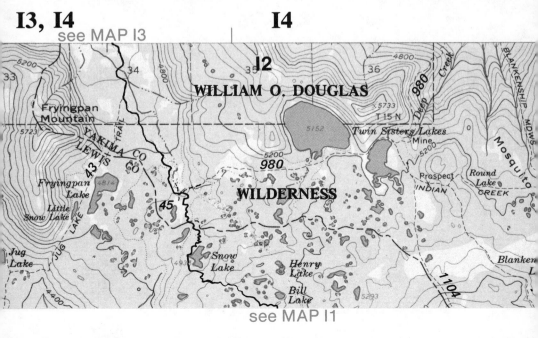

see MAP I1

the PCT as it tops the rise and then descends, first abruptly and then in a long traverse past a tarn, to Highway 410's fairly steady traffic at Chinook Pass (5432–2.7). Water can be found at a picnic area ⅓ mile south from here, but it must be treated. From this pass it's 68 miles east to Yakima, 41 miles northwest to Enumclaw, and 34 miles southwest to Paradise, the starting point for the challenging "standard" route to the top of Mt. Rainier.

Beyond the footbridge over the highway, the PCT turns north onto an old roadbed, crosses a bench and then as a trail approaches traffic as it makes a rising traverse. This steep slope supports a scrubbier flora than that at Chinook Pass proper. Fireweed, huckleberry, manzanita, pearly everlasting and bedraggled Alaska-cedars, hardy plants all, testify to tougher conditions. The gradual ascent turns up a ravine and then steepens into a couple of switchbacks before reaching Sheep Lake (5750–2.2), a popular spot for day hikers and overnighters. After following the lakeshore for a bit, our trail starts upslope, weaving and switchbacking generally northeast across meadowy bowls and

up into ptarmigan and pika country. It then traverses under small crags to Sourdough Gap (6440–1.2). The name of this saddle, as well as other features to the north, recalls the gold and silver prospectors who worked this region until not so long ago.

Admiring Mts. Adams and St. Helens, we can savor here the start of another long stretch of high traverse, which is wonderfully scenic if the weather is good. Skidding down scree off the gap, we come to an unsigned spur at the first switchback, and after another hairpin we settle into a long, gently descending traverse near treeline. Placer Lake comes into view 600 feet below as you approach Bear Gap, where you'll find a major trail plexus (5882–2.1). Here Silver Creek Trail 1192 drops northwest to civilization at Crystal Mountain Ski Area, Hen Skin Lake Trail 1193 starts a traverse southwest, and Bear Gap Trail 967 comes up from Morse Creek and Highway 410 to the east. We, however, take the PCT in a slant across the gap and then contour north, viewing ski lifts and condominiums well below, until we turn southeast on our way around the steep flanks of Pickhandle Point.

I5, I6   I6

Tarn near Chinook Pass

Next we angle back across the crest at Pickhandle Gap and promptly meet an obscure trail, signed FOG CITY and GOLD HILL, dropping east (6040–1.1). Then we rise along the open south slopes of Crown Point and, at the breathtaking crest between Crown Point and Gold Hill, reach the southern boundary of Norse Peak Wilderness. Here we meet two other trails (6200–0.3). One is unsigned, following the ridgecrest east to Gold Hill, and the other is Union Creek Trail 956, dropping north off the crest 50 yards west of where we gain it. We follow the PCT on a steady climb west and then north around Crown Point, before long coming onto the narrow watershed divide at Blue Bell Pass (6390–0.4).

From this saddle the trail contours north and, as it approaches the spur dividing Pickhandle

234 THE PACIFIC CREST TRAIL

and Bullion basins, it intersects an unsigned path. The lower track drops steeply into Bullion Basin, while the upper one climbs to the top of summit 6479. We contour around this summit, which takes us to narrow Bullion Pass. Balancing astride this narrow saddle, we first meet a steep, unsigned trail crossing the ridge, then meet Bullion Basin Trail 1156 (6150–0.9), descending to the west. As the crest rises to a summit again, we ascend along its west flank in a long, meadowy traverse to Scout Pass (6530–1.5). This presents us with a view across Lake Basin's gentle parkland bossed over by one of the area's larger crags.

A gentle descent leads one across the head of Lake Basin, and you pass first an unsigned and eroding trail that beelines down into the basin, then a designated trail (6390–0.6), which descends to excellent camping at Basin Lake, ½ mile below. Next you round the northeast spur of Norse Peak and descend into Big Crow Basin. As you near the bottomland at the head of this basin, you pass 30 feet above a welcome and reliable spring (6290–0.4). Some 40 yards beyond this you meet the junction with Norse Peak Trail 1191, which climbs west, and Crow Lake Way 953, which passes an old shelter ½ mile away on its eastward descent. Next the PCT passes a campsite as it rounds Big Crow

Basin, and then it rises along a bench and back to the crest at forested Barnard Saddle (6150–0.8). After weaving through a couple of small crestline ravines, passing an unsigned track that drops west in the first, it returns to the east side of the divide at Hayden Pass (6150–0.3) and we get a view over Little Crow Basin.

We make a steep slant down into this basin, and then gradually descend across its upper glades and fir forest to a sign, LITTLE CROW BASIN (5930–0.4). Twenty yards before this sign one can drop off the trail 75 yards to an established campsite. In a draw another 100 yards below and south of this site, water trickles much of the summer.

The PCT soon crosses an avalanche gully and continues slanting down out of Little Crow Basin, and then it traverses northeast for some time before making a brief climb up to Martinson Gap (5720–1.4). Beyond this gap the track turns northwest to angle up the slopes of Peak 6373, passing the "ghost trees" of an old burn. Next the trail pivots and arcs around the south and east slopes of 6373, recrosses the crest, and gradually settles onto the broadening Cascade divide, still presenting Mt. Rainier's massive white dome through the scattered and stunted subalpine firs. Along this stretch the trail intersects Arch Rock Way 1187 (5930–2.1)

I6
Lake Basin and Basin Lake

I6, I7, I8

see MAP 15
see MAP 16
see MAP 13

which, on its way west to Echo Lake, descends past nearby Saddle Springs. Although these springs are convenient to the PCT user, many years they trickle only into midsummer. However, beyond this junction an unsigned spoor (5700–0.5) drops east ¼ mile to a packer camp known as Morgan Springs, a more enduring water source.

Beyond this path, easy walking for ¼ mile takes us to Cougar Valley Trail (5780–0.3),

which heads east along a spur ridge, and more strolling along the crest brings us to an unsigned trail junction (5920–0.5), at the base of an open rise. We avoid the fork that climbs directly up this broad summit and take the one contouring to the east, passing through more blends of forest and meadow on our way to the spur trail (5760–0.8) to Arch Rock shelter. At the end of this 200-yard-long spur one finds a perennial spring trickling from a pipe, as well as an old four-sided

18, 19

19

shelter. Camp spots can be found in the forest below.

Beyond the turnoff the PCT descends past the northern access to the shelter, and then it crosses a seasonal branch of South Fork Little Naches River. Well sheltered now under silver fir and western hemlock, the route loses elevation along the broad crest to Louisiana Saddle (5220–1.5), from where obscure Middle Fork Trail 945 traverses east. Our trail continues descending through deep forest to Rods Gap (4820–1.1), from where it abruptly gains back 400 feet. Near the top of this climb a poetic sign warns that the wrath of the ghost of Mike Urich, a trail worker in this area during the '40s and '50s, will fall on anyone who harms the area's trees. One must imagine that Mike's ghost has his hands pretty full trying to catch up with the loggers who've worked not far to the north! After leveling out for a bit, our forest trail gently descends northwest and meets Maggie Way Trail 1186 (4850–1.6), heading west for a deep drop to the Greenwater River. Not much farther northwest our descent takes us out of Norse Peak Wilderness and ends

Shelter at Camp Urich

at perennial Meadow Creek. After fording this we momentarily arrive at Camp Urich (4720– 0.8). Here we find a rough shelter with an excellent wood stove, a large camping area, and a privy, all set on the west edge of expansive Government Meadow.

From the shelter we continue north on a broad track, and we promptly come to another Mike

I9, I10

I10

Hikers on an andesite rock outcrop west of Green Pass

Blowout Mountain, viewed from the north

Urich warning and an old wagon wheel. The latter recalls the first wagon train to cross the Cascades east of Puget Sound. In 1853 the party, headed by David Longmire, rested here before starting a rough descent into the Greenwater River canyon. By 1855 a military road was completed through this area, crossing gentle

I10

Mt. Rainier, from above outcrop

Naches Pass, ½ mile to the east. Just beyond this spot the PCT crosses this historic road (4800–0.2), which dirt bikers now know as jeep road 942. A VEHICLES PROHIBITED sign a few yards beyond this track shows us the way up a gentle rise to near the edge of Burlington Northern land. Loggers have been at work here in recent years, and it appears that a "temporary" PCT detour has become established. We drop east a short distance to meet a logging road, then follow this uphill for ½ mile, past an iron gate, and return to a northbound, crest-top path where the road bends southwest (4840–1.1). More logging and detours in the future are likely in this section.

Staying on or just west of the crest now, our level trail soon comes to a spur trail, which climbs 0.4 mile to the top of Pyramid Peak—an excellent vantage point. The PCT itself gives excellent vistas of Mt. Rainier as it contours around the peak's steep west slopes to Windy Gap (5200–1.4). Along this saddle it follows a jeep road for 30 yards before branching east off it and starting a long traverse. Eventually the path rounds a spur ridge, then descends for 0.5 mile and passes 20 yards above a delicious spring, where a couple of small camp platforms have been hewn (5180–2.1).

I10

Mostly well shaded by silver firs and Douglas-firs, the PCT continues contouring a couple of hundred feet below the ridgecrest that divides the Little Naches and Green rivers. After some time, though, the crest drops and meets our generally level tread. At this spot (4890–2.4) a dirt road that follows the divide forks, and we cross its branch just below the ridgecrest and continue heading east. A brief climb now introduces a vista south of splintery Goat Rocks, then we have a rollercoaster section of trail, which takes us back to the crest and across the ridgetop road (5000–1.1).

Brushing against wild rhododendrons in the shady fir forest, we rise above the road and then follow the crest into a gentle descent past a dry campsite (in early season water *can* be found downhill from here). The PCT enters brushy terrain thick with huckleberries and invading fir saplings, and coasts along Green Pass (4940–0.5). Next we face the first significant climb in many miles—up the west ridge of Blowout Mountain. We follow a couple of switchbacks and then, viewing Goat Rocks and much of the broad Naches River drainage to the south, we slant up to the ridgecrest, from where the obscure but signed West Fork Bear Creek Trail (5340–1.0) drops off to the south. The PCT continues climbing, switching back once and entering a small stand of subalpine firs, where we meet a sign pointing out obscure Granite Creek Trail 1326 (5480–1.0), bound for Mt. Clifty and Quartz Mountain.

*   *   *   *

A bench on the northeast side of Blowout Mountain cups a marshy pond and contains a spring that, by mid-July in most years, provides what can be the only water at all convenient to the PCT for 6 miles to the south and over 17 miles to the north. Granite Creek Trail 1326 is the southern end of a 1.2-mile alternate route that thirsty PCT hikers can take past this oasis, reconnecting with the PCT just north of Blowout Mountain. To do this, turn onto hard-to-follow Trail 1326, traverse east, and descend, first steeply and then more reasonably, to a saddle on the east ridge of Blowout Mountain. Here, 0.4 mile from the PCT, you meet Manastash Ridge Trail 1388. Take this trail north 0.3 mile to the pond and its adjacent campsites. To rejoin the PCT, climb north on eroding 1388 to crest the east-west ridge north of the pond's bench. Turn west here on Blowout Mountain Trail 1318 and

I10, I11

I6

953

1191

Shelter

6406

6433

6544

Big Crow Basin

Norse Peak

6856

NORSE

Lake Basin

Shelter

5200

Basin Lake

Scout Pass

6400

Creek

7166

Crystal Creek

4400

4400

6000

5200

4800

6000

Cement Basin

6601

5600

Cement

PEAK

6776

JEEP TRAIL

4254

5200

CRYSTAL

JEEP TRAIL

1156

6400

5200

5600

956

Union

4800

Crystal Mtn

T.R.

Mine

JEEP

SKI

LIFT

4583

Bullion Basin

Bullion Pass

Prospect

5600

Hill

5600

MOUNTAIN

5600

1192

5200

Elizabeth Creek

6479

Pickhandle Basin

Blue Bell Pass

Crown Point

WILDERNESS

Gold

6295

6383

Miners Lakes

Elizabeth Lake

6000

Hen Skin Lake

133

BM 5882

Mine

Pickhandle Point

Pickhandle Gap

Prospects

5600

SKI AREA

PIERCE CO YAKIMA CO

Bear Gap

967

4800

Mine

376

MRNP

6796

5200

Morse

Campground

Creek

BM 3900

4400

BM 4013

Placer Lake

5810

Mines

3640

Mors Cam

969

Sourdough Gap

6515

4800

BM 4320

River

Falls

Mesatche

968

see MAP I5

5200

BM 4577

Fork

4000

4000

BM 4859

Rainier

4400

410

5

TRAIL

4400

6000

WILLIAM O. DOUGLAS WILDERNESS

5623

5270

4400

3680

5200

5200

A clearcut lying north of Blowout Mountain

see MAP 19

18

Heliport
5879
Corral
Pass

7174

Saddle
Springs

Morgan
Sprs

7187

1176

Hidden
Lake

5406

Spring

5600

5200

NORSE

PEAK

WILDERNESS

Cre
La

see MAP 17

see MAP 18

17

951

MTN

TRAIL

River

6373

6127

NORSE

PEAK

953

Greenwater

Martinson Gap

PIERCE CO

YAKIMA CO

5600

6658

6546

953

Castle
untain

7188

Crow

Creek

4800

6703

6000

Little
Crow Basin

Hayden
Pass

WILDERNESS

4800

6220

Reese
Lake

6290

5200

Goat
Lake

6000

Barnard
Saddle

953

see MAP I10 | see MAP I11

see MAP I8

you'll join the PCT in 100 yards. PCT hikers coming from the north, or north-bounders not wanting to hassle route-finding along obscure Trail 1326, can branch off at 1318 and follow this description in reverse to the pond.

*　　　*　　　*　　　*

From the Granite Creek turnoff we climb a bit more to the crest of Blowout Mountain, where we get the most expansive view in some time, once again seeing Mt. Rainier dominating the central Washington hinterlands. Now we follow the trail along a narrow summit ridge, and look east down to the aforementioned pond, which could be our last water source for a *long* way. We then round the north summit of Blowout Mountain and switchback down through a dense fir forest to Blowout Mountain Trail 1318 (5260–1.1), the northern access to the pond.

North from the junction a steep ridgeline descent ends our hiking through extensive unmarred terrain, as we emerge onto a vast clearcut landscape. One's first reaction might be revulsion at ridge after ridge riddled with roads and shaved down to soil, but PCT hikers might consider that hiking the PCT is more than just a pleasant walk through beautiful scenery—it is a

I11　　　　　　　　　　　　**I11**

see MAP I11

see MAP I9

coming to know the Pacific Crest, its condition and goings-on. Hikers can see for themselves how the high rate of cutting here far exceeds the rate at which the trees will grow back, and can know that current practices will never allow them to grow to even nearly the size of their magnificent ancestors.

For quite some time the trail keeps on or near the ridge dividing the Yakima and Green rivers. At first it is barely east of deforested private land, but then it follows the flat but narrow ridge across a section line back into fully forested

government land. Our track eventually emerges from the woods just east of the crest, where one can see the PCT rising around barren Point 4922, ahead, at the end of a logging road. The route barely touches this road, then contours before climbing 50 yards onto the adjacent crest. From this it then switchbacks down, crossing two roads on its way to a major saddle (4400–2.8).

From this saddle we traverse around the east side of Point 4922, then re-enter forest and make a long, lazily switchbacking descent to

see MAP I12

see MAP I10

see MAP I9

Tacoma Pass (3460–2.7). Road 52 crosses this pass, and we jaywalk this logger's thoroughfare to ascend northwest into clearcut land again. to arc northwest into clearcut land again. With Mt. Rainier in full view, we now stride northwest along the divide as we cross one old logging road and then follow another one downhill for 30 yards before crossing it.

Now in forest, we cruise across Sheets Pass (3720-1.4), and then we climb and contour through pleasant woods to a campsite and a seasonal creek (3860-0.4). This rill might carry

water into mid-August of a *wet* year. From here the route turns south and climbs around the south ridge of Bearpaw Butte. Climbing in and out of the next clearcut, we find the trail a bit grassy and overgrown, but we follow short hairpins trending northwest. As we leave the hairpins and traverse northwest, we spot a stagnant pond about 300 feet below the trail, which the truly desperate might find refreshing.

Our climb takes us to the crest, which we follow northwest across an old log landing, across an old road, and then across another landing.

I12

I12

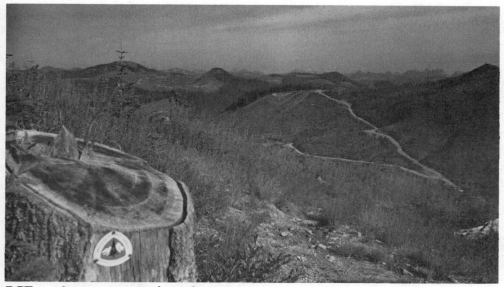

PCT marker on a stump in a clearcut

Shortly we drop a few yards south to avoid a ridgetop road and, as we traverse toward Snowshoe Butte, we make the short climb back and cross the ridgetop road where it curves. Next the trail turns north along the east slope of Snowshoe Butte, and passes through a corner of forested public land into more razed earth on the butte's north ridge. A switchbacking descent takes us in and out of this clearcut across one road and then lands us on a second road. We follow this second road 250 yards northeast downhill, and then leave it from the same side we entered it to walk back into the forest onto a broad saddle (4200-3.8) littered with blowdowns.

As we then follow the low crest from here, we branch left, north-northeast, at a trail junction back into a clearcut and, at the crest of a small knob, turn east onto a bulldozer track. We follow this for 200 yards past an old slash pile and continue east more or less directly up the adjacent ravine, passing a glade of corn lilies before we reach the edge of the clearcut near the crest of a knob. Here the trail turns north, past a row of fallen trees that, without their neighbors' shelter, have succumbed to storm winds. Our track traverses just east of the knob's summit, then descends just east of the rounded divide to a pass, where fast-growing grasses and shrubs, especially huckleberries, partly obscure the trail. Huckleberry and blueberry bushes favor

cleared and burned land, and so they cover a great deal of this country. By mid-August most PCT hikers here develop a purple tongue from sampling the abundant fruit. At the low point of the pass (4290-2.3) we cross a road, not far west of a flight navigation complex.

From here we make a short climb up the next knob north before starting a descent toward the Stampede Pass weather station, visible ahead. Steep switchbacks take us across a bulldozer track, then across a more substantial road. The last switchback brings us into dense forest, where an overgrown 4WD track might lead some hikers astray. White diamond trail blazes help us head nearly straight down the divide to a dry campsite at a notch, and then we rise and traverse around the east side of the next knob. We emerge from forest at a powerline cut, then soon reach another with old log poles. Deep beneath this latter line runs the Northern Pacific railway tunnel.

A short distance farther we cruise behind the weather station, cross its access road (3950-1.8), and then cross another powerline cut. With the maze of human disturbances that could lead one off route in this area, we depend a great deal on the stubby PCT posts that point the way across *almost* every road and powerline cut. We follow the low Cascade divide as it turns west, crossing another road and then another power-

see MAP I15

I14

SPILLWAY ELEV 2517
Keechelus Lake

Intake Tower
BM 2475
Gaging Sta

Mile 214.5 end

KEECHELUS

PACIFIC

Crystal Spring Forest Camp

Swamp Lake

Gravel Pit

Whittier

Mosquito

Stampede Pass

Lizard Lake

Weather Sta

Lookout

TUNNEL

Martin

Mile 210

INTERSTATE 90

Y A K I M A

Tall Cr

Cedar

R I V E R

NORTHERN

STAMPEDE

KITTITAS CO

PACIFIC

BM 2678

BM 2587

BM 247

see MAP I14

see MAP I12

I13

KACHESS LAKE 1 MI.

CLE ELUM 13 MI.

line cut, on our way through a regrowing forest of silver fir, Douglas-fir, lodgepole pine, white pine and western hemlock. A gradual descent then takes us down to Stampede Pass Road 54 (3680-1.0), a couple of hundred yards south of the pass proper. About 0.2 mile south down this road lies Lizard Lake, a swampy, fetid pond with a fouled campsite on its south shore. Unpleasant though it may be, next to crackling powerlines and an abandoned auto, any campsite with water near the trail is rare along this stretch of PCT, and the author (Selters) camped here and drank the water, after boiling it for 10 minutes or more, without any ill effects.

From Road 54 the PCT next strikes steeply uphill, switchbacking through the adolescent second-growth forest. Soon after it crests the rise, the trail turns north, parallel to a logging road, and enters a more recent clearcut. After a slight climb the trail cuts west across the divide and cruises through huckleberry prairies and across two logging roads on its way to the forested headwater ravine of Dandy Creek, which might carry water through July. The trail barely descends into the ravine before contouring south out of it, and then it slants southwest down through thick fireweed and other pioneers of clearcuts. It crosses a logging road and then empties onto and follows the same road to a hairpin (3840–2.1), where a rill might trickle through July. Dropping from the road here, the trail descends gradually, switchbacking across another logging road before reaching Dandy Pass (3680–0.3).

Here we enter forested public land and circle halfway around a hill under the shade of a magnificent forest of giant old-growth hem-

locks. This mile-long arc is a now-rare glimpse at the quality of tree for which the Pacific Northwest is famous, and with which the lumber industry made its killing. Eventually we cross the section line and enter brushy country again just shy of a saddle. Here we turn north and skirt the saddle to cross and then parallel a logging road, and in a few minutes we come to a creek (3600–1.9), which probably cascades year-round. A rough, rocky traverse north from here, paralleling and then dropping across a road, brings us to an even more certain stream, Stirrup Creek (3480–0.8). Along the south bank of this stream Meadow Creek Trail 1338 runs ½ mile through a clearcut up to Stirrup Lake, where one can find a pleasant campsite barely in the trees.

Climbing gradually from here among tall cedars, the trail crosses a well-graded logging road and rounds a ridge, and then strikes northwest on a level traverse. In 1989 this area was being logged, and PCT hikers had to detour some distance on the aforementioned road. Future logging and detours are likely. Eventually the trail re-enters forest at the Forest Service boundary and traverses to the dribbling headwaters of Meadow Creek (3660-2.1). From here we work up a couple of hairpins, gaining 350 feet to a ridgeline that overlooks the mostly clearcut headwaters of North Fork Cedar River, a major feeder into Seattle's water supply. At the valley's head we see Yakima Pass cupping Twilight Lake, which, at the bottom of a massacred amphitheater, looks like a forlorn island of natural beauty trying to hide behind a relict forest curtain. We slant down to the pass, crossing a logging road en route, and skirt Twilight Lake along its west shore (3575-1.4).

I13, I14
Lizard Lake and Mt. Rainier

I14

Mt. Rainier, from Dandy Pass

Campsites can be found in the scant trees on the east shore.

From the pass—part of an old Indian route—we strike northwest directly uphill, cross a road, and then cut northeast to ford the creek that issues from Mirror Lake. Just beyond this first ford the PCT turns across the end of a logging road and then climbs steeply to cross and recross the outlet creek on our way to Mirror Lake (4195–0.9). Suddenly we've entered a refuge of undisturbed mountain landscape; craggy Tinkham Peak looks over the sapphire waters that periodically ripple with feeding trout, and the rimming fir forest invites secluded access to a scenic swim, in warm weather anyway.

After passing a number of campsites on our way around the east shore of the lake, we exit the lake basin and meet Mirror Lake Trail 1302 (4220–0.4), coming up from the Lost Lake trailhead only a mile to the southeast. Here the PCT merges with Twin Lakes Trail 1303, continuing north for a bit and then climbing some steep hairpins to a spur of Tinkham Peak. Trail 1303, here signed as Cold Creek Trail, drops north from our route (4500–0.5), which goes west on a hillside, below andesite bluffs. Soon we cross a small creek on our way down to a soggy bowl with a couple of tiny ponds and a rug of marsh marigolds. Next we turn north and pass unmaintained Garren Ridge Trail 1018, which climbs west, and then we start a very steep, rocky climb of our own as we traverse on the slopes of Silver Peak. This climb takes us to a tiny side valley, behind a knob, from where we make a steep, then a moderate, traversing

descent among silver firs to a perennial creek (3900–2.5).

After crossing this creek we continue north, soon entering a clearcut that allows a view of Chair Peak and its satellites across the gash of the Snoqualmie River valley, and then we descend to and follow Olallie Creek. We cross a road and then a feeder of Olallie Creek, and finally cross to the east bank of Olallie Creek itself (3620–0.8). Along the creek we pass through a patch of forest and then break back into logged land, hearing the roar of Interstate 90 some 1400 feet below. Soon we follow a logging road a few yards north before descending from it, and then we traverse under powerlines and drop onto the powerline access road (3350–0.7). This we follow west downhill for 0.4 mile, past a spur road climbing east, and then we drop beside Rockdale Creek, which tumbles under a canopy of maples and firs. Across the creek we turn north under powerlines, proceed across talus slopes dotted with vine maple, and then enter deep fir-and-cedar forest for a long, flat traverse.

Eventually the steep slope we traverse levels into a bench, and the path skirts a small pond where an unsigned track branches northwest. Quickly, our trail then comes to a sign pointing out a 100-yard spur to Lodge Lake (3180–2.0). Down this spur one finds the lake's campsites, some close to the PCT, although a number, popular with overnighters, are set around the shallow, muskeg-rich lake. The PCT rises as it rounds Lodge Lake's bowl, then traverses slopes up past a creek ford to cross a forested saddle and enter a swale holding Beaver Lake (3480–

Peaks north of Snoqualmie Pass, l. to r.: Guye Peak, Red Mountain and Kendall Peak

0.8). Here the trail passes under one of the newer ski lifts of the Snoqualmie Pass ski area before starting a long, descending arc down the groomed ski slopes. The trail slowly curves far to the west, presenting views of Interstate 90 and the complex of cute buildings at Snoqualmie Pass below the craggy peaks across the valley. The latter promise a more ruggedly scenic and pristine section of PCT to the north. A final switchback ends by a huge parking flat at the northwest end of Snoqualmie Pass (3030–1.0). The amenities here await in the village ⅓ mile to the southeast. From the I-90 underpass nearest the ski area, the northbound PCT heads for Stevens Pass.

I15

The Pacific Crest Trail in Section J

—N—

0   1   2   3   4   5 miles

This section's PCT
Other trails
Hwys and major rds
Other roads
Campgrounds ▲

LEAVENWORTH 35 MI.

J8
Stevens Pass

HIGHWAY

HIGHWAY 2

Tye River

Scenic

Foss River

68

6830

6840

68

Mt Sawyer
1058

1062

Terrace Mtn

Deception

1060

Trap Pass
Trapper Cr

J7

Thunder Mtn

1567

1568

1569

1582

1551

1551

Surprise Mtn

Prospect Cr

J6

Deception Pass

1059

1066

Icicle Creek

WILDERNESS

French Creek

1595

Mt Daniel

Cathedral Rock

1376

LAKES

Dutch Miller Gap

J4

1337

Spinola Cr

J5

Fish Lake RS

1005

5620

Snoqualmie River

Middle Fork

J2

ALPINE

Escondido Ridge

Waptus Lake

1310

1310A

Trail Creek

1322

4330

J1

Chikamin Pk

Chikamin Ridge

Alaska Mtn

Red Mtn

Alta Mtn

3238

1320

1323

J3

1329

Waptus River

1310

4330

Snoqualmie Pass

1012

1013

1312

1331

Mineral Creek

1313

1323

295

4613

KLUM RIVER

INTERSTATE 90

PCT

4930

1312

46

CLE

Keechelus Lake

5480

5480

5483

49

INTERSTATE 90

49

54

Kachess Lake

4308

4310

903

Cle Elum Lake

903

PCT

54

Section J: Interstate 90 at Snoqualmie Pass to Highway 2 at Stevens Pass

Introduction: From high traverses along craggy crests, to meadowland tours past swimmable lakes, to forest walks near churning rivers, Section J bisects a spectacular variety of Cascade backcountry, making for a classic week-long backpack. This is the land of Alpine Lakes Wilderness, an area that was so designated after one of the 70s' most bitter wilderness battles.

From Snoqualmie Pass the PCT climbs directly to the crest-top crags and boldly traverses right among them. Confronted by Chikamin Peak and brutal Lemah Mountain it relinquishes the divide, swerving east to where summer storms generally dissipate into clear skies. On this stretch the route dips into and climbs out of two major watersheds, Lemah Creek and the Waptus River. It then works back to and weaves along the descending divide, visiting a number of memorably scenic lake basins on its way to Stevens Pass. In all, Section J will challenge your legs, lift your spirits, and probably confirm your reasons for backpacking.

Declination: 19½°E

Mileages:

	South to North	Distances between Points	North to South
Interstate 90 at Snoqualmie Pass..................	0.0		74.5
		7.0	
Ridge Lake and Gravel Lake	7.0		67.5
		8.2	
Park Lakes campsites...........................	15.2		59.3
		6.5	
Lemah Creek.................................	21.7		52.8
		9.8	
Waptus Burn Trail.............................	31.5		43.0
		4.8	
Waptus River.................................	36.3		38.2
		7.7	
Deep Lake...................................	44.0		30.5
		3.2	
Cathedral Pass................................	47.2		27.3
		5.3	
Deception Pass	52.5		22.0
		3.4	
Deception Lakes outlet creek	55.9		18.6
		4.0	
Glacier Lake campsite	59.9		14.6
		6.5	
Hope Lake...................................	66.4		8.1
		3.8	
Lake Susan Jane...............................	70.2		4.3
		4.3	
Highway 2 at Stevens Pass	74.5		0.0

Supplies: Two restaurants, a burger stand and a post office are found at Snoqualmie Pass, where Greyhound offers daily bus service from the east or west. Also at the broad pass is a bed and breakfast inn that has become a special gathering place for PCT hikers. Showers, laundry, reasonable rates, and shared stories make this place a treat, and the owners will pick you up and drop you off if you call 434-6540 from the phone at the post office. At section's end, Stevens Pass, there are no facilities. The closest town and post office to this pass is at Skykomish, about 14 miles west.

Wilderness Permits: None are required along this section, but the Forest Service asks that all hikers self-register at the post just beyond the Snoqualmie Pass trailhead.

Problems: Snow typically lingers through mid-August on some of the steep traverses during the first 15 miles, making for some treacherous gully crossings.

Snoqualmie Pass, at 3127 feet, is the lowest gap in the Washington Cascades. Its name comes from the local Indian term for the moon, which the natives' legends held to be the life source of their tribe. Hikers starting from here should turn off I-90 at the westernmost turnoff, signed ALPENTAL ROAD. The first right on the north side of the freeway branches right again to the trailhead parking lot. The actual PCT heads up the roadcut from the Alpental overpass and in 100 yards merges with the trail coming from this lot.

Embarking east from the parking lot, we promptly meet trails coming from the equestrian lot to the north and from the highway, and then reach the trail register. With fir and hemlock above us, and bunchberry, spring beauty, huckleberry and devil's club at our feet, we cross an abandoned road and before long start climbing three long, well-graded switchbacks. They lift us around a ridge away from the freeway noise and into the valley of Commonwealth Creek. As we traverse above this valley's floor, we cross a tributary right below a spraying waterfall, and then we come to Red Mountain

Trail 1033 (3820–2.7). Heading up Commonwealth Creek, this is the old Cascade Crest Trail, and it used to keep PCT hikers west of the divide until they reached Dutch Miller Gap. From the junction we resume climbing on the newer PCT, heading for high country that was seldom visited before the completion of this PCT segment in 1978.

To the west and north, Chair Peak, Snoqualmie Mountain, Red Mountain and other summits already hint at the alpine terrain awaiting as we next switchback south. Returning into deeper forest, we continue climbing steadily on another switchback leg, up to the divide between the Snoqualmie and Yakima rivers. Along here we glimpse Kachess Lake, to the southeast, then immediately angle back onto the west flank of the steepening divide and continue our ascent.

Before long the route emerges onto talus, and the high country opens up all around us. Besides the craggy, multicolored peaks to the west, Mt. Rainier rises like a huge apparition to the south. Even if bad weather obscures this view, we can still find our spirits lifted by brilliant pockets of paintbrush, columbine, spiraea, valerian, tiger

J1   J1

Red Mountain, from PCT in Commonwealth Basin

Mt. Rainier, from above Commonwealth Basin

lily, and other flowers. The PCT continues rising gradually, with dwarfed mountain hemlocks clinging to trailside craglets, while more peaks come into view to the north, including Mt. Thompson and distant Mt. Stuart. We cross to the east side of the crest (5440–3.2), from where level hiking shows us Chikamin Ridge at the head of Gold Creek Valley, and Alta Mountain and some amazing cliffs of Rampart Ridge draw our eye across the valley.

Water might seep from late snow patches on this trail, but otherwise this airy section, often

just a ledge blasted from the rocky crest, is fairly dry. Soon the trail rounds a narrow spur ridge well above glistening Alaska Lake, and then it cuts down to the crest saddle (5270–1.1) between Ridge and Gravel lakes. Campsites away from the west shore of Gravel Lake, the northwestern of the two lakes, are the last sites until Park Lakes, 8.2 miles distant. Camping is not allowed at well-worn Ridge Lake.

From the north side of Ridge Lake our trail takes off on a talus traverse around the rim of the cirque holding Alaska Lake, and then climbs

J1   **J1**

PCT, outlying fir and Snoqualmie Mountain

see MAP J2

see MAP I15

see MAP I15

see MAP J4

see MAP J3

see MAP J1

KACHESS LAKE 2 MI.

ALPINE LAKES WILDERNESS

ALPINE LAKES WILDERNESS

Overcoat Peak

Avalanche Lake

Iceberg Lake

Leman Mtn

Chikamin Lake

Chikamin Peak

Needle Sit Gap

Huckleberry Saddle

Huckleberry Mtn

Chikamin Ridge

Glacier Lake

Spectacle Lake

Delate

Prospect

Chikamin Pass

Park Lakes

Three Queens

Three Queens Lake

Alta Pass

Alta Mtn

Lila Lake

Rachel Lake

Mineral

Box

Looking over Ridge Lake toward distant Mt. Stuart

some as it rounds the sharp east ridge of Alaska Mountain. Next, steep switchbacks that hold snow into August take us down the north slope of this peak, and then a traverse leads us to a narrow, forested saddle (5030–2.2), between Joe and Edds lakes. These lakes lie, respectively, 400 feet below us to the east and 800 feet below us to the west.

We slant off the saddle into a meadowy ravine, and then rise across the open, rocky south flank of Huckleberry Mountain. As we turn north around the east side of this peak, which is a summer pasture for wary mountain goats, we enter a beautiful hanging vale. Here, with a full view of Mt. Rainier, we meet a stream that cascades among rock slabs and heather gardens. At the head of this ravine you'll pass a couple of small pools before coming to the crest at Huckleberry Saddle (5560–1.5), which is a broad pass with a fragile carpet of bilberries. This scenic gap has remained nearly pristine largely because the Forest Service prohibits camping at it.

Short switchbacks among dwarfed hemlocks take us above the saddle, allowing one to view Mt. Index and the Olympic Mountains in the distant northwest. This climb then leads to a traverse below the tip of a crag to Needle Sight Gap (5930–0.6). After a glimpse through this

notch beyond the Burntboot drainage to distant Glacier Peak, we turn southeast for a long alpine traverse along the meadowy and rocky southwest face of Chikamin Ridge. Whole platoons of marmots may whistle loudly and then scurry from our approaches as we make our way across this headwall of Gold Creek, from which we can admire the placed sheen of Joe Lake, the twin thumbs of Huckleberry Mountain and Mt. Thompson, and the miragelike dome of Mt. Rainier. On the way the trail crosses a few steep chutes that usually shelter slippery tongues of snow well into midseason.

After climbing gently on the last third of this traverse, we reach Chikamin Pass (5780–2.5), where we can look across Park Lakes' basin to Three Queens, Box Ridge and, in the distant northeast, the granite pyramid of Mt. Stuart. Now we brake down a couple of switchbacks into the lake basin, where mosquitoes swarm in the subalpine meadows much more thickly than at the breezy crests we leave. Once on gentler ground the route passes campsites, then southbound Mineral Creek Trail 1331, and finally an access spur (4960–1.4) that leads to more campsites. Weaving through this hummocky plateau, which actually straddles the divide between Mineral Creek and Delate Creek, we follow the PCT generally east and then north-

J1, J2   **J2**

east around the bowl of the northernmost Park Lake. The lake behind us, we climb a pair of switchbacks to pass some ponds and gain a northwest spur of Three Queens (5350–0.8). Here you can look north over turquoise Spectacle Lake to the spiny metamorphic fangs, hanging glaciers, and alpine waterfalls of Lemah Mountain. The rolling Wenatchee Mountains rise in the more distant east.

Now we start a bone-jarring 2000-foot descent, twisting and pounding down literally scores of tight switchbacks—hairpins that continue from a chute on the east side of a knob down to the runout of Three Queens' avalanche slopes. As the trail drops into thicker forest we pass Spectacle Lake Trail 1306 (4440–1.6), which forks north, and below this we walk on a sturdy bridge across roaring Delate Creek (3920–1.2). Just beyond, we find the old, steeper Spectacle Lake Trail, branching up the drainage, and then find a small campsite (3800–0.3). The last series of switchbacks finally drops us onto a bottomland forest with fern glades, and we later cruise past eastbound Pete Lake Trail 1323 (3210–1.8).

Northbound, the PCT rounds a small knob and then gently descends northwest to the trunk stream of Lemah Creek (3200–0.8), where there are many sandy-gravelly campsites. From here the trail continues north, rising over a small moraine and then dropping to cross a bridge over North Fork Lemah Creek. Immediately after climbing out of this stream's ravine, our trail meets Lemah Meadow Trail 1323B (3210–0.7) which climbs northwest from Pete Lake. The PCT continues north past a couple of campsites (3240–0.1), gradually leaving Lemah Creek, then passes through forest and meadow and across a freshet. It then comes to a switchback (3370–0.7), from where an access spur descends ¼ mile to more campsites back at Lemah Creek's north fork. Here the PCT embarks on a 2200-foot climb to the top of Escondido Ridge, a climb best started early in the morning if it's to be a warm day.

Not far into this climb we cross a couple of seasonal streams, but beyond these we must count on vistas through the cedar, hemlock, and vine-maple forest to inspire us on. Brief though they are, these impressive alpine views of Lemah Mountain, Chikamin Ridge and Three Queens broaden with every switchback. Eventually the montane forest wanes, and smaller mountain hemlocks and subalpine firs spread around us as we turn up a ravine into a secluded cirque with a chilly tarn (5520–5.3). Camping is

J2   **J2, J3**

View across Joe Lake toward Alta Mountain and the Three Queens

Three Queens and Alta Mountain

prohibited here, but after we switchback once more and contour southeast 0.3 mile through subalpine parkland we come to some designated campsites.

Continuing around point 5984, we reach another cirque, where camping is also prohibited, and we cross the inlet (5300–1.3) of the lowest of a chain of crystalline tarns before starting a gradually rising traverse across the next ridge. From the top of this ridge the PCT arcs around a sheltered vale, jumping its creek and passing a campsite a few hundred yards farther southeast. Next we exit this meadowy glen and emerge onto the edge of Escondido Ridge, where we have a view over Waptus Lake and beyond to ever-closer Mt. Stuart. Not far along the ridge we find Waptus Burn Trail 1329C (5180–1.7), which continues down the ridge, whereas we switchback down and begin a 2200-foot descent to the Waptus River.

A grand alpine panorama oversees our well-graded switchbacks. Across the valley long waterfalls drain the lofty Mt. Daniel-Mt. Hinman massif, and at the valley's head, the impressive sedimentary slabs of Bear's Breast Mountain thrust skyward. As we stomp down the first switchbacks, pointy subalpine firs give way to open brush (a scar from the 1929 Waptus Burn fire), then we traverse north to the main bank of switchbacks, the last three touching a cascading stream.

Western redcedar droops over us as we empty onto the broad valley floor and come to a campsite at northwest-bound Dutch Miller Gap Trail 1362, but we don't find water until 0.1 mile later, at the Waptus River (3020–4.8). A girdered bridge gets us across this cold torrent, and we turn downstream alongside a *roche moutonnée*, a "dome" of rock that stood fast even though it was overridden by the glaciers that filled this valley. The PCT then winds northeast past a connection to the Dutch Miller Gap Trail and continues under Douglas-firs that rise above a carpet of ferns and vanilla leaf. As we start rising off the valley floor, we cross Spade Creek and meet Waptus River Trail 1310 (3070–0.8). This trail comes up from campsites ¾ mile away at Waptus Lake, and ultimately from the Cle Elum River, about 12 miles away.

Our trail proceeds on a gently rising traverse above the valley, well shaded under spruce, fir, and cedar boughs, but we get occasional blue glints of large Waptus Lake below. On the way our path crosses a couple of fairly reliable streams. Between them Spade Lake Trail 1337 climbs north, and at the second one there is a campsite (3400–1.5). Eventually our trail turns north into the Spinola Creek valley and meets Spinola Creek Trail 1310A (3440–1.1), which climbs about one mile from the outlet of Waptus Lake. Through alternating patches of forest, meadow and talus, our trail steepens some and

J3, J4   **J4, J5**

see MAP J6

J4

ALPINE LAKES

WILDERNESS

see MAP J2

see MAP J5

see MAP J3

see MAP J4

J5

J3

ALPINE LAKES

WILDERNESS

COOPER LAKE 1 MI.

Box Ridge, from the Park Lakes basin

even switchbacks in several places as it works up this valley, keeping some distance above the creek. A second series of switchbacks gets us around a knob and onto a bench, from where Cathedral Rock marks our direction.

Now in a meadowy subalpine realm, we continue north, and not long after crossing a feeder creek meet Lake Vicente Trail 1365 (4440–3.8), which ascends west. We immediately turn through a small gap and then follow the bank of now-quiet Spinola Creek, soon crossing another tributary at a campsite. A bit farther north we approach Deep Lake's indigo surface, only to fork from the lake's campsite access trail (4400–0.5) and turn east to wade its ankle-deep outlet. Now we head for the east side of Deep Lake's basin, to the start of a 1200-foot climb to Cathedral Pass.

Well-graded switchbacks take us far above the lake to the scraggly outliers of the subalpine-fir forest, where we get a new perspective of the alpine bluffs of Mt. Daniel. From the last hairpin, Trail 1375 (5560–3.0) forks northwest to Peggys Pond. Under the towering and resistant andesite of Cathedral Rock, we top a crest at Cathedral Pass (5610–0.2) for a view across the upper Cle Elum River valley to the gray alpine uplands of Granite Mountain.

From the pass, the Rainier View spur trail heads south down the ridge, while we descend briefly east onto a parkland bench with a few campsites and a few small tarns (5460–0.1). From here Cathedral Rock Trail 1345, the old PCT, drops south 2000 feet to the Cle Elum River. The Forest Service warns that the new PCT, in continuing north high above the Cle Elum, crosses a stream that can be treacherous at high water, and suggests taking the old route and climbing back up to rejoin the newer trail at Deception Pass. In the author's (Selters') opinion, however, for the average backpacker the stream crossing in question is rarely dangerous enough to warrant the lengthy 9½-mile detour. Still, we've drawn it on Map J6 for those who may want to take it.

Wandering around hillocks as it continues north, our trail proceeds in the shadow of Cathedral Rock along the edge of the scenic bench. It then starts twisting down a ridgeline, steepening as it goes until it traverses into montane forest, where we find a couple of longer switchbacks. These end at a bench that has shady campsites at a junction of two streams (4600–2.0). North from this bench the trail continues descending steadily across slopes forested in complex patches of mountain hem-

J5, J6   **J6**

lock and subalpine fir, then redcedar, Douglas-fir and alder. The route crosses one creek, and then comes to a second, which is the one the Forest Service warned of (3770–1.4). This stream, which drains Mt. Daniel's northeast slopes, is swift and cold, and you'll want to wear shoes or boots to cross its stony bed. However, the current is not capable of carrying a person away. Before the sun gets high or on a cloudy day the ford won't be more than a shin-deep swash for a few short strides.

From this ford the trail ascends steadily across avalanche swaths and two or three more streams. The last, where the trail turns east at the head of the Cle Elum drainage, will likely require another, less vigorous footbath (4180–

J6

J6

Lemah Mountain, from Escondido Ridge

see MAP J7

J6

see MAP J4

see MAP J5

1.0). The gradual climb turns north again in a forest of unusually large subalpine firs and tops out at Deception Pass (4470–0.8). A number of trail options confront the hiker here: the old PCT (now Trail 1376) comes up from the Cle Elum River and Hyas Lake; Marmot Lake Trail 1066 branches west; and Trail 1059 forks north for Deception Creek, meeting Highway 2 six miles east of Skykomish. Beyond these junctions, the PCT heads north-northeast.

Now we contour around a knob to drop to nearby Deception Creek, a small stream in a deep and eroding drainage. This gully is cutting along the Straight Creek fault, a major crustal weakness traceable from near Yakima well into British Columbia. In the past land to its west was shifted north, displaced 100–200 miles over the millenia. We continue out of the gully on a level track, getting a glimpse back to the glimmering heights of Mt. Daniel and its massive Lynch Glacier. Next we round a ridge and jump one stream and then, near a campsite (4400–1.9), we jump another as we continue through cedar-and-fir forest. The PCT starts a long, gradually rising traverse above the valley of Deception Creek, passing through the skeletons of an old forest fire, and eventually rounding a ridge to meet Deception Creek Trail 1059A, which

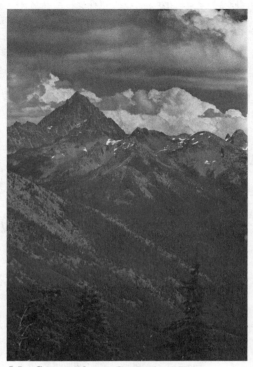

Mt. Stuart, from Cathedral Pass

J6, J7

Cathedral Rock, from the east

HIGHWAY 2 3½ MI.   HIGHWAY 2 and SCENIC 3½ MI.   see MAP J8

see MAP J6

Cathedral Rock and Mt. Daniel rising above Deception Creek valley

Pika

Glacier Lake, Surprise Lake and Glacier Peak

drops west. About 0.1 mile east of this junction we cross the outlet (5040–1.5) of Deception Lakes and then follow the west shoreline of the narrow lower lake. Although these lakes offer fine swimming and a pleasant rest, their accessibility has lured hordes who have beaten their campsites and much of their shorelines to dust.

Just as it nears the large upper lake, the PCT climbs northwest and enters a draw, at the end of which an unsigned and unmaintained trail drops off to the west. We, on the other hand, angle

northwest uphill and around a ridge to resume the ascending traverse high above Deception Creek. Now, however, we can see northwest beyond a checkerboard of clearcuts to the jagged teeth of Mt. Index, Mt. Baring and Three Fingers, as well as across the valley, where Lake Clarice nestles against Terrace Mountain. We

J7
Glacier Lake and Pieper Pass

J7

see MAP K1

see MAP J7

turn up a steep slope and with a few switchbacks surmount it at Pieper Pass (5920–2.0). From here the abandoned Cascade Crest Trail follows the ridgecrest north, but we turn east toward inviting Glacier Lake, and then drop off the pass for a braking descent.

Steep switchbacks take us down to a small bench with a tarn and a view of distant Glacier Peak, and then we wind among the granite

boulders of a lower bench before descending a talus slope to the cirque floor. From here we descend into the forest past a campsite (5000–2.0) that is above the southeast shore of Glacier Lake. Beyond this we cross a creek and hike around the bottom of a talus slope as we parallel Glacier Lake's glistening east shore 50–100 feet above it. We then continue away from the lake past a narrow pond, with another campsite, and

J7   **J7**

shortly meet Surprise Lake Trail 1060 (4840–0.8), which heads north for about four miles to meet Highway 2 eight miles east of Skykomish. At the junction the route pivots southeast to arc around the head of a ravine and start a rising traverse north.

This traverse takes us through forests and rocky fields, ever higher above Surprise Lake, ever closer to gnarly crags atop the crest. It ends where we join Trap Pass Trail 1060A (5080–1.0), in the middle of a bank of steep switchbacks, and we grind up the rest of these to the Cascade divide at Trap Pass (5800–0.9). With the blue disc of Trap Lake seemingly a straight drop below us, we switchback and traverse down and across its steep cirque wall to a sharply descending access trail (5350–0.8) to the lake. After leaving the lake's bowl, the PCT keeps to flowery avalanche slopes and shady forested slopes high above Trapper Creek. At a small bench it passes a campsite beside a seasonal creek (4970–1.2), and then climbs briefly to a notch (5210–0.7). From here we slant and switchback down through steep forest and across another bench, dropping before long to a gentle terrain at overused Hope Lake (4400–1.1). From here, at a curiously low spot in the Cascade crest, Tunnel Creek Trail 1061 drops 1.4 miles northwest to Road 6095, which descends 1.2 miles to Highway 2.

North from the turbid waters of Hope Lake we climb through fir-and-hemlock forest onto a somewhat swampy parkland plateau, on which we turn east to the north end of Mig Lake (4670–0.7). By midsummer this shallow lake warms to a pleasant swimming temperature. East from it, we drop to a crest saddle, round a knob, and curve around a swampy pond. Onward, we climb around a forested ridge, and confront steeper climbing beneath cliffbands, topping out at an unnamed crest saddle (5190–1.8). Here a slice of Swimming Deer Lake tempts one to drop 300 feet through very steep forest, but more accessible water is just down the trail, which contours east to a spur ridge, beyond which it drops along a rill in a grassy swale to the rim of Josephine Lake's cirque (4980–0.8). From here Icicle Trail 1551 descends around the cirque to the turquoise lake's outlet.

Swimmers at Mig Lake

From the Icicle Trail junction the PCT proceeds northwest down a ravine, then down a talus slope to the north shore of Lake Susan Jane (4600–0.5). With powerlines and the crest of Stevens Pass Ski Area in sight, and probably a number of overnighters at this pretty and accessible lake, a wilderness-accustomed PCT hiker strongly senses re-entry into civilization. Next the trail traverses west under steep but well-flowered bluffs, where snow lingers across the track into August. Soon after crossing a tumbling stream it passes a campsite near the edge of the swath cut for the immense powerlines overhead. These buzzing cables carry hydroelectricity from the rural Columbia basin east of the Cascades to the cities of the coast. A couple of rough roads run through the logged swath, and we depend on trail signs to follow our climbing, switchbacking path across the eroding roadbeds.

North of the powerlines our trail continues climbing, taking long, meadowy switchbacks up to the Cascade crest at a saddle (5160–2.2) near the top of a chairlift. Steeper, tighter switchbacks then take us down beneath this and other chairlifts to lower-angled slopes, from which we make a long descending traverse north, crossing a creek on our way to four-lane Highway 2. The trail empties onto a parking area (4060–2.1) a couple hundred yards northeast of the Stevens Pass Ski Area village, which in 1985 lacked summer services.

J7, J8   **J8**

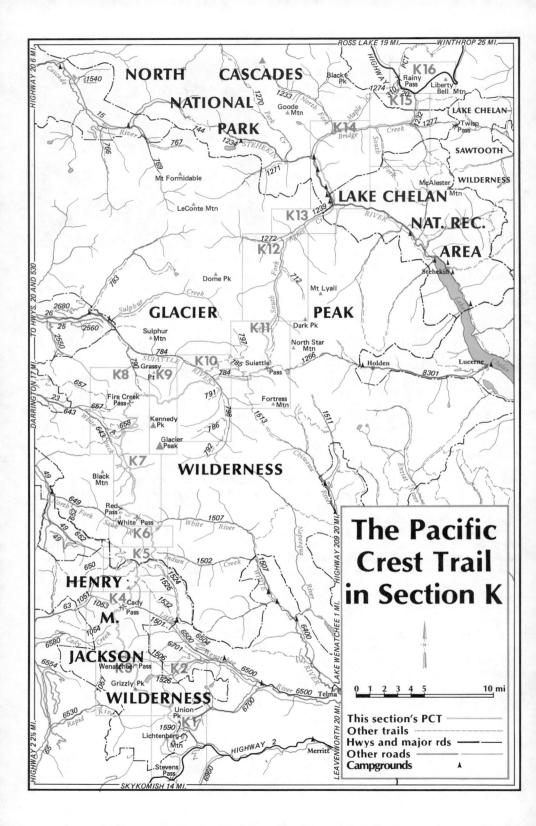

The Pacific Crest Trail in Section K

N

| 0 | 1 | 2 | 3 | 4 | 5 | | 10 mi |

This section's PCT
Other trails
Hwys and major rds
Other roads
Campgrounds ▲

Section K: Highway 2 at Stevens Pass to Highway 20 at Rainy Pass

Introduction: In this section you will traverse along a very rugged section of the North Cascades. This hike ranks second only to Volume 1's John Muir Trail section in difficulty. Traversing around Glacier Peak, the hiker brakes down to, then labors up from, a number of deep-floored canyons that radiate from the peak. Unfortunately, a nice, contouring trail, such as the one around Mt. Adams, is impossible to route around Glacier Peak proper, for such a trail would be too snowbound and too avalanche-prone.

Not only does this section have rugged topography, but it sometimes has dangerous fords, cold, threatening weather and persistent insects. Why then do thousands of backpackers flock to the Glacier Peak Wilderness? Well, perhaps because it is a *real* wilderness and not, like so many others, a wilderness in name only. It provides a definite challenge to modern-day man, who is so protected from the elements. This area's intimidating, snowy terrain, which is contrasted with lovely, fragile wildflower gardens, will draw you back time and time again.

Declination: 19¾°E

Mileages:	South to North	Distances between Points	North to South
Highway 2 at Stevens Pass	0.0		117.5
		5.5	
Lake Valhalla	5.5		112.0
		4.0	
Janice Cabin	9.5		108.0
		7.1	
Wenatchee Pass	16.6		100.9
		1.3	
Trail 1057 to Pear Lake	17.9		99.6
		10.0	
Lake Sally Ann	27.9		89.6
		4.7	
Indian Pass	32.6		84.9
		3.9	
White Pass	36.5		81.0
		1.9	
Red Pass	38.4		79.1
		7.3	
White Chuck Trail	45.7		71.8
		1.6	
Kennedy Ridge Trail	47.3		70.2
		7.2	
Fire Creek Pass	54.5		63.0
		4.0	
Milk Creek Trail	58.5		59.0
		5.3	
Dolly Vista campsite	63.8		53.7
		7.5	
Suiattle River access trail	71.3		46.2
		4.9	

Mileages:

	South to North	Distance between Points	North to South
Miners Creek	76.2		41.3
		3.0	
Railroad Creek Trail to Holden	79.2		38.3
		6.5	
Hemlock Camp	85.7		31.8
		7.0	
Five Mile Camp	92.7		24.8
		5.0	
Agnes Creek trailhead on Stehekin River road	97.7		19.8
		5.3	
Bridge Creek trailhead on Stehekin River road	103.0		14.5
		6.2	
Six Mile Camp	109.2		8.3
		8.3	
Highway 20 at Rainy Pass	117.5		0.0

Supplies: See "Supplies" in Section J for the facilities at Stevens Pass, our section's starting point. There are no other on-route supply points. However, upon reaching the Stehekin River near the end of the section, you can take a Park Service shuttle bus, $1.00 in 1985, over to Stehekin, which has a resort, post office, hiker-oriented store and information center. If you need new boots, clothes, or other special items, you can take a ferry from Stehekin to Chelan, then return again.

Wilderness Permits: In 1989 the Park Service implemented a backcountry-site reservation system for North Cascades National Park. Now 50% of the park's campground sites along the Stehekin River can be reserved up to a month in advance by writing to the Wilderness District Office in Marblemount, WA 98267. Also, sites at Fireweed Camp (p. 297), along Bridge Creek, can be reserved. Fortunately the Park Service does not require PCT hikers to obtain wilderness permits.

About 200 yards northeast from Stevens Pass on Highway 2, our route starts as a closed road that contours north across granitic terrain. On this open, bushy stretch, we pass an assortment of aster, bleeding heart, bluebells, columbine, fireweed, lupine, monkey flower, paintbrush, parsnip and Sitka valerian before curving west into a forested environment. We reach a 3-yard-wide tributary (3850–2.5) of Nason Creek, beside which one could camp, but elect to continue up to a meadow (4220–1.0), through which Nason Creek flows. Here among the cinquefoil, shooting stars, red heather and grass are good campsites. Mosquitoes and several species of biting flies, common in northern Washington through midsummer, will not bother you if the day is cold or misty.

Now within Henry M. Jackson Wilderness we climb up the trail to a second meadow, where one could camp, then switchback up to a saddle (5030–1.7), from which we can look down at beautiful Lake Valhalla and across it at the challenging west face of dark gray Lichtenberg Mountain (5844). Descending north from the saddle, we reach meadow campsites and a spur trail (4900–0.3) that descends southeast 200 yards to the northwest shore of deep, cool, sparkling Lake Valhalla (4830).

Lake Valhalla and Lichtenberg Mountain

K1

Our trail now climbs east to a saddle, snowbound through late July, then steadily descends northeast to Union Gap and a junction with Smithbrook Trail 1590 (4700–1.8), which descends eastward 0.7 mile to Road 6700. From the gap, our trail descends northwest along a lower slope of Union Peak (5696) before turning north and ascending to a delightful, singing cascade (4200–1.8). Tree frogs and evening grosbeaks join in a dusky chorus as we approach the large Janice Cabin (4150–0.4) beside shallow Lake Janus (4146), which is somewhat disappointing after Lake Valhalla. The warmer temperatures of this semiclear lake, however, do allow you a comfortable dip. Just northwest of the shelter is the clear outlet creek, but, judging by all the horse manure around the lake—despite the posted 200-foot restriction against horses—we feel you should treat the water before drinking it.

Beyond this creek, the PCT switchbacks west up to a gully, on your left, in which you could camp. In ¼ mile the trail reaches the crest (5180–1.6), traverses a short, northeast slope with a view due north of distant, regal Glacier Peak (10,541), and then reaches a saddle. A moderate descent northwest takes us to a meadow (5070–0.8), from which a faint trail leads 40 yards northeast, then descends a moderately steep gully toward Glasses Lake (4626). At the west end of the meadow, our trail passes a good, designated campsite, then follows a winding crest route up past outcrops of mica schist before it reaches the upper west shoulder (5580–2.1) of Grizzly Peak (5597).

From it we hike north along the ridge, round another summit, then come upon a designated but poor campsite on a saddle. Leaving it behind, we descend moderately across a west slope, pass well above shallow Grizzly Lake (4920), cross the crest (5120–1.4) and reach a good but shadeless campsite (5030–0.2) on a grassy flat. Descending north on a moderate-to-steep, sometimes soggy trail, we reach the crest again, then switchback down it to broad, forested Wenatchee Pass (4230–1.0), where there is another good campsite. Climbing north to a flat, we reach a junction with Top Lake Trail 1506 (4570–0.6), which curves east one-half mile to that lake (4590). You can camp 50 yards southwest of this junction, but with Pear Lake next on the itinerary, you'd be foolish to stop here if you can still make it to that lake by dusk.

Your trail heads west to a gully whose west side is composed of large boulders. Gushing from them is the outlet of Pear Lake, which is dammed behind them. We climb several short

K1, K2   K3, K4

Glacier Peak, from atop Grizzly Peak

see MAP J8

switchbacks, pass through a saddle with a view of Glacier Peak, then climb a few more hairpins to a ridgeline, the edge of Pear Lake's cirque (4880-0.7). From here Trail 1057 (formerly the PCT) heads west down to excellent campsites at the nearby, cliff-backed lake.

The late '80s PCT climbs northwest just below the crest of the ridge (a moraine),

allowing glimpses down to the aquamarine lake, then it weaves between mossy boulders atop the moraine. Next a switchback drops us to a notch where we leave the cirque and start a traverse around Peak 5548. Scattered hemlocks stand over us until we round 5548 and hike on a path blasted through huge granitic talus blocks. With pikas sounding off at our passage, we continue

K4

K4

our traverse to a tier of tight, steep hairpins that work past a cliff and up to the crest (5350-1.6).

On the west side of the crest we climb a bit more, then settle into a contouring ramble. As we round the meadowy bench of a point (5504) we can see the country ahead, through Saddle Gap to Skykomish Peak and Glacier Peak, and to the west to the Monte Cristo peaks. For a stretch we hike right below the scattered trees and glades of the crestline, and then we angle downslope into denser forest, passing one more talus slope before weaving down some switchbacks. From these we resume a contouring course and reach a pair of adjacent, fairly reliable creeks (4800-2.4). Beyond these the PCT climbs northwest gradually across steep slopes to a campsite, where a sign claims water is available not far downslope. Just up the trail from here we reach Saddle Gap (5060-0.7).

Beyond the gap we follow our northward-curving path down to a junction with West Cady Ridge Trail 1054 (4930-0.3), which climbs north-northwest. After descending north toward a prominent knob of metamorphic rock, we follow long switchbacks down to a fair campsite west of 10-foot-wide Pass Creek. Immediately after crossing it on stepping stones, we meet Pass Creek Trail 1053 (4200-1.0), which descends north alongside the creek. Our trail climbs northeast and shortly arrives at Cady Pass, where Cady Creek Trail 1501 (4310-0.4) departs northeast before dropping to that creek. At this forested pass is a dumpy, dry campsite that we would recommend for emergency bivouac only.

A long ascent—a taste of what's to come—now begins as the PCT switchbacks north up to a metamorphic ridge and reaches an exposed campsite at its crest (5470-1.9). This strenuous ascent does reward us, near its top, with scenic views to the south and east. After descending slightly to a granitic saddle, our trail rounds the east slope of a knob (5642), then reaches another saddle. Beyond it, trailside snow patches can last into August.

Now we contour across the east slope of rugged Skykomish Peak (6368), where minor PCT reroutings leave unsigned, paralleling tracks. Our twisting, contouring course takes us around granitic knobs and into ravines—a couple with creeks—and eventually brings us to Lake Sally Ann (5479-1.7). This beautiful lake has attracted many over the years, and the Forest Service has lined off much of the beaten-down spots, built a privy, and laid revegetation netting. Camping here is a privilege that, if abused, could be banned by the Forest Service.

PCT below Skykomish Peak

Beyond the lake the PCT curves down past creeklets to a junction with Cady Ridge Trail 1532 (5380-0.4), on which you can descend 200 yards to a suitable campsite on an open saddle.

Beyond this junction our sometimes snow-bound trail climbs northwest across a slope of greenish mica schist, glistening white-vein quartz and speckled adamellite before it switchbacks up to Wards Pass (5710-0.7). Turning north, we then hike along a crest route that takes us down to the soggy, volcanic soils of Dishpan Gap, where North Fork Skykomish Trail 1051 descends west and, just beyond, Bald Eagle Trail 650 (5600-0.6) veers north-northwest. Our route veers right and crosses the southeast slope of Peak 5892 to a ridgecrest campsite (5450-0.5) on an open slope of grass, cinquefoil and fawn lilies. Should you camp here or at a similar open site, don't be surprised to see deer come around and graze beside your tent.

Following the crest east across this glaciated country, we quickly arrive at a junction with Little Wenatchee River Trail 1525 (5440-0.3), which contours southeast. We diagonal up the northwest slope of a triangular summit, then

K4, K5   **K5**

reach a saddle from where a spur trail (5500-0.2) contours south to Trail 1525. The PCT heads north toward Kodak Peak (6121), then climbs east across its flowery, picturesque south slope of metamorphic rocks, where the distant view includes Mt. Rainier, Chimney Peak, Mt. Daniel, and the Stuart Range. Upon our arrival at Kodak Peak's east ridge (5660-0.7), Glacier Peak comes into view to the north. Little Wenatchee Ridge Trail 1524 strikes east-southeast along this ridge, the southern boundary of Glacier Peak Wilderness and the northern boundary of Henry M. Jackson Wilderness.

Our trail turns northwest and descends across open slopes, July snowfields, and a couple of rivulets before it curves north, and switchbacks

past stalwart hemlocks down to Indian Pass (5020-1.3). From here you can follow a spur trail 0.1 mile west to a good campsite, then another 0.1 mile to a boggy spring. Ascending to the PCT from the southeast is faint Indian Creek Trail 1502. From its junction we arc northwest up to a southwest spur of Indian Head Peak (7442), then climb northward to an adequate campsite at the north end of shallow, murky Kid Pond (5320-1.0). The location of this pond and the nature of its surrounding rocks of garnet-graphite-mica schist both indicate that it fills a slight depression behind avalanche deposits.

The PCT proceeds north to a ridge where we meet an older trail, which traverses the north slopes of Indian Head Peak. Then our trail descends to Lower White Pass (5378-0.7), from

K5   ## K5, K6

see MAP K4

Lake Sally Ann

see MAP K1

K4

1053

1501

Cady Pass

Bench Mark Mtn

1054

Saddle Gap

HENRY M. JACKSON

WILDERNES

Little Fish Lake

1057

Fortune Ponds

Frozen Finger Gap

Fortune Mtn

Pear Lake

1506

Top Lake

Peach Lake

Grass Lake

see MAP K3

which the old Cascade Crest Trail once descended northeast. Nowadays, the trail is called White River Trail 1507. An adequate campsite lies 30 yards east of this junction. Our trail climbs a ridge north to good campsites on the west and southwest shores of semiclear Reflection Pond (5560-0.3), then traverses across snowbound northeast slopes up to a junction at White Pass (5904-1.9). Here a trail begins a

curving traverse northeast to Foam Basin, with a campsite, about ¼ mile away. Another spur leads west down to good camping 200 yards from the ridgecrest, where snowmelt is reliable. No camping is allowed along the crest at White Pass.

Continuing along the PCT, we follow its contouring path west-northwest to a fork from where North Fork Sauk Trail 649 (5950-0.6)

K6, K7   **K7**

The Black Mountain glacier, from north of Baekos Creek

K6

Reflection Pond

Lower White Pass   BM 5378

GLACIER PEAK WILDERNESS   Kid Pond   Indian He Peak

5945

5703

652

see MAP K5

descends steeply westward. The meadow here has such an abundance of flowers and insects, it's no wonder that birds fly north to feast on them. Flycatchers hover and snatch insects from midair as we start a steady climb west-northwest. The trail becomes dusty as we approach a small summit (6650), affording an excellent panorama of the Monte Cristo massif and of prominent Sloan Peak. The path then turns north and shortly reaches the gray, garnet-biotite gneiss rocks of marmot-inhabited Red Pass (6500-1.3).

The view from here is nothing short of spectacular. Above us and 5 miles to the northeast is a towering volcano, Glacier Peak (10,541), which last erupted about 12,500 years ago. Below us is the perennially snowclad upper can-

yon of the White Chuck River. To the distant south is lofty, glistening Mt. Rainier (14,410), cloaked in snow, giving it the appearance of a giant stationary cloud that reigns eternally over the distant forest. If you're heading south, you'll definitely remember your climb up to this pass.

Our trail first switchbacks, then descends along the base of the east ridge of Portal Peak. When this section of trail is snowbound, most hikers slide directly down the steep, but safe, upper snowfield, then head east down-canyon until they reach the visible trail. Keeping north of the headwaters, the PCT descends toward a lone, three-foot-high cairn (5700–1.4) on a low knoll, turns northward, and then descends to campsites at a saddle (5500–0.3) between a 20-foot-high hill to the east and a high

K7   K7

PCT traversing southeast from slopes of Peak 6203

slope to the west. Better sites are on the hill. Just 230 yards north, we pass another campsite; then, farther down, we can see numerous campsites along the banks of the rumbling White Chuck River, below and east of us.

We may spot a blue grouse and its chicks as we descend alongside a swelling creek that we cross three times via log bridges. Hikers have camped beside each crossing. Leaving the last crossing (4700–1.5), our trail switchbacks down toward the White Chuck River, parallels it above its west bank, and then crosses it (4000–1.0) eastward via a wide, planked horse bridge. We leave the river's side, follow an undulating

K7   K7

route north, then descend to a good campsite just before a log crossing of cold, roaring Baekos Creek (3990–1.0), whose north bank contains much green mica schist. We follow the base of its high north bank downstream a short way, switchback over it, then descend to level ground and a number of log crossings over small creeks. Mountaineers intent on climbing Glacier Peak (10,541) usually leave the PCT between Baekos and Kennedy creeks. Should you try, bring rope, crampons and ice ax.

Near a campsite beside the north bank of Chetwot Creek (3730–1.3), the vegetation opens enough to give us views southwest to broad Black Mountain glacier, which spreads across the upper rim of a deeply glaciated side canyon. Continuing northward, we reach Sitkum Creek, make a precarious log crossing of it, then find ourselves at an excellent campsite (3852–0.8), with a raised fire ring and an isolated pit toilet.

* * * *

From a junction by this creekside campsite you can take a 3¼-mile alternate route that goes by inviting Kennedy Hot Spring. To take it, follow White Chuck Trail 643 as it first tra-verses northwest, then switchbacks down a crest to a junction beside Kennedy Creek. Here, on a spur trail, you curve southwest immediately over to the White Chuck River and, near a ranger station, bridge the river and hike 80 yards upstream to Kennedy Hot Spring (3275), a cubical, neck-deep hole in the ground. Many hikers used to skinny-dip at this 94°F soda spring, but its increasing popularity in the 1960s led to a ban of this fun in the early '70s. From the bridge, you can follow the river's west bank a short way down to campsites on a gentle slope. When you are ready to leave—if ever, considering what's ahead—retrace your steps to the Kennedy Creek junction, cross the creek, follow Trail 643 ¼ mile downstream, then climb 1¼ miles up Kennedy Ridge Trail 643A to the PCT.

* * * *

From Sitkum Creek a long climb lies ahead of us. After an initial 250-yard climb north, we reach an adequate campsite. One-quarter mile later, we reach a better one beside Sitkum Creek, and then we cross an unmapped creek just before reaching a moraine ridge. Enjoying a short-lasting descent northeast, we pass by small outcrops above us that are quartz-and-

K7, K8   K8

Glacier Peak, from slopes above Pumice Creek; Glacier Ridge is in the mid-ground, Kennedy Peak on the left skyline; Kennedy Glacier (left) and Scimitar Glacier (right) descend the flanks of Glacier Peak.

Too often, clouds roll in and obscure views; Glacier Peak, to the south, is the pointed peak left of center.

biotite-rich, Miocene-age granitic intrusions. The slopes above them are composed of andesitic lava flows from Glacier Peak. We reach chilly, glacier-fed Kennedy Creek (4050–1.2), a 10-yard-wide torrent that sometimes has to be forded, since bridges built across it have a tendency to be wiped out by avalanches. Without a bridge, the ford can be treacherous. Around July 11, 1975, one such avalanche tore down this creek and nearly overwhelmed the Kennedy Hot Spring area, 1½ miles downstream.

After crossing the creek, we climb southwest up a path cut through unstable morainal material that is in turn being undercut by the creek. Soon we reach a junction with Kennedy Ridge Trail 643A (4300–0.4), down which you can head west toward Kennedy Hot Spring. Its warm water indicates that molten magma is relatively close to the surface.

Now the real climb begins as we ascend six short, steep switchbacks past huge andesite blocks to the lower crest of Kennedy Ridge. This we struggle upward, stopping several times to catch our breath and to admire the scenery around us. In spots, this crest is no wider than the trail. The gradient eases off and we eventually reach an excellent campsite by Glacier Creek (5640–1.9), which occasionally has an

avalanche roar down its canyon, destroying all the trees in its path. Nevertheless, mountaineers and hikers alike camp in its track. For mountaineers, the shortest climb to Glacier Peak's summit begins here.

Leaving the creek, we switchback north, then climb northwest past adamellite boulders to a junction with Glacier Ridge Trail 658 (6050–0.7), which is a six-inch wide footpath that descends that ridge westward. After a short, steep descent northeast, we contour in that direction to jump-across Pumice Creek (5900–0.5), whose bed contains metamorphic, granitic and volcanic rocks. You might try to identify all three types and decipher their stories. A fair campsite is beside the north bank. Our trail descends west, then contours over to a ridge (5770–1.6). North of it, we descend even more, then cross a branch of Fire Creek (5370–0.8) just below its fork upstream. On an open meadow atop a bluff 20 yards north of it is your last good campsite this side of Fire Creek Pass. Now we make one final effort, and *voila!* a magnificent panorama of the North Cascades unfolds around us as we gain access to Fire Creek Pass (6350–1.7).

The North Cascades of Washington contain 756 glaciers, which account for about half of all the glacier area existing within the conterminus

K8   **K8**

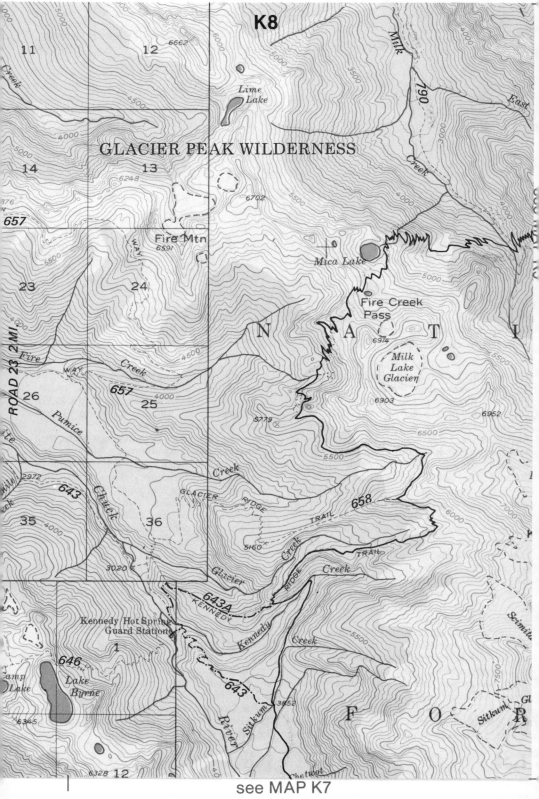

K8

11 12 6662

Lime
Lake

Creek

Milk

790

East

4000

5000

6000

3500

3000

Creek

GLACIER PEAK WILDERNESS

14 13
6248

6702

5500

4000

657

Fire Mtn
6591

Mica Lake

N A T I

Fire Creek
Pass

6974

23 24

Milk
Lake
Glacier

6903 6952

Fire

WAY

Creek

657

5779

6500

ROAD 23 2 MI.

26 25

4000

Pumice

5500

6000

Creek

GLACIER RIDGE

658

643

Chuck

36

TRAIL

2972

35 4000

5160

Creek

TRAIL

3020

Glacier

Creek

Creek

Scimitar

643A
KENNEDY

Kennedy Hot Springs
Guard Station

1

RIDGE

Kennedy Creek

5500

646

7500

Camp
Lake

Lake
Byrne

643

Sitkum

3852

F O R

6345

River

Sitkum

Sitkum Gl

6328 12

Chetwot

see MAP K7

United States. The range's great number of fairly high summits coupled with a year-round barrage from storms accounts for its vast accumulation of ice and snow. Chances are that you'll encounter at least one storm, lasting only a few days if you're lucky, before you reach the Canadian border.

At Fire Creek Pass, the trail goes between two large cairns 30 yards northwest of an emergency campsite. Our usually snowbound route switchbacks down a ridge north-northeast to a ford of the outlet of perpetually frozen Mica Lake (5430–1.1), whose cirque wall of dark metamorphic schist is intruded by light pegmatite dikes. From its shore, you can see dozens of unappealing switchbacks you'll have to climb to surmount the next ridge. As we descend farther, we must boulder-hop across wide, shallow Mica Creek, just east of which is a good, but open, campsite (5110–0.5) on a small bench. We continue to switchback eastward and reach a basin, another creek and a good, obvious campsite (4400–1.1). From it our unrelenting descent takes us down to deep, 5-yard-wide Milk Creek. A log crossing existed in 1973, but was replaced with a $40,000 "permanent" bridge in 1974. This, however, was wiped out by an early-summer avalanche in 1975. Another bridge was built and was still standing in 1977, but there's no guarantee a bridge will be there when you reach the creek.

Immediately beyond this crossing, we meet Milk Creek Trail 790 (3800–1.3), descending north, which the old Cascade Crest route used to follow before the train of switchbacks to the east of us was constructed. Snowfields and avalanche hazards probably prevented the construction of a trail that would contour around Glacier Peak at the 6000-foot level.

When you leave the creek and an adjacent campsite, take your time switchbacking up the east wall of this canyon. If the day is drizzly, you'll find that the "fog drip" on the flowers of this heavily vegetated slope will saturate you from the thighs down. Ahead of you grow miles of this inconsiderate vegetation that you must switchback through. Rationalizing your fate, you can observe that in this weather there are no flies or mosquitoes around to bother you. When you finally finish your creekless ascent and reach the ridgecrest (5750–2.5), you may be greeted by a marmot. If not, at least you can expect a rest at an open campsite.

After a short, negligible climb, we contour the east slope of our ridge and leave behind its outcrops of densely clustered, light-colored

K8, K9

Miocene dikes, sills and irregular masses. As we enter the deeply glaciated East Fork Milk Creek basin, these outcrops give way to ancient, metamorphic rocks. Along the south wall of this basin, our trail passes just below a small knoll (5860–1.5), 100 yards below which is an adequate campsite. Beyond this point, we shortly cross a hundred-yard-wide boulder field that is laced with creeklets. Our route now climbs gently northeast to another ridge (6010–0.6), from which we can see an open campsite at the base of a ridge knoll 10 feet below and 100 yards north of us. The trail switchbacks slightly up the ridge, contours southeast across it, then starts the first of 59 switchbacks down to Vista Creek. After a few of these, we reach the Dolly Vista campsite (5830–0.7) beneath a few, protective mountain hemlocks. A pit toilet is immediately north; water is found by traversing about 100 yards southeast.

From the campsite, our path switchbacks northeast down through open forest to a saddle (5380–0.5) on Vista Ridge, where we reach a dry, open campsite. Northeast of us this resistant ridge is composed of Miocene intrusive rocks that are capped with remnant Quaternary

andesite flows from Glacier Peak. Starting down into deep, glaciated Vista Creek canyon, we're grateful that we're descending the last 38 switchbacks rather than ascending them. By the time we reach the last one, 50 yards from the creek, we've left most of the "rain forest" behind, and we hike 100 yards northeast to a large, signed campsite (3650–2.6) beside Vista Creek. From it, our trail descends into a Douglas-fir forest that has an understory of huckleberry, ferns and Oregon grape.

The trail curves east and the gradient eases as we approach a log crossing of wide, silty Vista Creek (2877–2.1). On its southeast bank is a good campsite with a fire ring and pit toilet. Now we contour east across a gentle slope to a crossing of Gamma Creek (2910–0.8). Part of its flow is derived from the 140°F., sodium-chloride-bicarbonate-rich waters of Gamma Hot Springs (5000), about three miles upstream. Our trail gradually curves southeast and arrives at a junction with Suiattle River Trail 798 (3028–0.7), which first bears southeast before climbing south up-river. The PCT descends north, switchbacks down to a 50-yard-long horse bridge across the silty-gray Suiattle

K9

K9, K10

The Ermine Glacier spreads out across Glacier Peak's lower flanks; viewed from switchbacks just below Vista Ridge

see MAP K9

see MAP K11

K10

Miners Ridge

Image Lake

Lookout 6210

BM 2481

784

E R

3000

4000

3000

Suiattle

BM 2848

784

BM 1834

MINERS CR TRAIL

5430

4000

795

TRAIL

3000

Miners Creek

Middle Ridge

Mile 35

4036

2877

2798

Lyman Camp

3500

Creek

3028

791

Creek

5387

Creek

4928

3472

River

Small Cr

798

Gamma

Vista

4000

5336

L

4500

5000

Gamma Hot Springs

5500

Gamma Ridge

5885

Creek

798

River

GLACIER PEAK WILDERNESS

Gamma

Dusty

7009

Gamma Peak

6000

6500

4500

Mile 39.8 end

4000

798

792

Glacier

Chocolate

Creek

Glacier

5500

6000

View northeast from upper Vista Creek canyon: Plummer Mountain and Fortress Mountain stand above smooth, dropping Middle Ridge

River, then immediately reaches a junction with the Suiattle River access trail (2860–0.8).

From here you can follow a trail southeast ⅓ mile upstream to Lyman Camp. Its large, flat site is a nice place to camp, once you get used to the horse manure. If you turn left (northwest) and follow this trail downstream, you'll pass by some campsites, then after 330 yards reach a good shelter and a separate toilet both above the south bank of Miners Creek.

Our next trail segment, straight ahead, makes long, easy switchbacks up to the lower edge of Middle Ridge, then climbs east up its north slope to a junction with the Buck Creek Pass trail (4580–4.4), which climbs five miles south to the pass. From this junction you can follow the old PCT route, which makes an initial steep descent north, bridges a sluggish creek, and then quickly arrives at a very good campsite on the south bank of Miners Creek—a 0.4-mile side trip. However, the new PCT continues ¼ mile east to a creek, then ¼ mile north to Miners Creek (4490–0.5). You can camp nearby. From the creek's horse bridge, the PCT makes an initial jog downstream, then passes more than half a dozen creeks and creeklets as it climbs east. Switchbacks ultimately take you 400 feet higher to a junction with the old PCT route (5280–1.5). You continue to climb eastward, soon getting southwest views of majestic Glacier Peak and southern views of Fortress Mountain and the deep, glaciated canyon below it. The route turns north and soon reaches a spur trail (5790–0.7) that goes about 150 yards east to a two-tent site.

Climbing, we reach a second trail in 0.1 mile, this one a footpath northeast over to the Railroad Creek Trail, which vaults Cloudy Pass. Immediately before Suiattle Pass, we meet a minor trail that climbs to the crest above the PCT. On the crest (5990–0.3), we meet an abandoned trail that starts east across the pass.

Switchbacks, often accompanied by snow patches, take us down to a creeklet (5730–0.3), from which a spur trail climbs north-northwest to a hemlock/meadow campsite. More switchbacks take us down to a junction with the Railroad Creek Trail (5550–0.2). If you've been having snow problems, you may want to start down this trail, which forks in about 0.1 mile. The north banch, down Agnes Creek, is the old PCT route, and although it is supposedly unmaintained, it was very hikeable in 1982.

The new PCT takes you on a fairly scenic rollercoaster route in and out of two deep side canyons. Your route is downhill all the way to the first of these (4980–1.3), which in August 1982, had a signed campsite—under snow! Leaving this cirque and its giant, rockfall boulders, which have buried the creek, we switchback (needlessly?) high up on the Agnes Creek canyon wall. After a northward traverse, our trail bends into the second side canyon, and we immediately encounter a spur trail (5450–1.4). This one climbs 110 yards to a poor, heather-bound, one-tent site. In 100 yards, the PCT gives rise to two more spur trails, one descending 60 yards to a two-tent site. The other climbs 90 yards to another poor, heather-bound, one-

K10, K11   **K11**

Canyon
Lake

Cr

Canyon

7435

CHELAN CO
SNOHOMISH CO

7419

Sitting Bull
Mtn

7759

Big Spruce Camp

North
Star Mtn

W E N A

Cloudy Peak

7509

797

Plummer
Mtn

7870

Miners

Ridge

NATIONAL RANGE

Suiattle Pass

5983

BM
6438

Cloudy Pass

5605

12

784

Glacier Peak Mines

BM 5488

5549

1279

6835

Lyman
Lake

5587

Forest

Miners

BM 4483

Creek

5500

4648

5000

5000

GLACIER PEAK WILDERNESS

W

Middle

BM 5402

6655

9197

Ridge

8386

6000

2052

5279

Small

Creek

Fortress
Mtn

8674

To HOLDEN and LAKE CHELAN

K12

1272

WENATCHEE

Agnes
Mtn

N A T I O N A L

F O R E S T

Swamp Creek
Camp

GLACIER

PEAK

712

Spruce Creek Camp

WILDERNESS

Mount
Blankenship

Needle
Peak

Saddle Bow
Mtn

Hemlock
Camp

tent site. A trickling creeklet flows between these three exposed sites.

Up to a dozen more creeklets are passed as we descend to a bridged creek on the floor of the second side canyon. About 300 yards past it, we meet yet another spur trail (4810–1.6), this one climbing 140 yards to a sheltered, two-tent site, with view and spring-fed creeklet. The PCT then drops east, briefly switchbacks west, turns east again and in 60 yards reaches the last spur trail (4680–0.2). This crosses the adjacent creek and ends at some small sites among firs of a nearby ridge.

Now we have a generally moderate descent to Agnes Creek, the forested route being punctuated with some bushy, wildflowered patches that present views. At last we bridge Agnes Creek and in about 150 yards reach Hemlock Camp (3560–2.0). If you've taken the old PCT route, which is considerably shorter, you'll meet the new route here. The camp comes equipped with benches, a table and a fire ring.

Continuing north along our near-the-creek route through a forest of western hemlock, Engelmann spruce, western redcedar, Douglas-fir and western white pine, we descend past Mt. Blankenship (5926) to the west and Needle Peak (7885) to the east before reaching Spruce Creek Camp (2900–2.7). At this site, you'll find only log stumps around a fire pit, but it's still quite a nice camp.

Our canyon grows ever deeper as we trek northward, catch a glimpse of the blue-green waters of the South Fork, and then contour over to well-equipped Swamp Creek Camp (2780–

1.3). Here, beside the seven-yard-wide torrent, Swamp Creek Trail 712 begins a three-mile climb up the creek toward Dark Glacier, which is tucked in a deep amphitheater below Dark Peak. Leaving this very good campsite, we cross the creek on a sturdy horse bridge, progress north to the rim of the inner gorge of the South Fork (2570–1.6), then gradually curve down to a junction with West Fork Agnes Creek Trail 1272 (2160–1.4), which descends west-north-west to that creek. Several fair campsites are just west of this junction, but much better ones are at Five Mile Camp, about 100 yards east, above the west bank of Pass Creek. These are the last campsites we'll see within Glacier Peak Wilderness. Hiking northeast, we'll soon leave the granitic rocks of the Cloudy Pass batholith behind and walk upon schist and gneiss that date back to Jurassic times or earlier.

The overpowering canyon which we hike through bears a strong resemblance to deep Kings Canyon in the Sierra Nevada of California, except that this one supports a much denser growth of flowers, shrubs and trees. We pass by seasonal Trapper Creek (2070–1.2), then approach Agnes Creek which, like its South Fork, possesses an inner gorge. Our undulating trail goes right out to its brink at several spots, then descends to switchbacks that take us down to a massive bridge 40 feet above roaring Agnes Creek (1550–3.6), which, at this point, is larger than most rivers we've seen along the Pacific Crest Trail. Now within the Lake Chelan National Recreation Area, we cross the 27-yard-long bridge, climb a low ridge, then contour

K11, K12   K12, K13, K14

Glacier Peak, viewed from near Suiattle Pass

see MAP K14

K13

N P

LAK
CHEL
NATION
REC AR

GLACIER PEAK WILDERNES

see MAP K12

northwest to a trailhead at a bend in the Stehekin River Road (1650–0.2). Just 35 yards up the road is High Bridge Campground, with a shelter and outside tables. Water can be obtained by walking back down the road to the high bridge and then descending steep, short switchbacks northward to the west bank of the Stehekin River.

You can descend the road 200 yards to the High Bridge Ranger Station, which is immediately northeast of a bend in the Stehekin River. During the 1989 summer, shuttle buses from the

K14
Five Mile Camp

Stehekin resort area, 10.6 miles downstream, departed daily at 7:30 A.M., 9:00 A.M., and 2 P.M., arriving at the High Bridge Ranger Station about an hour later. The buses continued from this station north to Cottonwood Camp, 11.4 miles up-river, before returning to Stehekin. From the High Bridge Ranger Station, the buses in summer 1989 left for Stehekin at 10:45 A.M., 12:45 P.M., and 6:00 P.M. However, these departure times, like those from Stehekin, have changed in the past and could change in the future. In 1989 the bus fare was $4 per person, each way, so you could leisurely ride up and down 22 miles of the Stehekin River canyon and decide which of its nine campgrounds was best for you. A one-way trip from High Bridge to Stehekin was $2.

If you're like most hikers, you'll be weary by the time the PCT reaches the Agnes Creek trailhead, and you'll welcome the opportunity to relax overnight in Stehekin. The North Cascades Lodge dominates the Stehekin complex, providing good meals and accommodations. The old Golden West Lodge has been transformed into the National Park Service Information Center, at which you can get wilderness permits as well as information. There are also a gift shop, a packer station, a small, limited general store, and—perhaps most important—a post office.

You'll find camping ¼ mile north of the complex at Purple Point Campground. It is possible, though very unlikely, that you'll encounter western rattlesnakes here, for they are quite common in the Stehekin area though become less common up-canyon. More likely, however, you'll meet black bears, which have become an increasing nuisance as they've grown bolder in recent years. You can expect to see them at any of the nine roadside campgrounds. Be sure you know how to "bearbag" your food.

Many backpackers hiking from Stevens Pass through the Glacier Peak Wilderness to High Bridge end their hike there and take the shuttle bus to Stehekin. They then take the Lady of the Lake ferry ($13 one way in 1989) along 50-mile-long Lake Chelan to the city of Chelan, at the lake's far end. (In its deepest spot, this huge lake is 1486 feet deep, or in other words, its deepest point is 386 feet below sea level and is therefore the lowest land surface in the western United States. Glaciers certainly performed an impressive excavation!) The advantage of ending at Chelan rather than at Rainy Pass is that you are much closer to Stevens Pass, your starting point. The drive from Stevens Pass to Chelan is 90 miles, but it is an *additional* 103 miles to Rainy Pass. For non-through PCT Hikers, that additional shuttle is not worth the generally viewless hike along the last stretch of Section K.

To complete this stretch from the Agnes Creek trailhead, you walk down to the nearby bridge over the Stehekin River, immediately beyond which you'll find another trailhead by

Recommended minimum distances for bearbagging your food

the High Bridge Ranger Station (1600–0.1). Take this trail, which starts initially east, then switchbacks up to a granitic bench with a trail junction (1860–0.4). The trail southeast descends to the Cascade Corral, on the Stehekin River Road. The PCT climbs northward, topping a low, bedrock ridge and reaching a junction at the west arm of swampy Coon Lake (2180–0.7). From it, a rigorously switchbacking

K14

K14

View up Lake Chelan, from Stehekin resort

1233

NORTH CASCADES

Bridge

Creek

North Fork
Camp

N A T I O N A L   P A R K

Waddell

Waddell
Lake

Creek

Storm

Creek

Mine
Bridge Creek
Campground

Bridge Creek
Ranger Station

Mile 14

STEHEKIN

Shady
Campground

Creek

Creek

McGregor
Mtn

Salt Creek

Glacier

McGregor

Bridge

RIVER

Buzzard

Creek

Dolly Varden
Campground

Coon
Lake

L A K E   C H E L

Tumwater Bridge

Tumwater
Campground

Creek

N A T I O N A L   R E C R E A T

High Bridge
Campground

High Bridge
Station

Mile 16

STEHEKIN

Cabin

RIVER

Mile 8

trail climbs about 7 miles to the top of McGregor Mountain. The PCT heads northwest, passing two seasonal creeklets on a mostly descending grade to yet another junction (1940–0.8). Here we meet the Old Wagon Trail, which winds 200 yards west down to the Stehekin River Road. Dolly Varden Campground, with two sites, lies 0.4 mile up it.

The PCT coincides with a stretch of the Old Wagon Trail, and we cross two seasonal creeklets before climbing to McGregor Creek (2195–0.6). Our ascent abates, then soon we ford Buzzard Creek (2260–0.4), and later, two-branched Canim Creek (2160–0.7). In about ⅓ mile we leave the Old Wagon Trail and make an undulating traverse that ends about 50 yards

K14

K14

before Clear Creek, roughly opposite the Bridge Creek Ranger Station (2105–1.3), and just beyond it pass Bridge Creek Campground with its shelter. After a few more minutes of walking, we arrive at the PCT Bridge Creek trailhead (2180–0.3), located 240 yards southeast of Road 3505's crossing of Bridge Creek.

Back on a trail again, we climb up a wandering path that takes us past a small lily-pad pond, on a bench, then winds to the edge of the Bridge Creek gorge and climbs its slopes to jump-across Berry Creek (2720–1.7). Watching out for western toads, we climb a little higher on the slope before we descend to a sideplanked horse bridge above wild, roaring Bridge Creek (2540–1.0). Climbing a few yards north of the bridge, we reach the dusty, rustic North Fork Camp atop a rocky bluff that overlooks the junction of the North Fork with Bridge Creek. The camp's resident landlords—golden-mantled ground squirrels—may exact "rent" from your backpack while you're not looking.

From this site we switchback east up to a junction with North Fork Bridge Creek Trail 1233 (2810–0.3), which climbs northward. We climb east up a bushy, aromatic slope, reach a point several hundred feet above Bridge Creek, and take in gorgeous views below us as we descend slightly to a small, stonewall campsite imme-

K14

View up South Fork Bridge Creek canyon

Inner Gorge of Agnes Creek

diately before a saddle. Beyond it, we descend north to wide, alder-lined Maple Creek (3070–1.5), which has a suspension bridge crossing it 25 yards upstream. Be careful climbing the talus boulders to and from the bridge. We then follow our level, relaxing path east and come to a 250-yard-long spur trail (3130–1.7) that descends southeast, steeply at first, through a meadow of tall cow parsnips, to Six Mile Camp, a well-furnished site designed with horseback riders in mind.

Not far beyond this spur trail, the Rainbow Lake Trail (3240–0.7) peels off from the PCT, descends southeast, and climbs up South Fork Canyon to Pass 6230, immediately west of domineering Bowan Mountain (7895), and Rainbow Lake south of the pass. Just 330 yards down this trail is South Fork Camp, beside Bridge Creek. From the junction, our route continues east through alternating forest and brush

K14, K15

see MAP L1

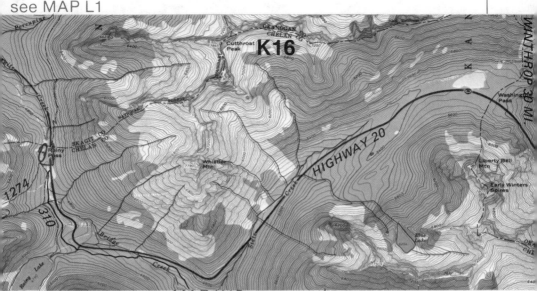

see MAP K15

cover, then reaches a junction with a 110-yard-long spur trail (3510–1.5) that descends first southwest, then southeast to the loveliest Bridge Creek campsite: Hide-Away Camp. Strictly for backpackers, this shady, creekside campsite has a table, log stumps and a fire ring.

Continuing east within hearing distance of the creek, we leave this campsite and eventually turn northeast just before reaching a junction with Twisp Pass Trail 1277 (3635–0.9), which curves east and bridges Bridge Creek after 70 yards. Forty yards east-northeast from this crossing, a right fork veers southeast 30 yards to the large, flat, dusty, but well-furnished Fire-weed Camp.

Our trail climbs moderately northeast and in ⅔ mile passes an old log cabin with good camping, then leaves North Cascades National Park just before a series of creeks, *not* just after them. Our trail then reaches a shallow, wide ford of Bridge Creek (4145–2.2), but a foot-trail bypass route begins about 100 yards before the ford. From where the foot and horse paths reunite, we climb to the nearby Crocker Cabin Historical Site, with a campsite, and immediately past it reach Stiletto Peak Trail 1232 (4250–0.2), which leads east-northeast. After a few minutes' walk, we make a log crossing of State Creek, pass an adequate campsite on its

west bank, and then continue north toward the traffic we hear on the highway above us. We quickly encounter abandoned Washington Pass Trail 1275 (4420–0.5), on our right (east), which was desecrated when the North Cascades Highway (State 20) was paved over it. This new road, completed in 1972, lessened the wilderness experience at least to the same extent that the new Tioga Road in Yosemite National Park diminished that park's High Sierra wilderness character.

Our trail arcs northwest up to a spur trail (4510–0.5) that forks right (west) 50 yards to a parking lot beside the highway at a point 0.1 mile below its crossing of Bridge Creek. Our trail, also called Bridge Creek Trail 419, bears west-southwest 35 yards to a bridge across Bridge Creek, then parallels the highway west up to the outlet creek (4705–0.7) of Rainy Lake. From it, our path climbs gently north, levels off and strikes a course through the soggy headwaters of Bridge Creek before reaching a junction with Rainy Lake Trail 310 only 20 yards before our trail reaches a large trailhead parking lot. No camping is allowed at Rainy Lake. Immediately past the lot we cross a road, built in 1978, which cuts across Highway 20's Rainy Pass (4855–1.1), and bends north to nearby rest areas, one on each side of the highway.

K15   # K16

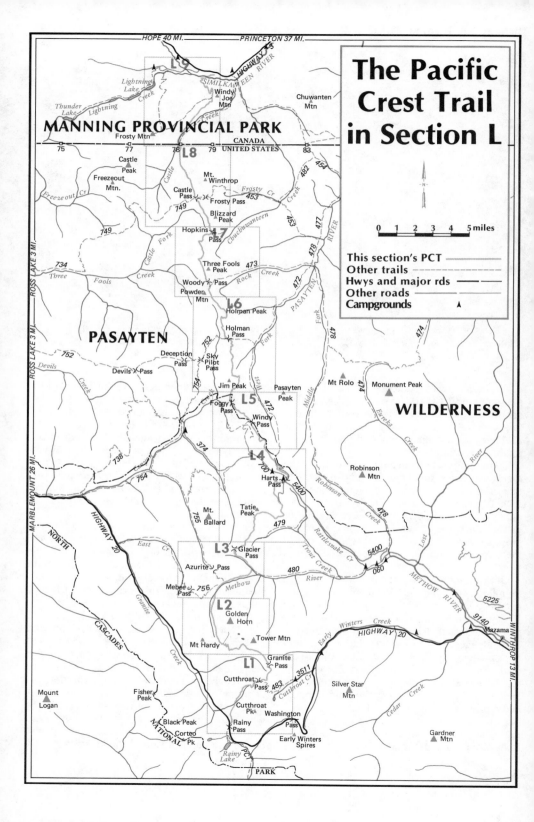

The Pacific Crest Trail in Section L

-N-

| 0 | 1 | 2 | 3 | 4 | 5 miles |

This section's PCT ———
Other trails ————
Hwys and major rds ━━━
Other roads ━━━
Campgrounds ▲

HOPE 40 MI.   PRINCETON 37 MI.

L9

Lightning Lake
Thunder Lake
Lightning Creek
Windy Joe Mtn
Chuwanten Mtn

MANNING PROVINCIAL PARK

Frosty Mtn   CANADA
75   77   78 L8 79 UNITED STATES   83

Castle Peak
Freezeout Mtn.
Freeze out Cr
Mt. Winthrop
Castle Pass
749
Frosty Pass   453
Frosty Cr
482 454

L7
Hopkins Pass
Castle Fork
Blizzard Peak
Couchbwanteen
473   477   478

734
Three Fools Creek
Three Fools Peak
Woody Pass
Powder Mtn
Rock Creek
472

PASAYTEN

752
Deception Pass
Devils Pass
Devils Creek
Sky Pilot Pass
Holman Peak
Holman Pass
West Fork
754

L6

Jim Peak
Foggy Pass
L5
Windy Pass
472
Pasayten Peak
Middle Fork
Mt Rolo
Monument Peak
474

WILDERNESS

374
L4
Harts Pass
5400
Robinson Mtn
478
Robinson Creek
Eureka Creek

738
754
Mt. Ballard
755
Tatie Peak
479
Rattlesnake Cr
5400
060

NORTH
HIGHWAY 20
East Cr
L3
Glacier Pass
Azurite Pass
Mebee Pass 756
Metbow
Trout Creek
480
River
5400
METHOW RIVER
5225
9140
Mazama

CASCADES
Granite Creek
L2
Golden Horn
Mt Hardy
Tower Mtn
Early Winters Creek
HIGHWAY 20
WINTHROP 13 MI.

Mount Logan
Fisher Peak
L1
Granite Pass
Cutthroat Pass
483
3511
Cutthroat Cr
Silver Star Mtn
Cedar Creek

Black Peak
Corteo Pk
Cutthroat Pk
Rainy Pass
Washington Pass
Early Winters Spires
Gardner Mtn

NATIONAL
Rainy Lake
PARK

MARBLEMOUNT 26 MI.
ROSS LAKE 3 MI.

Section L: Highway 20 at Rainy Pass to Highway 3 in Manning Park

Introduction: The final leg of the Pacific Crest Trail leads from the North Cascades Highway (Washington 20) at Rainy Pass to Manning Provincial Park, British Columbia. In this relatively short trek, there is vehicle access only at Harts Pass (30 miles north), where gravel Road 5400 crosses the crest to serve a turn-of-the-century mining district.

In this entire section, the Pacific Crest Trail is well east of much of the Cascade Range. To the west, Mt. Baker, Mt. Shuksan and the Picket Range receive the brunt of any bad weather. Overall snow accumulation along the PCT route here is much less than it is at Mt. Baker, and PCT hikers may enjoy sunshine when Puget Sound and the western mountains are cloud- and rain-bound. Nonetheless, until midsummer, hikers should be prepared for a snow-covered and icy trail. After the snow melts, the mosquitoes have a heyday, so the most pleasant month to hike this section is, usually, September. Typically the winter snows do not start in earnest until at least October (but beware the exception!).

Near Rainy Pass the scenery is spectacular, and many mountains are crowned with craggy spires of Golden Horn granodiorite. Consequently the PCT only occasionally follows the crest of the Cascades exactly: much of the mileage is in long traverses and river valleys. Even if backpackers were as surefooted and agile as mountain goats, they would not choose a route true to the divide. Then, as the intrusive rocks give way to lower Cretaceous graywackes, the terrain becomes hilly, so the PCT can follow the crest more closely than before.

North of Harts Pass the PCT offers a variety of scenery and terrains. High meadows, wooded slopes and valleys, as well as rugged, precipitous ridges make up the bulk of this section, which traverses the backbone of the 790-square-mile Pasayten Wilderness. In good weather the views are frequently spectacular, particularly in the fall when larch, spruce and scrub maple splash gold, green and red across the slopes.

Declination: 20°E

Mileages:

	South to North	Distances between Points	North to South
Highway 20 at Rainy Pass	0.0		69.1
Cutthroat Pass................................	5.1	5.1	64.0
Methow Pass	10.6	5.5	58.5
Glacier Pass.................................	21.2	10.6	47.9
Harts Pass	30.5	9.3	38.6
Windy Pass	35.7	5.2	33.4
Holman Pass	44.3	8.6	24.8
Woody Pass.................................	50.2	5.9	18.9
Hopkins Pass................................	55.3	5.1	13.8
U.S.-Canadian border at Monument 78	61.9	6.6	7.2
Highway 3 in Manning Park	69.1	7.2	0.0

Supplies: No supply points are found until northbound hikers reach trail's end, in Manning Provincial Park. In it, just west of the trailhead, you'll find Manning Park Lodge, with food and lodging, and the park headquarters, where you can get information. Greyhound Bus service is available to and from Vancouver, B.C.

Problems: Very early and very late season hikers should be ready for treacherous, precipitous snow slopes, avalanche hazards and dangerously exposed hiking along parts of this PCT section. It is also wise to acquaint yourself with the border-crossing information on page 21 of this book to avoid unpleasant hassles associated with customs and immigration regulations of both the United States and Canada.

Black Peak (right) stands high above Granite Creek canyon

Hartline

see MAP K16

A large, off-road rest area, equipped with "plush" toilet facilities has been built west of the North Cascades Highway. Ample trailhead parking for horse packers and hikers parallels the shoulder of the road. Nearby outhouses are smaller than those in the rest area. Our north-bound path bisects the narrow peninsula of wilderness between the highway and an eastern parking lot. At the north end of the parking lot we enter Douglas-fir forest to begin a climbing, northward traverse. One creek, draining Cut-throat Peak (7865) cascades across our path even in September and October. Numerous other streams are of nuisance value early in the season, but typically dry up by late August. The grade levels as we near Porcupine Creek (5080–1.5), which we bridge. Then we turn northeast to parallel it and resume our ascent. A pair of switchbacks lift the path away from the stream bed and guide us onto a steep, open slope where avalanches sweeping down from Peaks 7004 and 7762 may threaten May and June hikers. After traversing higher to contour around the headwaters bowl of Porcupine Creek, we switchback up the steep, glacier-formed basin wall. Deciduous larches, the poetic tamaracks, add foreground to the rugged panorama un-folding before us. Black Peak (8970) and Corteo

L1

Peak (8100), across the highway, front the more distant North Cascades. Scrub huckleberry and heather compose the basic ground cover which "springtime" (July) flowers eloquently embroider.

We pass campsites which are inviting, though lacking late-season water, as the PCT levels to the west of grassy, granitic Cutthroat Pass (6820–3.6). Here Cutthroat Lake Trail 483 forks east to begin its traversing descent to Cutthroat Lake (4935), visible in the valley below. Liberty Bell Mountain (7720), a favorite rock climb, peaks above the ridge across the lake. We head northeast to arc around two bowls, contouring across steep scree slopes beneath precipitous cliffs. Before leaving the second cirque we choose the upper and more traveled of two trails. The lower trail dead-ends on the ridge 100 yards ahead. Climbing slightly, we reach a crest and pause to enjoy a picturesque view of Tower Mountain (8444).

Our route continues northward, balancing precariously across a precipice before executing several short, tight switchbacks down the rugged north ridge. Avoiding the rock walls above Granite Pass, we descend south to zigzag above beautiful, glacier-carved Swamp Creek valley. Then, at Granite Pass (6290–2.4), we reach "terra flata" and are welcomed into a sheltered camp. Don't expect convenient late-season water here.

From the camp our route to Methow Pass makes a long traverse of the open lower slopes of Tower Mountain. Scrub subalpine fir, western white pine, mountain ash and heather provide little protection for sun-beaten or windswept walkers. Outcrops of the Golden Horn granodiorite are clearly exposed by the trail cut. Upon reaching the bowl below Snowy Lakes, we lose some precious elevation as we drop into an idyllic park, where a bubbling stream, grassy flowerlands, larch and spruce all recommend a large campsite (6300–2.2). Shedding our packs and donning our sweaters, we settle in. Firewood in this delicate alpine valley is in limited supply, and is better left unburned. A cross trail from the campsite heads north, up-valley, to Upper and Lower Snowy Lakes in a higher cirque.

From the camp a pair of switchbacks help us climb out of the bowl to set up the approach to Methow Pass (6600–0.9) (pronounced METhow). Views of Mt. Arriva (8215) and Fisher Peak (8050) are the last we'll have of the mountains west of Granite Creek. Mt. Hardy (7197), just west of the pass, and Golden Horn (8366), to the north, will stay with us during our trek down the valley of the Methow River's West Fork. Like most high-elevation "campsites," Methow Pass is waterless when it is not swampy.

Leaving Methow Pass on a northward traverse, we spy below us a backpackers' campsite on a level bench with an uncertain water supply. Now zigzagging into the valley, the PCT crosses a few infant streams, then straightens to parallel the West Fork of the Methow. From here, at sunset, Golden Horn glows spectacularly against the deep blue-black of the eastern sky. A long,

L1
View southeast from Cutthroat Pass

L2

Hartline

slight but steady downgrade brings us to Golden Creek and Willis Camp (4570–4.2). Nimbly rock-hopping the stream, we have only a short stint before bridging the West Fork Methow River (4390–0.7). A small camp by the bridge on the east bank is the best trailside camp between here and Brush Creek. Within 200 yards the level path enters the first of several avalanche paths.

At a PCT mileage sign we merge onto the route of the old Cascade Crest Trail (now Trail 756) (4380–0.8). Westbound, this overgrown trail climbs out of the Methow Valley via Mebee Pass to descend along East Creek, pass the Gold Hill Mine, and meet Granite Creek and Washington Highway 20. This trail also extends diagonally 0.2 mile downhill to riverside Horse Heaven Camp. The PCT, bending east and crossing what the map calls Jet Creek, reaches a junction with Mill Creek Trail 755 (4380–0.2), which looks like a rocky stream bed in the grass of the clearing. Almost immediately we cross signed Jet Creek, dry in late season.

The scree fields change in character and composition as we head east out of the granodiorite body and into a zone of lower Cretaceous graywackes ("muddy" sandstones), conglomerates, argillites and shales. Then our trail turns northeast to enter the mouth of Brush Creek's canyon. After passing a small campsite, we cross Brush Creek on a bridge and in 50 yards meet West Fork Methow Trail 480 (4280–1.9). Here we zig once and start climbing in earnest along steep, brushy Brush Creek. A few small campsites line the trail in this fairly hospitable and picturesque valley, and high in the west some small glaciers cling between the rugged upper cliffs of Azurite Peak (8400). A few switchbacks ease the grade of the final climb to Glacier Pass (5520–2.8), where campsites without nearby late-season water are found in the forest-sheltered gap. Two trails, the first heading north, the second trending west, are separated by 100 PCT trail yards.

Ambling on, we gear down for a long, zigzagging climb to a grassy pass. Dwindling scrub subalpine fir, spruce and larch accompany us up the slope. Pausing for breath, we appreciate the view of three little lakes nestled near the head of South Fork Slate Creek's

L2, L3

L3

Tower Mountain, from above Tower Pass

Hartline

glacial valley, as well as the broadening panorama of the North Cascades. At last we top off the climb and descend slightly along the ridge into an alpine-garden pass (6750–2.6) above South Fork Trout Creek. Here the trail begins a long traverse north-eastward. Beyond the first ridge we round is a pleasant trailside campsite with water (6600–1.0). Continuing, we climb to a windy, viewful pass (6900–0.9) on the southwest shoulder of Tatie Peak (7386). As our trail contours around the peak we pass stratified outcrops of alternating shale and conglomerate, then approach a knife-edge saddle above Ninetynine Basin, beyond which the Slate Peak Lookout Tower (7440) is prominent. A descending traverse guides us around Peak 7405 through a gap in a side ridge. Both the Harts Pass Road and the Brown Bear Mine house remains can be seen from here.

Angling down, we pass below the sites of the mine tunnels, not obvious from the trail, and approach dirt Road 500. Twenty yards short of the road (6440–2.8), PCT emblems guide us onto a newer stretch of trail that avoids it. In 150 yards we cross the jeep-trail access to the Brown

L3, L4

see MAP L4

L3

see MAP L2

see MAP L5

see MAP L3

Bear tunnels, and then continue to traverse above Road 500. A trail from the road joins us as we approach and then thread a minor gap (6390–0.7). Beneath exposed outcrops of banded argillite and gray sandstone, we traverse north along a steep hillside before our trail turns

to traverse down to Harts Pass (6198–1.3). An infrequently manned Forest Service Guard Station, on the east side of Harts Pass Road 5400 across from a parking lot and car-camping area, sometimes has a backcountry register for hikers to sign. The small community of Mazama is

Climbing toward Glacier Pass

Tatie Peak, from Slate Peak area

18.7 miles east on Road 5400. Also at the pass, a road branches east-northeast from Road 5400 to parallel the PCT for 1.3 miles before switch-backing up to Slate Peak Lookout.

The Slate Creek mining district was a relatively rich mining area in the State of Washington. Boom camps were fairly populated in the early 1890s until word of the Klondike bonanza lured all the miners away. Del Hart, who owned some mines near Slate Creek, commissioned Charles H. Ballard in 1895 to survey a road from Mazama to the mining area. The pass through which the road was routed now bears Hart's name. The road today is a favorite summer-recreation route and one to the best access roads to the Pasayten Wilderness, which we will soon enter. Gold, silver, copper, lead and zinc are among the metals whose ores were mined in the Slate Creek District. An interesting sidelight to the history of this area is that the first hydro-electric power plant in the high Cascades was installed here. O. B. Brown designed, paid for and supervised construction of the 350-kilowatt plant that he located on the South Fork of Slate Creek.

From the PCT crossing of Road 5400, a scant 35 yards north-northwest of the pass proper, we proceed east-northeast through partly open

L4

spruce-fir woods parallel to a Forest Service road and about 100 feet below it. Beyond a meadow our trail switchbacks up onto a small shoulder with an adequate camp, where we come to a junction (6880–1.4) with a spur trail to the road. It is about 0.1 mile east-southeast down this spur to parking spaces.

Continuing west-northwest on the PCT, we ascend gradually past scattered Lyall larches, common on this small shoulder. Soon the shoulder gives out, leaving the trail hanging on the side of Slate Peak, with spectacular views down the Slate Creek valley, dominated by Mt. Baker (10,778) and other peaks to the west. Mt. Baker is a living volcano, and in March 1975 it increased its thermal activity, which lead many to suspect it would soon erupt. Since the end of the Ice Age, about 10,000 years ago, it has erupted violently at least four times, and on at least four other occasions it has produced enough steam to melt glaciers and trigger large mudflows. Some future PCT hikers may just witness a full-scale eruption.

Passing occasional outcrops of gray and green slate, we descend gradually to the pass (6700–2.2) just above Benson Creek Camp. Still on the west side of the divide, we climb up around an arm and descend past Buffalo Pass (6550–0.7) to Windy Pass (6257–0.9), from where a trail crosses ours to descend south-southwest to Indiana Basin. In about 35 yards we pass a sign heralding our entrance into the Pasayten Wilderness.

The PCT continues north-northwest, leading us out of true-to-its-name Windy Pass and around to the northeast cirque of Tamarack Peak (7290)—clad in tamarack, or larch. After crossing a small basin with water and an adequate camp, the trail switchbacks up to and over an arm of Tamarack Peak, descends the open north cirque, and finally traverses the northwest arm of the mountain to Foggy Pass (6180–2.2). From this pass we cross to the west side of the divide for a brief wooded hike to Jim Pass (6270–0.7). Then, back on the east side of the divide, we traverse around Jim Peak (7033) to

L4 **L4, L5, L6**

Silver Star Mountain, viewed from Harts Pass area   *Hartline*

Windy Pass   *Hartline*

see MAP L6

see MAP L4

the rocky shoulder called Devils Backbone (6180–1.3). Descending into the north cirque of Jim Peak, the PCT crosses the head of Shaw Creek and ascends gradually for about a mile before plunging down switchbacks to a junction with Trail 752 at Holman Pass (5050–4.4). This pass is heavily wooded and not particularly nice for camping, although wildlife abounds in the vicinity.

We climb northwest out of Holman Pass, crossing the outlet stream from Goat Lakes in about a mile, and switchback up a grassy knoll to

L6

see MAP L7

L6

see MAP L5

a never failing spring (6200–2.4) and a good but much used camp. From here the trail traverses up the steep, grassy slopes bounding Canyon Creek to Rock Pass (6491–1.2). Our trail bypasses the precipitous east-wall traverse of Powder Mountain (7714), climbs over the divide about 300 yards southeast of Rock Pass and descends southeast out of Rock Pass to switchback into the avalanche-swept valley of Rock Creek. The PCT next traverses northwestward, crossing an unreliable creek (and/or snowfield) draining the northeast cirque of Powder Mountain. We then climb the beautiful garden slopes of a small ridge, past nestled camps and a trail leading northeast via Coney Basin down to the Pasayten River, as we follow the PCT into misnamed, rock-strewn Woody Pass (6624–2.3).

From here our trail traverses open slopes with a few wooded fingers, the least spectacular side of Three Fools Peak (7930), until it rounds the south arm of the cirque that cradles Mountain Home Camp, a flat, grassy bench with good camping. Beyond, the trail begins to climb steadily as it traverses the grassy headwall of the cirque. Shortly after we arc to the north, climbing through occasional stands of scrub conifers, a faint trail (6800–2.5) takes off down a more or less open gully to the flat bench of Mountain Home Camp, now 400 feet directly below us.

Continuing on the PCT, a short switchback brings us to the crest of Lakeview Ridge, on which a short spur trail takes us to an enticing view of a nestled lake 1000 feet below, and the valley of Chuchuwanteen Creek beyond. The PCT continues along the crest for a short

L6, L7

L7

see MAP L8

see MAP L6

distance before it is forced to the west just long enough to switchback once more before climbing to an unnamed summit (7126–0.7) on Lakeview Ridge. From here we have views on all sides, weather permitting: to the south, the very rugged Three Fools Peak; to the north our first glimpse of Hopkins Lake; and farther north and west, the rugged Cascades of Washington and Canada.

Now heading down toward Hopkins Pass, we stick to the ridge crest most of the time until we are forced by Peak 6873 on the ridge to pass east of it. Then our route switchbacks around the north side of the amphitheater for which

Hopkins Lake is the "stage." Several short switchbacks and two longer ones bring us down nearly to the level of the lake, to where a trail (6220–1.7) to dependable campsites at Hopkins Lake (6171) takes off to the southwest. We continue almost eastward for a few hundred yards to Hopkins Pass (6122–0.2), where the old trail down Chuchuwanteen Creek linking up with the Boundary Trail is marked ABANDONED.

The Pacific Crest Trail continues north-northwest from Hopkins Pass, traversing the mostly wooded west slopes of Blizzard Peak (7622). After a mile we reach a stream and its clearing, then re-enter woods and continue our

L7   **L7, L8**

see MAP L9

see MAP L7

see MAP L8

traverse about 0.4 mile before starting a gradual descent toward Castle Pass. Shortly before the pass we join Boundary Trail 749, turn sharply left and follow it around a small hummock to Castle Pass (5451–2.5), where we might lunch in the sunshine of a small open area. Then, after meandering northward down a quarter mile of lush alpine gardens, the trail becomes firmly established on the east slope of the Route Creek

watershed. We cross two seasonal streams and two avalanche paths, one from the east and one from the west. A reasonable camp lies 200 yards off the trail on the edge of one avalanche track; don't stay there if there is still much snow on the slopes above. Continuing the traverse, we come to two reliable streams in about a mile, then leave the woods for more-open slopes with rounded granite outcrops.

L8   **L8**

Monument 78 on U.S.-Canada border

After passing two more streams and a stock gate across the trail, we finally pound down the last four switchbacks to Monument 78, on the United States-Canada border (4240–4.1). After shooting several pictures of the scaled-down, 4⅔-foot-high, bronze "Washington Monument" (with a lift-off top for notes within), we leave the Pasayten Wilderness for the final leg of our trip. Welcome to Canada! (See the section on border crossing on page 21).

Just north of the monument is a junction with the Castle Creek/Monument 78 Trail, veering right. This provides a mostly downhill route out to Highway 3, but you end up about 2½ miles east of Manning Park Lodge (though only ½ mile southwest of Hampton Campground). However, this trail is often boggy and can be in poor shape after too much horse use. Plunging into the dense, wet, valley-bottom woods, we quickly reach a late '80s horse corral and an adjacent backcountry campground. Not far past it, just ¼ mile into Canada, we bridge seasonally raging Castle Creek. Still in the woods, we wind through a dense spruce-fir forest and soon begin a mostly viewless climb steadily but gently northeast. As the path climbs, we cross from granite to slate and back again, plod up a short switchback leg, cross a few ravines, jump a few creeklets, and arrive at the southwest base

L8, L9

A long-sought goal: trail's end in Manning Park

Playground by Manning Park Lodge

(5070-3.7) of Windy Joe Mountain. From a spring here the PCT turns north and climbs briefly to a saddle and a junction with the Mt. Frosty Trail (5120-0.1), which starts to climb southwest.

From here the PCT makes an undulating traverse north across Windy Joe Mountain's west slopes. We soon hear the traffic on Canada's main east-west thoroughfare, Route 3, cutting a swath through the dense forest on the unseen, deep canyon floor below us. Our trail ends at a hairpin turn on the closed Windy Joe fire access road (5220-0.7), and we follow the road, first north and then south, down to a creek crossing. We immediately recross the creek, descend ½ mile, and then cross it for the last time (4500-1.2).

The moderately descending road soon winds down gentler, still viewless slopes to a bridge over the major branch of the Similkameen River, then in 200 yards crosses a smaller branch (3780-1.1). Here the fire access road curves left and climbs 250 yards up to Highway 3.

From the bridge, two trails start down-canyon, and we take the one that climbs east up a 20-foot-high bluff. It then winds northeast, almost touching Highway 3 near a sewage plant, then parallels the highway east to the Beaver

Pond parking lot (3800-0.4), which marks the end of the long trail—or the beginning, if you are going south. (If you are going south, you'll find the spur road leading to this lot begins about 0.3 mile east from the park headquarters road, or, 0.9 mile east from the east entrance to Manning Park Lodge.)

If you've hiked a good portion of the Pacific Crest Trail, or perhaps just one rainy day's worth, you'll want to stop at the lodge to shower and get a warm meal. It also has tempting accommodations, but they are beyond the budget of most backpackers. From the Lodge the economy-minded backpacker can trek one mile west on Highway 3 to Coldspring Campground, then later catch a bus from Manning Park Lodge west to Vancouver, B.C.

We hope you arrived in good spirits and in good health. And we also hope that your hike through Section L was, despite the odds, warm, dry and insect-free. If you have hiked all or most of the way from Mexico to Canada, won't you please write us and tell us about your experiences and about the usefullness of this guidebook. The letters we received from your predecessors helped make this edition more useful for PCT trekkers, and we'd like to see the tradition continued.

L9   **L9**

Recommended Reading and Source Materials

Pacific Crest Trail

Clarke, Clinton C., *The Pacific Crest Trailway*. Pasadena: The Pacific Crest Trail System Conference, 1945.

Gray, William R., *The Pacific Crest Trail*. Washington, D.C.: National Geographic Society, 1975.

Green, David, *A Pacific Crest Odyssey*. Berkeley: Wilderness Press, 1979.

Ryback, Eric. *The High Adventure of Eric Ryback*. San Francisco: Chronicle Books, 1979.

Schaffer, Jeffrey P., and Ben Schifrin, Thomas Winnett, Ruby Jenkins, *The Pacific Crest Trail, Volume 1: California*, 4th ed. Berkeley: Wilderness Press, 1989.

Sutton, Ann, and Myron Sutton. *The Pacific Crest Trail: Escape to the Wilderness*. Philadelphia: Lippincott, 1975.

Backpacking and Mountaineering

Beckey, Fred, *Cascade Alpine Guide, Climbing & High Routes, Volume 1: Columbia River to Stevens Pass*. Seattle: The Mountaineers, 1974.

Beckey, Fred, *Cascade Alpine Guide, Climbing & High Routes, Volume 2: Stevens Pass to Rainy Pass*. Seattle: The Mountaineers, 1978.

Beckey, Fred, *Cascade Alpine Guide, Climbing & High Routes, Volume 3: Rainy Pass to Fraser River*. Seattle: The Mountaineers, 1981.

Darvill, Fred T., M.D., *Mountaineering Medicine*, 12th ed. Berkeley: Wilderness Press, 1989.

Fletcher, Colin, *The Complete Walker III*, New York: Knopf, 1984.

Hargrove, Penny, and Noelle Liebrenz, *Backpackers' Sourcebook*, 3rd ed. Berkeley: Wilderness Press, 1986.

Manning, Harvey, *Backpacking: One Step at a Time*, 3rd ed. New York: Knopf, 1980.

Molenaar, Dee, *The Challenge of Rainier*, 3rd ed. Seattle: The Mountaineers, 1979.

Peters, Ed, ed., *Mountaineering, the Freedom of the Hills*. Seattle: The Mountaineers, 1982.

Schaffer, Jeffrey P., *Crater Lake National Park and Vicinity*. Berkeley: Wilderness Press, 1983.

Thomas, Jeff, *Oregon Rock: A Climber's Guide*. Seattle: The Mountaineers, 1983.

Wilkerson, James A., M.D., ed., *Medicine for Mountaineering*, 3rd ed. Seattle: The Mountaineers, 1985.

Winnett, Thomas, and Melanie Findling, *Backpacking Basics*. Berkeley: Wilderness Press, 1988.

Geology

American Geological Institute, *Dictionary of Geological Terms*, rev. ed. Garden City, New York: Doubleday, 1976.

Bacon, Charles R., "Eruptive History of Mount Mazama and Crater Lake Caldera, Cascade Range, U.S.A." *Journal of Volcanology and Geothermal Research*, vol. 18, pp. 57–115; 1983.

Baldwin, Ewart M., *Geology of Oregon*, 3rd ed. Dubuque: Kendall/Hunt, 1981.

Crandell, Dwight R., *Surficial Geology of Mount Rainier National Park, Washington* (U.S. Geological Survey Bulletin 1288). Washington, D.C.: U.S. Government Printing Office, 1969.

Crandell, Dwight R., *The Geologic Story of Mount Rainier* (U.S. Geological Survey Bulletin 1292). Washington, D.C.: U.S. Government Printing Office, 1969.

Crandell, Dwight R., *Recent Eruptive History of Mount Hood, Oregon, and Potential Hazards from Future Eruptions* (U.S. Geological Survey Bulletin 1492). Washington, D.C.: U.S. Government Printing Office, 1980.

Dole, Hollis M., ed., *Andesite Conference Guidebook* (Oregon Department of Geology and Mineral Industries Bulletin 62). Portland: Oregon Department of Geology, 1968.

Harris, Stephen L., *Fire and Ice: The Cascade Volcanoes,* Seattle: The Mountaineers, 1976.

Howell, David G., "Terranes." *Scientific American,* vol. 253, no. 5; November 1985.

Jones, David L., *et al,* "The Growth of Western North America." *Scientific American,* vol. 247, no. 5; November 1982.

Luedke, Robert G., and Robert L. Smith, *Map Showing Distribution, Composition, and Age of Late Cenozoic Volcanic Centers in Oregon and Washington* (U.S. Geogical Survey Miscellaneous Investigations Series Map I-1091-D). Washington, D.C.: U.S. Government Printing Office, 1982.

McKee, Bates, *Cascadia: The Geologic Evolution of the Pacific Northwest.* New York: McGraw-Hill, 1972.

Pough, Frederick H., *A Field Guide to Rocks and Minerals,* 4th ed. Boston: Houghton Mifflin, 1976.

Staatz, Mortimer H., *et al, Geology and Mineral Resources of the Northern Part of the North Cascades National Park, Washington* (U.S. Geological Survey Bulletin 1359). Washington, D.C.: U.S. Government Printing Office, 1972.

Tabor, R.W., and D.F. Crowder, *On Batholiths and Volcanoes . . . North Cascades, Washington* (U.S. Geological Survey Professional Paper 604). Washington, D.C.: U.S. Government Printing Office, 1969.

Wells, Francis G., and Dallas L. Peck, *Geologic Map of Oregon West of the 121st Meridian* (U.S. Geological Survey Misc. Geol. Investig. Map I-325, 1:500,000). Washington, D.C.: U.S. Government Printing Office, 1961.

Biology

Arno, Stephen F., and Ramona P. Hammerly, *Northwest Trees.* Seattle: The Mountaineers, 1977.

Burt, William H., and Richard P. Grossenheider, *A Field Guide to the Mammals,* 3rd ed. Boston: Houghton Mifflin, 1976.

Franklin, Jerry F., and C.T. Dyrness, *Natural Vegetation of Oregon and Washington* (USDA Forest Service General Technical Report PNW-8). Washington, D.C.: U.S. Government Printing Office, 1973.

Hitchcock, C. Leo, and Arthur Cronquist, *Flora of the Pacific Northwest; an Illustrated Manual.* Seattle: University of Washington Press, 1973.

Horn, Elizabeth L., *Wildflowers 1: The Cascades.* Beaverton, OR: Touchstone Press, 1972.

Ingles, Lloyd G., *Mammals of the Pacific States.* Stanford: Stanford University Press, 1965.

Keator, Glenn, *Pacific Coast Berry Finder.* Berkeley: Nature Study Guild, 1978.

Larrison, Earl J., and Grace W. Patrick, William H. Baker, James A. Yaich, *Washington Wildflowers.* Seattle: Seattle Audubon Society, 1974.

Murie, Olaus J., *A Field Guide to Animal Tracks,* 2nd ed. Boston: Houghton Mifflin, 1975.

National Geographic Society, *Field Guide to the Birds of North America.* Washington, D.C.: National Geographic Society, 1983.

Niehaus, Theodore F., and Charles L. Ripper, *A Field Guide to Pacific States Wildflowers.* Boston: Houghton Mifflin, 1976.

Peterson, Roger T., *A Field Guide to Western Birds.* Boston: Houghton Mifflin, 1972.

Stebbins, Robert C., *A Field Guide to Western Reptiles and Amphibians.* Boston: Houghton Mifflin, 1966.

Sudworth, George B., *Forest Trees of the Pacific Slope.* New York: Dover, 1967 (1908 reprint with new Foreword and Table of Changes in Nomenclature).

Watts, Tom, *Pacific Coast Tree Finder.* Berkeley: Nature Study Guild, 1973.

Whitney, Stephen R., *A Field Guide to the Cascades & Olympics.* Seattle: The Mountaineers, 1983 (published simultaneously in Canada by Douglas & McIntyre, Ltd., Vancouver, B.C. under the title of *A Field Guide to the West Coast Mountains*).

Index

The italic letter-number combinations (*A1, B1,* etc.) refer to this book's topographic maps.

Use these next four pages for hitchhiking.

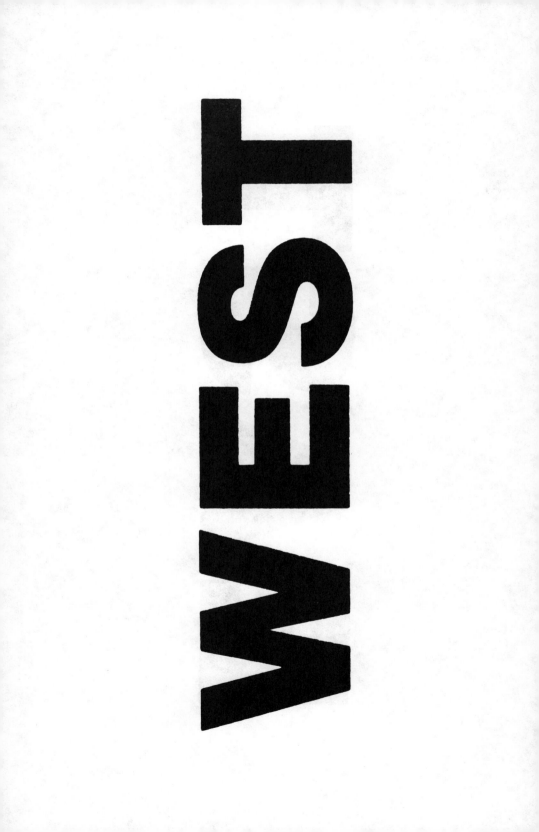